ROUTLEDGE LIBRARY EDITIONS:
HEGEL

Volume 3

THE BRITISH HEGELIANS

THE BRITISH HEGELIANS
1875–1925

PETER ROBBINS

LONDON AND NEW YORK

First published in 1982 by Garland Publishing Inc.

This edition first published in 2020
by Routledge
2 Park Square, Milton Park, Abingdon, Oxon OX14 4RN

and by Routledge
52 Vanderbilt Avenue, New York, NY 10017

Routledge is an imprint of the Taylor & Francis Group, an informa business

© 1982 Peter Robbins

All rights reserved. No part of this book may be reprinted or reproduced or utilised in any form or by any electronic, mechanical, or other means, now known or hereafter invented, including photocopying and recording, or in any information storage or retrieval system, without permission in writing from the publishers.

Trademark notice: Product or corporate names may be trademarks or registered trademarks, and are used only for identification and explanation without intent to infringe.

British Library Cataloguing in Publication Data
A catalogue record for this book is available from the British Library

ISBN: 978-0-367-37331-3 (Set)
ISBN: 978-0-367-81731-2 (Set) (ebk)
ISBN: 978-0-367-40995-1 (Volume 3) (hbk)
ISBN: 978-0-367-41007-0 (Volume 3) (pbk)
ISBN: 978-0-367-81421-2 (Volume 3) (ebk)

Publisher's Note
The publisher has gone to great lengths to ensure the quality of this reprint but points out that some imperfections in the original copies may be apparent.

Disclaimer
The publisher has made every effort to trace copyright holders and would welcome correspondence from those they have been unable to trace.

THE BRITISH HEGELIANS
1875–1925

Peter Robbins

 Garland Publishing, Inc.
New York & London ★ 1982

© 1982 Peter Robbins
All rights reserved

Library of Congress Cataloging in Publication Data

Robbins, Peter, 1940–
  The British Hegelians, 1875–1925.

  (Modern British history ; 6)
  Bibliography: p.
  Includes index.
  1. Philosophy, English—19th century. 2. Philosophy, English—20th century. 3. Hegel, Georg Wilhelm Friedrich, 1770–1831—Influence. I. Title. II. Series.
  B1615.R63 1982   192   81-48366
  ISBN 0-8240-5162-9

All volumes in this series are printed on acid-free, 250-year-life paper.
Printed in the United States of America

PREFACE

The focus of this study is the social and political, and to a lesser extent the moral and metaphysical, thinking of an informal school of philosophy which had a clearly ascertainable and relatively well-defined impact on British academic life as well as a more diffuse influence on British public opinion, social practice and policy-making for two or three decades prior to World War I. Such recent works as Peter Clarke's <u>Liberals and Social Democrats</u> and Peter Gordon's and John White's <u>Philosophers as Educational Reformers</u> indicate an awakening of interest in the latter dimension of British Hegelianism. The present work has something to say about the "social gospel" of British Hegelianism; but it is primarily concerned with the sources of British Hegelian thinking, the lines of its development and intellectual relationships among members of the "school."

It is not a study of British Idealism, nor of neo-Hegelianism in Britain. Although the British Hegelians are sometimes referred to as neo-Hegelians, this is, strictly speaking, a misnomer. I would argue that neo-Hegelianism, like neo-Marxism, is a comparatively recent development and that both are products of the "young Marx" industry, that vast and still growing enterprise – mainly but by no means exclusively European – dedicated to exhaustive research into <u>vormarz</u> Germany, Left, Right and Centre Hegelians, all their antecedents, Rousseau, <u>Sturm und Drang</u> and Scottish Enlightenment, and of course everything that Kant, Fichte and Hegel ever wrote. In addition, this work has expanded its range of sources to include twentieth century Marxians who pioneered the move "back to Hegel," such as Gramsci and Lukacs. The present intense and widespread interest in Hegel centres on his phenomenology and his earlier writings rather than on the logic and the later writings which engaged the attention of the British Hegelians.

There are very few British Hegelians of the old school left, either writing philosophy or in positions of academic influence. G.R.G. Mure, who recently retired as Warden of Merton College, Oxford, must be one of the last. I do not know enough about the current state of affairs at Scottish, Commonwealth or American universities to comment further about any Hegelian remnant in the professoriat. But certainly the fascination with Hegelian ontology is generally considered regrettable and as remote and difficult to comprehend as the Victorian crisis of religious doubt which first occasioned it.

As for British Idealism, it has a distinct history running from the Cambridge Platonists through Coleridge to Collingwood – and beyond. This stream of thought was for a time swept along by strong Kantian and Hegelian currents before returning to its characteristically English meanderings.

Unless otherwise indicated in the text, "idealism" and "idealist" are here used to refer to philosophical idealism.

In footnotes on their first being introduced, I have provided brief biographical sketches of the principal British Hegelians and of minor figures whose labours in some way, however small, paved the way for Hegel's entry into British philosophy. Some others have received the same treatment because, even though peripheral to Hegelianism, they are important in other contexts, but their names may be unfamiliar to the general reader – if such can be found for a work of this nature.

In chapters 10 and 11 I have quoted fairly liberally from McTaggart's <u>Studies in Hegelian Cosmology</u>, because it is, compared to Green's <u>Principles of Political Obligation</u>, Bradley's <u>Ethical Studies</u> or Bosanquet's <u>Philosophical Theory of the State</u>, difficult to come by either in whole or in part.

The bibliography includes a chronologically ordered list of English translations of Hegel's writings.

This book began in 1963-64 as a doctoral dissertation at the London School of Economics and Political Science. I would like to take this opportunity to express my gratitude to Professor Elie Kedourie for his supervision and guidance of my graduate work at LSE, while entering the customary disclaimer on his behalf with respect to any errors, omissions or lapses herein, for which, of course, he bears no responsibility whatever.

After being submitted as the written requirement for a doctorate from the University of London in 1966, this work lay untouched until the summer of 1980. As a result, considerable re-thinking has occurred and extensive re-writing has been necessary. The process began with my first year of university teaching, and I thank the 1967-68 honours political science class at the University of Victoria for a profound "learning experience." In particular, I would express my appreciation to Garry Curtis for his friendship, counsel and unfailing belief that something would come of my labours on Green, Bradley, Bosanquet and the rest. Two former colleagues at the University of Victoria, Richard Powers and Mark Sproule-Jones, have continued to encourage me in this and other scholarly endeavours.

Over the years of <u>The British Hegelians</u>' gestation, birth, limbo and rebirth, my parents have assisted in a variety of ways. In addition to their financial aid, my mother has typed the thing at least once, and my father has given me the benefit of knowledge gained from his long and scholarly devotion to nineteenth century English literature.

Of all those who have had to put up with the "thing," the one who has borne the brunt from first to last and who deserves first prize for tolerance and good humour - and for timely prodding - is my wife, Juliet. A more than honourable mention goes to my three children.

Latterly, as publication deadlines approached and pressure mounted for the final revision, my colleagues on the staff of <u>Hansard</u> have suffered my abstracted air and mutterings about obscure fragments of British cultural history. Two of them, Jo-Anne Brookman and David Greer, have devoted many hours of their own time to helping me with the production of final copy.

ABBREVIATIONS

The following abbreviations have been used for works cited often:

Bosanquet, Bernard	The Philosophical Theory of the State, 4th edition	PTS
	The Principle of Individuality and Value	PIV
Bradley, F.H.	Collected Essays	CE
	Ethical Studies, 2nd edition	ES
Green, T.H.	Lectures on the Principles of Political Obligation, 1941 reprint	PPO
	Prolegomena to Ethics, 5th edition	PE
McTaggart, J.McT.E.	Studies in Hegelian Cosmology	SHC
	Studies in the Hegelian Dialectic	SHD

TABLE OF CONTENTS

Preface		i
Abbreviations		iii
Introduction:	The Hegelian Enterprise	1
Chapter 1	Idealist Political Theory and the Victorian Frame of Mind	9
Chapter 2	The Prehistory of Hegelianism in Britain	17
Chapter 3	Religious Resistance to Hegel: From Coleridge to Personal Idealism	26
Chapter 4	J.H. Stirling: Kant as the "Secret" of Hegel	38
Chapter 5	Hegel and Classical Scholarship at Oxford	42
Chapter 6	The Principle of Utility from Hume to Sidgwick	50
Chapter 7	F.H. Bradley: The Organic Theory of Society	57
Chapter 8	T.H. Green: The Pursuit of the Common Good	65
Chapter 9	Bernard Bosanquet: The Idealist Theory of the State	72
Chapter 10	Idealism, "Evolutionism" and Utilitarianism	81
Chapter 11	Idealism as a Substitute Religion	91
Chapter 12	R.B. Haldane: Hegelianism with "Dirty Hands"	98
Chapter 13	The Decline of British Hegelianism	102
Bibliography		110
Index		122

INTRODUCTION

> For the principle in system is not the simple
> exclusion of all that does not fit, but the
> perpetual re-establishment of coherence.
>
> Oakeshott, Introduction
to Leviathan, xv

The Hegelian Enterprise

There has always been a substantial body of philosophical opinion which has felt that the coming of Hegel to Britain was like the introduction of some exotic foreign drug designed to confound native clarity and common sense. During the little more than a century of the English-speaking world's cognizance of Hegelian philosophy there has been one period, dating roughly from the 1880s to World War I, when those who felt otherwise prevailed. From shortly after World War I until very recently Hegel has been the object of Anglo-Saxon suspicion or disdain.[1] The reasons for this disfavour were not quite the same as those which operated in the middle years of the nineteenth century. Very few twentieth century philosophers have cared to condemn Hegel as irreligious, although some British Hegelians "defected" on some such ground. Neither individualist ethics nor existentialist Christianity has been aimed directly against the Hegelian version of idealism - although they have detracted from its influence. Accusations of political reaction, immorality and Greater German nationalism have all been thoroughly discredited - though not eliminated. Charges of bad logic and overweening metaphysics have had to be laid with increasing care and circumspection, and have, more often than not, completely misfired.

The basis for such charges has been, primarily, the dualist or realist view of the world. This is the metaphysical foundation which gives the positivist and empiricist opposition to idealism its force and penetration. It goes to the very core of Hegelian philosophy and it has been the most trenchant and enduring criticism of it. The opposing monism, philosophical materialism, languishes as low as does philosophical idealism. After all, the view that mind and matter, or mind and body, are two separate kinds of ultimately irreducible stuff which somehow interact is the obvious and commonsense one.

A fully and finally satisfactory explanation of mind-body interaction remains an elusive goal. C.D. Broad has distinguished 17 possible theories of the relationship between mind and matter. Some would say that a solution to this hoary problem is inherently impossible and content themselves with the dogmatic assertion that mind and body obviously do interact and that there is no more one can meaningfully say on the subject. Others would say that everyday linguistic usage talks about a dualistic world, and that that is sufficient. However, most dualists continue to seek for an explanation of interaction, usually on the basis of some

---

[1] In the fourteenth edition of Bertrand Russell's A History of Western Philosophy (New York, 1964) Hegel is still labelled an "enemy of analysis" (p. 744), and his unity of thought and being, in the guise of the theory of internal relations, "a mistake, and from this mistake arose the whole imposing edifice of his system." To which, characteristically, Russell adds: "This illustrates an important truth, namely, that the worse your logic, the more interesting the consequences to which it gives rise" (p. 746).

analogy which indicates the kind of thing that might occur, or which suggests a possible way of looking at instances of interaction between mind and body. Such analogies are frequently drawn from natural science, particularly from physics, in which a certain class of phenomena may require two contrary sets of explanation in order to account for all its observable behaviour - for example, the wave and corpuscular theories of light. Rarely does a contemporary philosopher attempt to reduce one of the interacting "stuffs" to the other, certainly not matter into mind. Experience would seem to guarantee the independent existence of a world of matter external to our minds. Yet it is precisely experience upon which the philosophical idealist such as Hegel has always taken his stand.

An examination of experience as a progressive development from sense-certainty to self-conscious reason shows, according to Hegel, that the external world is the product of mind, and that mind must so externalize itself. The identity of matter and mind is both the ground and the result of a continuous process of diremption and reunion. The end is implicit at the outset of any journey of experience undertaken by any consciousness, but it cannot be deduced a priori. The categories of thought are proved only in the continuing effort to order experience through them. One must reduce the flow of impressions impinging on one's consciousness - channelling, diverting, sifting and storing. This cannot be done without mental equipment. But the "forms" which mould our experience, while pre-established, are part of the flow of experience and, indeed, a late development. By themselves they are an abstraction, a skeleton without flesh or breath of life. The design of the force which draws things out and makes them manifest is not for us to posit; it is in and for us to create. Creating it is a process in space and time occupied by self-conscious human beings. There are still some things which we have not, for better or worse, created. However, nothing is inherently inexplicable, and if it can be grasped in and for itself, if its structure and principle can be understood, then it can be re-created, if only in thought. The process of re-creation was, for Hegel, contemplative, not active - for Marx, the signal failure of philosophical idealism. Hegel regarded his philosophy as the beginning of the end of the process whereby self-conscious reason brought "home" to the world the spirit of what it was and what it had done: thought would be adequate to being; mind would penetrate matter and there find forms of self-expression.

The logic of the process lies in the experience of it and only there. The Hegelian principle of identity is an identity-in-difference. In other words, it recognizes the externally related, the contingent and the accidental for what they are: real experiences. The unceasing efforts of many minds to establish non-contingent relations among the various elements of their combined experience produce results, although they also produce fresh dissonance and incoherence. The effort is always renewed and, in spite of losses, its results are cumulative. The ultimate identity of mind and its products, nature and history, is the absolute presupposition of our acquiring any grasp whatsoever of the world as we experience it.

Hegel has sometimes been said to be no philosophical idealist, because of his apparent disinterest in the problem of knowledge.[2] For one thing, he did not ask himself the epistemological question posed by such important predecessors as Berkeley, Hume and Kant: how can my sensations yield knowledge of whatever it is which occasions them? I am only aware of my own sensations and reflections on them, and I have no assurance that the sensations and reflections conveyed to me by others can confirm anything other than themselves, i.e. be evidence for the existence of others, because they are only further sensations of mine. A collapse into solipsism is the reductio ad absurdum of subjective idealism, and many who have followed that course have provoked an extreme reaction, even in their own thought, towards "radical publicism."[3] That sort of internal dialectic - the probing of the limits of a certain

---

[2] A.C. Ewing, Idealism: A Critical Survey, 3rd ed. (London, 1961), ch. 2, esp. pp. 60-62.
[3] J.N. Findlay, "The contemporary relevance of Hegel," Hegel: A Collection of Critical Essays, ed. A. MacIntyre (New York, 1972), p. 15.

line of argument by pushing it until it breaks down - was for Hegel the pursuit of truth. It is a method he made peculiarly his own in his analysis of any set of propositions about any area of experience, or thought about experience. Hegel's own starting point was the actual, living stream of experience, what the pragmatist William James called a "blooming, buzzing confusion." There is nothing outside our experience - until we start analyzing it, as we must. The problem of the existence of an external world is what we might call an academic one. No one not a lunatic behaves as if it did not exist. Theoretically, its existence is a useful hypothesis for a number of purposes, including the pursuit of natural science. But reality is to be found in the ebb and flow of experience, and in the dialectical turning of our experiences inside out and upside down. What we seek is not verification of this, that or the other thing, but an order and coherence in our experiences which will satisfy, among other things, the quest for truth.

Kant posited a transcendental schema, the synthetic unity of the manifold of apperceptions, as the ground of our knowledge of a causally related, spatially and temporally ordered phenomenal world. He retained, however, a world of things-in-themselves, inaccessible to the human mind. What the mind can know of an external, phenomenal world is the result of a degree of self-activity inconceivable to any empiricist philosopher. But Kant's philosophy is firmly dualist. The a priori conceptions apply only to sense data. They can yield no knowledge of a supersensible world; they are tied to sense-perception. The mind interacts with an external world which is an inexplicable noumenon. Essential reality, the thing-in-itself, eludes the mind because it is not adequate to the task of penetrating that reality which lies behind the phenomenal world. The pure forms of space and time are the rational, a priori framework within which the world of contingent phenomena necessarily moves, and without which we could have no experience whatsoever. They are not only the means whereby order and coherence are created in our experience. They are the sine qua non of experience. This framework, this schema is supplied by the understanding in conjunction with sense-perception. In addition, there are pure ideas - categories such as causality - which, when schematized by the infusion of empirical knowledge (i.e. knowledge given under the forms of space and time), further order our experience. These, again, only give substantive knowledge in conjunction with what is derived from sense-perception. They have a further regulative function, but in themselves they can contribute nothing to our knowledge of the external world. Even as regulative, they cannot be projected beyond experience without creating irresolvable antinomies. Only for the practical or moral reason can a pure idea have substantive status. The external world is both conception and perception, the conception empty without sense data, the perception shaped entirely by the conceptual framework.

Hegel contended that Kant's transcendental unity of apperceptions yielded merely subjective knowledge, with no guarantee of objective truth. He began with the assumption that we can know reality, that we are capable of knowing everything. The object is in thought as it is in reality, because reality is thought. This is no mere play upon words. Hegel meant that the categories of thought are those of reality. They are logically prior to reality externalized as nature and history, but knowing them is a moment of advanced self-consciousness, which is a product of that process of self-development and self-expression which the world as an idea must have gone through in order for us to have the sort of experience we, as human beings, do have. From reality being a species of self-consciousness it does not follow that truth is merely subjective or a product of introspection. On the contrary, from self-conscious reason being reflected in reality it follows that the truth about ourselves may be found in the world we have created and re-created. A journey into inner space must eventually become a journey into outer space. It begins and ends in common space, and each connection made is an intimation of cosmic necessity. In becoming aware of its own implications, the human mind explicates the whole of reality. It is a necessary presupposition of knowledge that reality is a thought process. It is equally necessary, in order that mind know itself as reality, that it externalize itself in the worlds of nature and human history.

The effort to understand the external world is mind's coming into its own. It must take in - literally comprehend - everything before it can affirm the identity of mind and matter, the underlying spirituality of the universe. The bare assertion of that identity is not sufficient; in fact, it is quite erroneous. The knowledge of physics, chemistry, engineering, animal husbandry, history - each in and for itself, each according to its own peculiar method and conforming to its own criteria of truth and adequacy - is necessary to that full self-knowledge which is the actualization of the spiritual principle of reality. One cannot evade the "patient toil of the negative."

In spite of Hegel's vehement opposition to any reduction of the universe to undifferentiated spirit, his positivist and realist critics persist in attacking him for disregarding essential distinctions, above all that between mind and an external world of matter or bodies in space and time. He certainly regarded the universe, the totality of things, as fundamentally spiritual in nature, and he did attempt to trace a progressive spiritual development in nature - with some rather absurd results from the point of view of the natural scientist. But he was certainly not purporting to construct nature a priori or deduce the whole of natural science from purely rational principles, as many of his critics have suggested. He set out to describe a fully intelligible world, one in which nothing is left out or disconnected, in which everything can be explained in terms of everything else because all is rational - there is nothing which the mind cannot penetrate and there discover a reflection of itself.

This world of Hegel's was neither an article of faith nor a mystical vision; it was the necessary outcome of finding the key to the understanding of the external world in self-consciousness. Self-consciousness was for Hegel the archetype of identity-in-difference. It was the perfect example, because the ultimate source, of the reconciliation of apparently irreconcilable contradictories.

If one were to alter the terms of the duality of mind and body and refer to them as subject and object, one would get a clue to Hegel's identification of them. The self is both the subject and the object of introspection. While one cannot jump out of one's skin and examine one's self as one would any external object, one can examine oneself objectively as if one were someone else as well as oneself. However, this does not seem at first sight to have much bearing upon the problem of the mind-body relationship. The mind, after all, is not a material object; and there are a large number of material objects without minds - and even more without self-consciousness. Hegel's approach to this problem was to point out that self-consciousness depends upon the same opposition of subject and object as does the consciousness of anything in the external world. Consciousness of self requires the objectification of self. Conversely, the consciousness of an external object requires that one somehow find oneself in that object. The object is and remains external; but in the process of coming to understand it, the mind sees it less and less as an alien object and more and more as a familiar and integral part of an expanding world of experience. At the stage of philosophy, the full spirituality of the object becomes explicit. However, the stage of sheer externality is not abolished. It is sufficient for natural science and practical life; and it is necessary for self-consciousness: the self becomes conscious of itself only in contradistinction to what is not itself, the external world of things and other selves. In the process of coming to full self-consciousness, the self brings with it the not-self, which it at first regards as something in bare opposition to itself.

The culmination of this process is a system of knowledge in which, although the sum is self-consciousness, every stage traversed in reaching it is preserved in it. Self-consciousness would not be full self-consciousness if it did not include the inevitable moments of diremption and duality. It was these moments of the self faced by an alien, irreducible other, rather than the introspective habit of standing outside oneself, that Hegel was referring to when he talked about self-objectification.

In talking about mind, Hegel was talking about any individual mind as a moment in the totality of human minds past and present. Self-consciousness is an individual thing; but even at its lowest level, that of sense-certainty, the germ of universal objective mind is at work. Self-consciousness can be consciousness of self only because the self is shared; each is a manifestation of intersubjective mind, and even the self's most individual characteristics derive from shared experience.

Our experience is neither an undifferentiated datum nor a series of data, nor is it "formed" in a synthetic a priori fashion as it is in Kant's transcendentalism. For a proper understanding of it, Hegel renovated an ancient notion which had fallen into considerable disgrace with the rise of modern science and mechanistic philosophy. This was Aristotle's theory of causation, particularly of the final cause or _telos_. What shapes and directs any process is its immanent or built-in purpose - its genetic code, to use a metaphor drawn from twentieth century science. It has to be remembered that this is only a metaphor, because Hegel has been all too easily made the butt of such stale anti-Aristotelian jokes as the one that the apple fell because of its inner drive, or _conatus_, to strike Newton on the head and initiate a chain of reasoning to produce the law of universal gravitation. The Hegelian version would be that a particular phase of the human experience was characterized by, among other things, looking at falling objects in a new light. There was a shift in intellectual vision, which was increasingly informed by an atomistic conception of matter in motion. Men of affairs as well as men of science conceived of the whole world as "push" because that afforded both an explanation which was simple yet cognitively powerful and an unprecedented degree of control over external forces. A new way of ordering experience emerged; and whatever it might have to say about physical causation, its own emergent structure was anything but fortuitous. It was the product not just of many minds, but also of many currents of thought. It was both cause and consequence of a new world view, whose most comprehensive, far-reaching and systematic expression was to be found in the philosophy of Hobbes. Like its representative philosophical expression, this confluence of ideas had its own "centripetal force" drawing into itself "numberless currents of thought, contemporary and historic."[4]

Explaining Hegel's (or any other) philosophy metaphorically can be misleading, especially in Hegel's case, because of his deliberate eschewal of the imagery of art and religion. Nevertheless, here is yet another metaphor: Hegel's history of philosophy is itself a philosophy. His account of how certain thinkers thought is part of the plan to whose unfolding those thinkers contributed. The end or final cause of all human activity is a fully self-conscious philosophy, one which knows the necessity of each particular in the implementation of the plan of the world. The plan, however, is neither a blueprint nor an oracle; it is an evolving hierarchy of being as experienced by all men. Philosophy may understand better than any other mode of experience what has happened and why, but its comprehension grows with the growth of experience as a whole. Philosophy is the most self-conscious fibre of being, but it is part of the natural history of being from rocks to religion. It is implicit in the life of each human being that he or she seek to make a distinctive contribution to the human experience of Being.[5] The integrating element is spirit at work in the world - or in New Testament language, _logos_, the word of God incarnate.

---

[4] Michael Oakeshott, Introduction to Hobbes' _Leviathan_ (Oxford, 1960), p. xii.
[5] I have tried to resist the creeping capitalization of philosophical terms, if only because Hegelianism has long been the chief offender in the eyes of those who take strong exception to the use of capitals to confer undeserved grandeur upon concepts. However, in this case at least, without capitalization confusion could arise. By _Dasein_, Hegel meant determinate being, which is pure being in a perpetual motion of becoming what it is not. What it is, is nothing. It must continuously negate itself in order to break itself up into determinate things, to acquire properties and qualities, to be something.

It was with the world spirit that Hegel sought to overcome Kant's dualism and the unknowable reality beyond the reach of human experience and conception. World spirit signifies more in Hegel's philosophy than common reason, but it is essentially, in all its meanings, a rational principle. The Hegelian term <u>Geist</u> can be translated as mind or as spirit, spirit being a higher and fuller level of mind; mind has more strictly intellectual connotations. Spirit is realized in art and religion as well as philosophy. In the Hegelian system philosophy is the crown of this trinity and can conceive what the emotive and aesthetic modes of experience cannot - that is, their respective roles and relations to the rest of experience. In addition to its place in the hierarchy of being as the highest form of self-conscious intellectual activity, philosophy is also the fullest expression of that rational principle which ensures the human capacity to "grasp" the world. As we now know, the whole world, the totality of things, is only explicable as the unfolding of what is, in human terms, the rational. While great play has been made during the past 150 years of the spirit of the age and similar notions which attempt to formulate the phenomena of the collective psyche, none of it truly addresses Hegel's philosophical problem. It was conceived in psychological terms only insofar as his phenomenology offered a descriptive analysis of recognizable psychological types. But they are treated primarily as logical types, in much the same sort of way that classical theorists of the social contract treated the state of nature. Hegel's purpose was philosophical: to explain the necessary forms of human experience; not to show how this or that historical form of social consciousness, politics or artistic endeavour embodied this or that idea.

Between various prototypes of psycho-history and Marx's historical materialism, the exact nature of the Hegelian enterprise has been obscured. One of the things that historical materialists (Marxist and non-Marxist) have been doing with increasing diligence since the 1960s is reading their antecedents backwards, i.e. from Marx to Hegel. One of the things they have discovered is that there is still a lot left on the agenda of Hegel's phenomenology, and that we are still wrestling with the contradictions of what Hegel called "the unhappy consciousness." As Charles Taylor has said in response to a question first posed by Benedetto Croce in 1907 - What is living and what is dead in the philosophy of Hegel? - Hegel's ontology may be a dead letter, but his account of modern man's predicament is as vital as ever.[6] Can we be at home in a world which is partly of our own making? Our making it is no protection against our being alienated from it - quite the contrary - and we have a collective propensity to rationalize what we have made, in the sense of finding reasons for that which has always been, or has become, bereft of any rational basis. Marx's theory of alienation and the false consciousness of capitalist society is the best-known elaboration of these ideas. Again, Hegel's distinctive purpose can be lost sight of. By inverting Hegel's conception of freedom, Marx thought he could project the final act of human emancipation onto the stage of history; the realization of rationality could become a plan of political action. For Hegel, true freedom lay in knowing that the freedom of all must be. Unfortunately for the unfree - and that includes everyone in various ways and to varying degrees - the idea of freedom cannot be imposed on events, nor can its actualization be foreseen. Anyone can now be free to the extent that he or she knows "what it's all about" and can reconcile his or her own self-realization with the general scheme of things. It's basically a question of finding one's identity and one's self-respect in the world as it is. What one finds are a lot of other individuals and groups who have sought or are seeking self-realization. To seek self-realization is to participate in the adventure of human reason, the most self-conscious moment in the spirit of the world. In quasi-religious fashion, Hegel depicts self-realization as a kind of self-abnegation. The self to be realized is always more than oneself. One finds a lot of what one is meant to be in interests and experiences which appear to be outside oneself.

It is important, in discussing Hegel on self-realization and the need for wholeness in our

---

[6] See Charles Taylor, <u>Hegel</u> (London, 1975), esp. ch. 20.

experience, not to attach too much weight to the prescriptive aspect and religious overtones of self-realization. For one thing, Hegel's philosophy was in part a reaction against the Romantic philosophers' holy war against the prevailing rationalism and materialism of the eighteenth century Enlightenment. The campaign's chief architect was Herder, who aimed at nothing less than a new science of man in the manner of Vico, based on the conception of man as a being who created, identified and established himself in the world, within each sub-group of humanity, in a variety of unique ways. Such ways lay in and through the development of diverse forms of linguistic and artistic expression. The attack, as it gathered momentum, culminating in the leadership of Fichte, was directed as much against constricting social and political forms as it was against rationalist culture. It sought a revolution in consciousness which would both complement and control the overthrow of the ancien régime. With Fichte it went even further, positing a moral will independent of everything else, an eternal categorical imperative to make the world over - the success of which endeavour would be self-destructive. Hegel accepted the need to rediscover spirituality in nature - to, if nothing else, see nature as a medium for human self-expression - but he rejected the increasingly central role in human experience assigned by the Romantics to a schwarmerei of moral indignation and mystical communion with nature. His basic objection to the radical freedom preached by Fichteans and so-called liberal nationalists was that it claimed too much for subjectivity in opposition to the world as structured by Enlightenment philosophy, and it entailed a "bad infinity." That is to say, Romantic idealism posed a good will in endless opposition to whatever was recalcitrant to it, in the impossible - and therefore morally corrupting - pursuit of the elimination of the contingent and the conventional. The proper conception of infinity, says Hegel, is circular. Self-realization rightly conceived is a search for oneself in the world which returns to oneself. The end is in the beginning; but the fulfilment occurs in and through the joys and sorrows, the enrichment and the loss of the intervening journey. Moreover, no matter how far one might soar above them, one cannot dispense with the "cake of custom" and social routine.

It bears repeating that Hegel's basic objective was metaphysical rather than moral: to demonstrate the necessary unity in diversity of the world; to overcome division between subject and object, between man and nature, between values and facts, because the world spirit demands it. The identity of identity and non-identity cannot be merely asserted, willed or projected; it has to be rationally explicated. However, it cannot be done by the kind of reasoning which is employed in either pure or applied science. This is designed to separate the human mind, as a disembodied set of rules, from the matter which it probes and manipulates, and it is well suited to its appointed purpose. Hegel terms this mode of reasoning Verstand (understanding), and distinguishes it very carefully from Vernunft (reason). The latter is the method and the result - the one implicit in the other - of the mind in search of ultimate explanations, of that reflection on experience which mediates (overcomes without discarding) the consciousness of diremption in nature and human history.

Hegel's vision of the identity of the autonomous individual with the rational plan for the world and everything in it was both logical and historical. The logic without the history was timeless, immutable truth, but entirely abstract. In order that spirit may be fully realized, mankind must "work it out." This means experiencing all the lower and more or less distorted forms of consciousness en route to the recovery of primitive unity. Of course, there are worlds of difference between the innocence of original man and the experience of self-conscious, reflective man. Going no further back than the unself-conscious harmony of Periclean Athens:
> "From the felicity of 'substantiality' ('so sind sie-so leben sie') the Western consciousness must endure its historical saeculum of 'alienation' or 'bifurcation.' However, this is the charge of freedom."[7]

---

[7] G.A. Kelly, Idealism, Politics and History (Cambridge, 1969), p. 325.

The philosophical anthropology which Hegel inherited from Kant was moralistic. Kant was primarily concerned to make room for man as a free moral agent in a world of external causation. He also explored the notion that the nexus of man and his world and the way to grasp reality lay in the aesthetic sense, that the model of truth is artistic appreciation of significant and therefore satisfying form. As with the self-legislating moral will, Kant owed much of the inspiration for his ideal human character to Rousseau's various attempts to construct an "image" of the good man - the self-possessed, self-directed person. Kant sought a ratiocinative conception of that form of individual human freedom for which Goethe and Schiller provided primarily literary expressions. Rousseau's <u>Emile</u>, especially the first part, is devoted to the cultivation of a sensibility which is part aesthetic, part moralistic. Emile's education is designed to produce an individual immune to "the historical pattern of corruption" by inculcating "the rhythm of the human heart."[8] The natural goodness of man - the residue of which may be found in agricultural village life - is a pleasing prospect. However, it cannot be recaptured, and sterner stuff than flights of literary fancy is required to make men moral: something both artistic and political, and therefore coercive; a quasi-divine, supernatural act of constitutional creation. Rousseau's political writings contain many strictures on fine art and the cultivation of feelings for their own sake. The crux of his objections was the classical republican commandment against poetry as a threat to civic virtue. In Kant's case, the antinomies of practical reason - the logic of the moral will - remain unresolved by the critique of judgment, so that we are left with the unconditional and unconditioned will to good as the most authentic expression of humanity. To be a true subject and not an object one must will the good, because the only intrinsically, independently good thing is the good will. The problem of autonomous, self-directed moral action, as it presented itself to Hegel, was to retain such freedom while avoiding the pitfalls of, on the one hand, amorphous feelings of goodwill - an intense sort of bonhomie - and the morality of impulse, and on the other, the impotence of a will to good which cannot achieve anything in the real world of human desires and needs without compromising its autonomy. Hegel's solution, the concept of <u>Sittlichkeit</u> (roughly translatable as social ethics), was a political one.

<u>Sittlichkeit</u> is not the set of values by which political life in the rational state can be judged. But it closely approaches that higher form of life by overcoming the inadequacy of the Kantian ethic - the highest achievement in its sphere - through an act of Hegelian mediation. It cancels and preserves the contradictions inherent in <u>Moralität</u>; it does not deny them. Similarly, the rational state "sublates" <u>Sittlichkeit</u>. The distinguishing feature of <u>Sittlichkeit</u> is that it is a set of internalized rules, which exist independently of the self-legislating subject. However, they have been freely internalized and are therefore not something set over against the subject. The political subject of the rational state, which expresses its rationality to a very high degree through the conduct of its citizens according to <u>Sittlichkeit</u>, is a subject in the sense of being a self-directed member of his community. Short of being a philosophical sort of person, a Platonic visionary, or a member of that "universal class" of higher civil servants whose function it is to understand the ethos of the community and its place in the unfolding of world spirit, the citizen of a well-governed state with good laws lives at the peak of human achievement. Furthermore, he obeys positive laws and social conventions, and not the golden rule of Jesus Christ or William Godwin. Hegel purported to find his standard of the rational state in what was actually happening around him, in the laws which were in place and in the political reforms which were in process. The underlying rationality of all that is actually happening is difficult to explain without falling into the trap of either the Whig interpretation of history or the simple-minded positivism that whatever is, is right. The conceptual device which allowed Hegel to demonstrate - to his own satisfaction at least - the historical reality of the rational was the teleological argument which Kant explored at length in his <u>Critique of Judgment</u>, found wanting and discarded.

---

[8] <u>Ibid.</u>, p. 45.

CHAPTER 1

Idealist Political Theory
and the Victorian Frame of Mind

The idea that nature is the result of a diremption within the world spirit is an unnecessary mystification for those who do not share Hegel's preoccupation with the rational ordering of all experience. There is, however, one area of human experience which lends itself particularly well to a Hegelian explanation - the social and the political. Here we are faced with an external world which everyone must to some extent agree is a product of the human mind. Just as the world of natural phenomena is, says Hegel, an externalization necessary to full self-consciousness, so is the world of custom and law. The crucial difference is that the human spirit is more deeply involved, more self-conscious and more purposive in the life of organized political society.

At this point we need to remind ourselves of the potential for misconceiving the spirituality which Hegel discovered in the world and all its doings as a sort of gnosticism. Hegel was talking about a necessary process of self-knowledge. It is a process of self-realization in that sense, as much as it is self-fulfilment. In explicating Hegel's political thought, we should think in terms of the dialectical, teleological mode of thinking which he called <u>Vernunft</u>, because the state, as the apex of moral and political endeavour, is neither a transcendental deduction nor a moral ideal in Hegel's philosophical system; it is the necessary historical expression of continuing and cumulative attempts to live the good life in a collective form. <u>Vernunft</u> may also be interpreted as intersubjective mind, as opposed to a narrowly rationalistic <u>cogito</u>. In this sense, it is a collective and substantive thing, and not simply an inference from any individual experience or the rules for thinking to indubitable conclusions. Reason is self-conscious thought. But, as we have seen, it is not esoteric; it is not what we would today call a second-order activity; it is not the preserve of the professional philosopher. It is part of the "cunning of reason" that it can fool the wise. The rational state knows that it is rational, and it knows through the experience of each of its citizens. Hegel's political theory describes the rational state in terms of an immanent potential which every state seeks to actualize. The fully rational state is one in which every citizen regards himself as in a position to fulfil himself because he is a member of the state. Teleologically, every state exists because its citizens are conscious to some degree that individual potential can only be realized within the state.

The idea that the state can be the agent of moral improvement and spiritual advancement, that it is more than a common denominator or an organization of material convenience, has deep roots. Particularly in the political part of his philosophical system, Hegel was self-consciously renovating a tradition of thought which has always drawn directly from Plato and Aristotle. The climate of opinion in early nineteenth century Germany was especially receptive to such theories, because of a comparatively recent but well-developed passion for the art and thought of classical Greece. It was almost a hundred years after German hellenism burst into bloom that a similar thing occurred in England.[1] The Roman model retained its hold

---

[1] The philhellenism of such English Romantic poets as Keats and Byron is well known, but they were superficial in their appreciation of classical Greek culture by comparison with Schiller and Hölderlin. Behind the extensive knowledge of and penetrating insight into classical Greek culture displayed by the German Romantics lay the pioneering philological work of Winckelmann. Their passion for things Greek was so exceptional as to be called by one commentator "the

on the English mind, but in late Victorian art history and literary criticism the Greeks overtook the Romans, due in part to the transmission of German classicism by such influential scholars as Benjamin Jowett and by the British Hegelians themselves. Hegel was an enthusiastic but discriminating hellenist with an intense interest in the Greek city-state. In it he found the prototype of the completely rational state, the state whose citizens are self-consciously at one with their social and political setting. The citizens of ancient Athens had been in quite unself-conscious unity with their laws, customs and gods. There had been a natural and immediate acceptance of the moral and political order. In fact, there had been for a brief period no distinction - and consequently no conflict - between the moral and political worlds. It was inconceivable that the political life of the city could be judged by any higher moral standard. As Hegel fully appreciated, it was so judged by Sophocles' Antigone. It was also judged - and found wanting - in the speeches and deeds of some of its most illustrious political leaders. It was a vital, dynamic form of political identity-in-difference, albeit inherently unstable.

The relatively unself-conscious harmony of the polis was no defence against an apolitical, individualistic moral creed. First Stoicism and then Christianity offered the individual release from the formalized social and political world which succeeded the city-state. A condition of alienation - alienation of the individual from his celestial as well as from his terrestrial city - lasted until the French Revolution, when a forcible assimilation of the two cities, and of the alienated individual to this ideal brought to earth, was attempted. The attempt was unsuccessful because the resultant state of absolute liberty was an empty proclamation. It lacked the concrete content, the diversity and particularity required to realize true freedom. The rational state, prematurely proclaimed by the French Revolution, must comprehend the intermediate phase of sheer individualism. It must give the subjective element its due.

In speaking of individualism in society, Hegel was fully aware of what was happening in the industrial towns on the Continent and in the most industrialized country, England. He also studied the work of British political economists, particularly James Steuart. What Hegel called "civil society" was basically the free market economy with a strong infusion of corporativism. This very energetic area of social life was seen by Hegel as being destructive as well as creative if not mediated by the state, by the political organ of that reason which grasps the proper place in the total scheme of things of the production of goods and services and the pursuit of wealth. The rational state does not repress economic activity or attempt to reverse its course, but it does contain and control it. It cannot merely reproduce the unself-conscious and (by modern standards) static community of the classical city-state.

One of the most important things which the French revolutionaries and their German philosophical counterparts left out of account was the complexity of the societies whose political organs they so easily removed. As has been said many times with the hindsight offered by Hegel himself and de Tocqueville, the seeds of the post-revolutionary regimes were not only present in the ancien régime but had germinated and sprouted there. The attempt to impose on French society, for example, a political ideal drawn from a Roman past or an imagined future was doomed to failure. A highly articulated social order functioned within the fossilized aristocratic regime. After the ravages of the Terror it reasserted itself. Arguably, it had to, because people cannot live without functional differentiation and the social sub-groups to which they attach themselves for their various special activities and interests. They cannot live in a continuous state of collective reformation euphoria.

---

tyranny of Greece over the German mind."
   Hegel's frequent allusion to themes from classical Greek drama is a striking feature of his work. This and other aspects of Hegel's hellenism are discussed in J.G. Gray, Hegel's Hellenic Ideal (New York, 1941).

For Hegel, the various "estates" of a modern organized society are necessary manifestations of embodied <u>Geist</u>. What Hegel failed to foresee was the sweep and dissolving power of the idea, not that all are free but that all must be free without distinction, rank or condition. On the other hand, he had more than an inkling of the anomie to be experienced by those who lived in homogeneous or homogenizing societies. Hegel was certainly not, like Burke, urging men to cling to their "little platoons" of habitual loyalty or extolling the prescriptive right of existing institutions. He did insist, however, upon the rationality of a society of differentiated - and unequal - parts. This was not to deny the changes, including future changes, wrought by social mobility and state action; but absolute freedom was quite impossible, and some sort of social order and articulation were indispensable.

In the rational state the individual citizen knows that he is free, and knows it in and through his participation in the rational will of the state. The rational will may be seen simply as an amplification of the general will, to the extent that Rousseau's "<u>moi commun</u>" is a universal "I," an element in the content of each particular consciousness which unites it with every other consciousness. Rousseau's general will was considered by some British Hegelians, notably Bernard Bosanquet, to be a prefiguring of Hegel's rational state. On Bosanquet's interpretation, Rousseau's general will is merely an area of agreement among particular individual wills; whereas Hegel's rational or objective will actually constitutes individual wills - they live entirely within it. Rousseau's state is a device to secure the private individual in the "natural liberty" which he brings with him to society. Natural liberty is the creation of bad social theory, a fiction, and the individual is an unreal abstraction apart from the society which creates and sustains him. For Hegel, the identification of the individual's moral will with the collective will of the social organism is the source and sustenance, not the denial, of personal freedom, and it is the necessary precondition for the fulfilment of individual spiritual needs and aspirations through a variety of socio-economic and cultural activities.

The notion of a social organism belongs more to the British Hegelians than to Hegel himself. It owed a great deal of its persuasiveness to the then recently developed Darwinian theory of the origin of natural species, which inspired much misguided "organic" political theory, in which the explanation of legal and other social obligations was distorted by excessive reliance upon the ideas of environmental conditioning and selective adaptation. The British Hegelians were at times led astray by the biological analogy. On the whole, however, their grounding in Aristotle - as with Hegel himself - provided them with a theory of development in which rational purpose played a large part and preserved them from the naturalistic distortions of uncritical social Darwinism. In part because of the popularity of pseudo-Darwinian theories of politics and society, in part because of their Hegelian version of naturalism, they did not simply dismiss the idea that, as a social <u>animal</u>, man is subject to a process of purely natural selection and that species survival can under certain, and not merely atavistic, circumstances shape our social norms and collective moral judgments. In spite of their ethical pitfalls, and the connotations of brutality, biological metaphors are almost inescapable in a discussion of the development of the individual moral will in a social context. It is less awkward - it "comes naturally" - to say "growth" rather than "development," which is itself indicative of the pervasiveness of the analogy. The so-called organic theory of society was well suited to explain the origin and nurture of the individual moral will. Most British Hegelians were also satisfied that it went a long way toward explaining the full nature of political man. In this latter respect they were misled, and Hegel's "rational state" and "rational will" are more appropriate headings. The distinctive feature of the fully rational state, says Hegel, is the self-consciousness of its members. They are not the member organs of an organism; they are capable of thinking themselves apart from society. They in fact do not exist apart from society, and cannot, but they are distinguishable, they lead individual lives, and they act for their community as opposed to merely carrying out its commands.

The analogy of organic growth was particularly congenial to the nineteenth century. It tied in very well with its historical studies, and the nineteenth century was pre-eminently an historical age, as the seventeenth was a scientific one. The notion that any particular national group possesses an historical development unique to itself was the great solvent of abstract social and political models. It became increasingly difficult to postulate universal conditions for order and progress. Yet the desire to find an order and a purpose within historical change itself remained as strong as ever. Hegel's philosophical system is historicist or developmental, in the sense that it recognizes actual historical differences not only as necessary but also as the working out of a single, all-pervading idea. Historical change is the medium of purposive growth. The end to which each and every one of the multiplicity of historical forms contributes is spirit's full self-knowledge, the explication of the world, which would be impossible without all the diverse forms and all the intervening stages. One of the highest of these stages is the social and political life of the rational state. Hegel regarded the Prussian limited monarchy in which he lived as the historical form most expressive of social and political rationality, but as by no means its consummation. There was nothing accidental about it, nor was it simply expedient or convenient. It was something which afforded spiritual fulfilment as much as art, religion or the pursuit of knowledge. Reason required it, and its imperfections did not detract from its essential rationality.

The notion that any political community is an indispensable self-manifestation of universal reason or the world spirit struck representative Victorian minds as extremely odd, if not bizarre. Native philosophical traditions of empiricism, "psychologism" and "common sense" realism strongly reinforced the moral and political theory of utilitarianism, and vice versa.[2] The affinity, if not the alliance, between these two streams of thought is made quite explicit in J.S. Mill's System of Logic (a work which, incidentally, had gone through nine editions and countless printings by 1875). The basic components of our experience are discrete units of sensation. From these we induce, by psychological association and assimilation, those "tendencies" amongst phenomena which further observation and experiment (if feasible) stabilize as the "laws" of the sciences of man and nature. The method of decomposition and recomposition, using the building blocks of our sensory experience, works in the theory of political reform equally as well as it does in theories of the physical universe.[3] A political community, according to classical utilitarianism, is a "fictitious body," nothing more than the individuals who compose it at any one time.[4] Continuity is a minor consideration. The institutions, the laws, the customs and rules which relate the members of a community to one another are a temporary convenience subject to unlimited alteration.[5] Parts are removable without reference to other parts or to the whole. The pieces of a social arrangement and the

---

[2] A closer examination of the chief theorists of utilitarianism is reserved till later. See ch. 6, pp. 50-56.
[3] Mill termed the proper method the "Concrete Deductive Method." (J.S. Mill, A System of Logic, 8th ed., p. 619). The Whig historian, T.B. Macaulay, was one of the first to point out that the utilitarians' method was a thinly disguised species of a priorism, and that the historical experience of government and political life in general, as captured in the theories and reflections of others, was cheerfully ignored by the utilitarians in applying their assumed "laws."
[4] Jeremy Bentham, An Introduction to the Principles of Morals and Legislation, ed. W. Harrison (Oxford, 1948), p. 126. Bentham italicized "body" and "member," presumably to indicate that they were untrustworthy metaphors of social structure.
[5] In Hobbesian fashion, Bentham claimed that the only law worthy of the name - authoritative law - is the command of the legislator (the sovereign, in John Austin's jurisprudence). There are, of course, limits to what the legislator can achieve; but these lie in his instruments, the pleasures and pains which govern human behaviour. Bentham's contempt for custom and common law is notorious: "...he who, for the purpose just mentioned or for any other, wants an example of a complete body of law to refer to must begin with making one." (Bentham, Morals and Legislation, p. 123.)

individuals who are pieces of those pieces are like the parts of a Meccano set. They may be assembled in a variety of ways, according to the design of any intelligent individual, regardless of his experience of materials and their behaviour in the real world of social construction.

The philosophical radicals, the utilitarians of the 1820s and 1830s, whose activities revolved around and gave direction to the Westminster Review, were breezily confident in the possibilities of social reconstruction. In marked contrast to their view, redolent of the eighteenth century Enlightenment, that mankind had no history, only a long and virtually unrelieved experience of misery and error, and that the human condition might be rapidly transformed by the application of a few simple principles to the problems of ignorance and injustice, was the (broadly speaking) "Anglican" view that progress was being made, that it would continue to be made, but that it would require careful cultivation of what had been slowly and painfully achieved in the past. This latter view may be called "Anglican" because it was the view of a broad spectrum of conservative reformers who, while they did not share the extreme Burkeans' belief that the aristocratic constitution of church and state was divinely ordained, nevertheless were greatly concerned that unless something was done to civilize the mass of Britons, the pressure for radical reform, which laissez-faire liberals, middle-class democrats and Chartist agitators were exerting with increasing urgency on a variety of institutions, would explode with such force that many cultural and spiritual values would be blown away with social and political privileges. The sense of social obligation, assumed yet alert, which characterized their viewpoint made them receptive to the general thrust and tone of the social and political thought of philosophical idealism. In particular, they found in the historicist rationalism and skepticism about individual liberty conveyed by idealism a friendly sign, a welcome marker in their navigation of a middle course between Whigs and Tories on the one side and "steam intellect" Radicals on the other.

The separation of the individual from his social matrix was a corollary of the Kantian theory of moral autonomy. Kant's preoccupation with the internal aspect of morality and relative neglect of intersubjective morality - what Hegel called Sittlichkeit - made him, in a limited sense, an ally of social and political atomism. This is not to say that in some devious way Kant was a utilitarian, nor that he believed that society is freshly created by each new political generation. On the contrary, he asserted the cumulative nature of society, its institutions and its mores, and also the necessity for a customary or habitual element in morality. Moreover, like Rousseau, Kant portrayed humanity as driven to construct a society of freedom under law by what he called "unsocial sociability."[6] Amour propre - envy and pursuit of "the bubble reputation" - is what poisons natural sympathy and necessitates the formation of a second human nature. Kant, again like Rousseau but without his despair, offers no solution to the "most difficult" problem of all: who or what will govern the governors of that best society in which all capacities are developed to the full but in which no one's freedom is inconsistent with anyone else's? The rulers, too, must be human, and therefore subject to amour propre and self-partiality. Kant was sanguine about the eventual realization of civic perfection - admittedly after "many vain attempts" - because "the history of mankind can be seen, in the large, as the realization of nature's secret plan to bring forth a perfectly constituted state."[7]

All this sounds a bit like Hegel's world spirit, and the List der Vernunft weaving its unexpected patterns in human history. However, Kant's political proposals were rationalistic projects of enlightened reform, the sort of thing which Hegel averred to be dangerously

---

[6] Immanuel Kant, Idea for a Universal History from a Cosmopolitan Point of View, trans. L.W. Beck, in Kant on History, ed. Beck (Indianapolis, 1963), pp. 11-26. See especially theses 4, 5 and 6.
[7] I. Kant, Universal History, p. 21.

unrealistic, an abstraction with no grip on actuality. In addition, his moral philosophy pulled him further toward the view that society is composed of self-legislating, strictly autonomous individuals. The individual cannot manufacture the content of his moral will entirely for himself; but the goodness of that will lies entirely in its self-consistency. The measure of morality is an internal one. The autonomous moral agent obeys a universal and impersonal law, paying no heed to subjective whims and inclinations or to the blandishments of mere propriety and taste. The principal defect of the good will, in Hegel's eyes, was its being unattached to time or place, to social conditions. It was an abstract universal. The moral actions of the possessor of a good will are motivated entirely by a sense of duty - duty to the moral law, which law requires that one legislate for oneself as if one were legislating for everyone. The good will is neither deflected nor reinforced by any other motive than that of acting in such a way that its action may become the basis of a universal maxim.[8] The Kantian individual obeys a bleak and stoical law which tends to cut him off from others. He is an end in himself, living in a "kingdom of ends." Every human being in this kingdom is an end in himself; no one is to be treated as a means to some other end. As Kant himself was aware, such a kingdom of ends-in-themselves is an ideal. All any existing society can do is strive to approximate to that ideal, since a society consisting of perfectly Kantian individuals would be an anarchy, with no need for any reserve of political power to enforce their social behaviour. They would be incapable of disregarding the rightful claims of each other; they would exist in rational harmony, undisturbed by self-interest. They would share no overriding common interest, because they could no more be the means to a common end than they could to each other. A community of people living according to the Kantian ethic would not really be a community. It was abstraction from concrete social and political conditions which Hegel regarded as the major defect in Kant's moral philosophy. Kant further failed to see that a common temporal interest permits the individual to realize himself as an end in himself, that it is the peculiar nature of a community to overcome the apparent opposition between ends and means in material as well as moral concerns. What Kant called a heteronomous end, one not freely chosen, is not therefore immoral or subversive of the good will. There is nothing immoral in being compelled to meet one's bodily as well as spiritual needs.

"The fact that man is a living being, however, is not fortuitous, but in conformity with reason, and to that extent he has a right to make his needs his end. There is nothing degrading in being alive, and there is no mode of intelligent being higher than life in which existence would be possible."[9]

In a well-governed community the satisfaction of needs is a cooperative pursuit, a common endeavour. The citizen of any state - because every state approximates in some degree to the rational state - is a means to an end which includes himself. His state may be very wide of the mark, it may be excessively devoted to the pursuit of material gain for its own sake, but he cannot fulfil himself by trying to destroy it or by withdrawing from it. However imperfect, it is for him the only available vehicle for the realization of rational freedom.

Hegel attempted to contain economic, political and cultural forces released or accelerated by the French Revolution and the Napoleonic wars within the framework of a political dispensation which, in the event, proved constricting and ephemeral, unequal to the task. His brand of liberal constitutionalism was an interpretation of events in Prussia which took a reactionary turn even before his death; and the explosive powers of democracy and nationalism were to prove a combination beyond the capacity of <u>Vernunft</u> and objective mind. New social forms - in industry, communications and urban life - broke out of the confines of traditional political structures or forced them to make radical alterations. That society and not the state

---

[8] "Every maxim that does not so qualify is opposed to morality." Immanuel Kant, <u>Introduction to the Metaphysics of Morals</u>, trans. J. Ladd, in <u>The Metaphysical Elements of Justice</u>, ed. Ladd (Indianapolis, 1965), p. 27.

[9] G.W.F. Hegel, <u>Philosophy of Right</u>, trans. T.M. Knox (Oxford, 1942), <u>Zusätz</u> to para. 123, p. 252.

was setting the pace of human development - and that it should do so - became the common contention of reformers and revolutionaries. That the Rechtstaat could harmonize the new forms of human endeavour, and direct their energies into purposes dictated by what Hegel called the "rational will," was either an anachronism or divination of the world spirit. What Hegel perceived most acutely was the potency of what his immediate predecessors had done to create a philosophical image of the self-possessed human being for whom nothing was impossible and whose highest standard was self-consistency. A fascination with will power was one of philosophical idealism's chief legacies.[10] Only Hegel offered a logic of the will to reconcile without neutralizing self-determination and the determinateness of the world. However, there was no returning to any conception of mankind as part of the chain of being. Kant's transcendentalism made it possible to conceive of human reason as the final arbiter of the world and the individual moral will as the only absolutely and unconditionally good thing.

Kant's kingdom of ends has continued to exert a powerful political appeal, both as a utopia and as a discipline for the culture of self-mastery. Kantian ethics owed much of its original "muscle" to German Pietism (a significant factor in Kant's personal background and development), and it found an echo in the English Puritan tradition of belief in salvation by self-improvement and taking the war between good and evil to the forces of evil. Many of the British Hegelians were products of that tradition and, as imperfectly "mediated" Kantians, they ranked the good will above the good society.

The British utilitarians saw a balance of interests in society. Kant postulated a regulative ideal sustained by a universal, passionless sense of duty. For the former, society was little more than a referee, and laws and institutions exceeding the minimum required to ensure civil peace, order and fair play were a mischievous obstruction; for the latter, society was a moral cocoon, superfluous to the fully rational individual. Both the utilitarian "fact" and the Kantian ideal portray the individual as morally self-sufficient and disregard the positive moral function of society - that of providing both the source and the fulfilment of the individual's moral being. Neither Kant nor the utilitarians could conceive of the whole of society - the conflicts of interest, the articulation of functions and classes, and the body of received law and custom - as the true expression of rational freedom. This conception was Hegel's most important contribution to social and political theory. His rational state was a necessary stage in the unfolding of the world spirit; it was a logical necessity in the special Hegelian, historicist usage of "logic."

It was not until the last quarter of the nineteenth century that philosophical idealism gained sufficient purchase on British thinking to be able to provide a systematic alternative to the incoherent but influential utilitarian consensus, whose authority was such that other theories effectively accepted its terms. Without a philosophy, the doubts and reservations expressed by mainstream social critics such as J.S. Mill and Matthew Arnold could prick but not get under the skin of native insularity. It was the British Hegelians who challenged the supremacy of the dominant theories of mind and nature - for example, associationist psychology and the crude inductivism which appeared to work so well in the triumphs of British applied science. Although they could not evict what Bradley contemptuously called "the school of experience," they soon succeeded in domesticating philosophical idealism. The Marxists failed dismally in their efforts to convince any but a minuscule number of British thinkers that their philosophy was anything but an alien intrusion, although much of the empiricism and materialism of Engels' "scientific socialism" was congenial to the nineteenth century English mind. It was competition from pragmatism and logical positivism - two philosophies of partially foreign provenance - which proved most damaging to philosophical idealism. In the process of naturalizing Hegel and giving him a new home, the British Hegelians lost sight of elements in

---

[10] It still fuels the debate between revolutionary and evolutionary Marxists, the former arguing that history can be made to fulfil its purpose by an act or acts of revolutionary will.

his thought which were subsequently re-appropriated by others, including some of his compatriots who had earlier rejected him. As part of the hardening and narrowing tendency, some minor British Hegelians propagated a somewhat preachy, Sunday-school version of Hegel, which was an easy target for critics. The main British rendition of Hegelianism, however, offered a solution to the liberal (and Liberal) dilemma - an almost subconscious, quasi-metaphysical attachment to rampaging subjectivity, combined with deep anxiety about the quality of life thus freely created - which did not involve any radical discontinuity or jettisoning of widely held values.

CHAPTER 2

The Prehistory of Hegelianism in Britain

The British Hegelians constituted an informal philosophical school whose lifespan was almost exactly fifty years, from the publication of the Green and Grose edition of Hume's Treatise of Human Nature in 1874 until the deaths of Bernard Bosanquet, F.H. Bradley and J.McT.E. McTaggart in 1923, 1924 and 1925 respectively. This school of thought must be called informal, because the British Hegelians, while all acknowledging a substantial debt to Hegel, vary considerably in the use to which they put Hegelian ideas. Bradley maintained that the "Hegelian School" existed only in "our reviews," and during the course of his philosophical career he gradually moved away from what he saw as the excessive intellectualism of Hegel's philosophy, although he never repudiated spiritual monism. The leading role which conscience plays in T.H. Green's moral and political philosophy was the result of a strong infusion of Kantian ethical principles. Andrew Seth (Pringle-Pattison), like Green, professed to be more Kantian than Hegelian. He and the personal idealists were alarmed by the tendency, as they saw it, of the Hegelian One to swallow up and extinguish individual personality. Some of them professed a sort of pragmatic humanism, and (ironically) attacked Bradley as the most intellectualist of the Hegelians. McTaggart's variation on the Hegelian theme was that the dialectic of categories, sound in itself, could be legitimately used to arrive at metaphysical conclusions far different than Hegel's, and that Hegel's moral and political philosophy had no necessary place in the dialectical process.[1] He shared the personal idealists' quasi-religious conviction that the most real thing, metaphysically speaking, was human personality, but not the Christian beliefs of most of them. Christianity proved one of the most stubborn obstacles to Hegel's being accepted in Britain, and the next chapter will review the theologically based resistance to Hegelianism.

Although German philosophical idealism shows a line of continuous development from Kant through Fichte and Schelling to Hegel, it did not come to Britain in easy stages, one preparing the way for the next. Certainly Kant was known of and discussed in Britain long before Hegel became an object of study, but it is a curious fact that, with the exception of Sir William Hamilton and the utilitarian, Henry Sidgwick, little serious and sustained attention was paid to Kant's philosophy until the British Hegelians launched their attack-in-depth upon empiricism and utilitarianism in the 1870s. Edward Caird's Critical Account of the Philosophy of Kant, the first important study of Kant's philosophy in English, appeared in 1877.[2] For their attack, the British Hegelians drew upon the full armoury of German philosophical idealism. For the first time in Britain - some eighty years after part of the first Critique had been translated - Kant's thought was being thoroughly examined and assimilated.[3] As in the case of Hegel, the initial period of misunderstanding was a prolonged one, although in Kant's case there was not

---

[1] McTaggart, in C.D. Broad's words, "pulls some intriguing rabbits out of the Hegelian hat."
[2] Caird's is the idealist interpretation of Kant, emphasizing his positive views, and severely critical of his negative strictures, on metaphysics. Caird regarded Kant as a precursor of Hegel, and Hegelianism as the consummation of the Critical philosophy. This interpretation was repeated in his Critical Philosophy of Immanuel Kant (1889). Hamilton's is the positivist, anti-metaphysical interpretation of Kant, an agnostic position on the nature of reality - or the Unconditioned, in Hamiltonian terminology.
[3] See chapter 1 of René Wellek's Immanuel Kant in England, 1793-1838 (Princeton, 1931) for a discussion of the pioneering efforts of Nitsch and Willich to interest the British in Kant's thought, and of the Kant translations by the Scot, John Richardson.

the same degree of second-hand condemnation and moral obloquy. The failure to appreciate and understand Kant was primarily a failure to recognize the central problem of his philosophy. In spite of the fact that it had first been raised by a British philosopher, Hume, the climate of philosophical opinion in Britain during the first half and more of the nineteenth century was such that Kant's statement of the problem and his treatment of it were largely ignored. Hume's empiricist successors had put together a makeshift solution, which, although it did not come to grips with the problem, satisfied all but the most pertinaciously metaphysical philosophers. As will be seen in subsequent chapters, the British Hegelians themselves tended to either see Kant through Hegelian spectacles or retreat from philosophical idealism to such an extent that in some cases their views on knowledge and its limits resembled those of Locke or Hume.

Hegel's initial reception in Britain resembles that of Kant insofar as both philosophers underwent a lengthy period of being treated with either blank indifference or irritated perplexity - added to which in Hegel's case was the prejudicial suspicion that something atheistic was afoot. The first abortive attempts by a handful of enthusiasts to bring Kant to the reluctant attention of the British philosophical community have been described in detail by Wellek. In this chapter Hegel's equally unpromising beginnings in Britain will be recounted. The remaining chapters will concern not the early and usually superficial transpositions of Hegel's philosophy, but the growth of the richest fruit of the Hegelian seed, a distinctively British form of Hegelianism.

Hegel's name is mentioned on several occasions by British commentators during the 1830s, 1840s and 1850s, but it is seldom more than a bare mention. The first time he was noticed in a philosophical context was in Sir William Hamilton's "The Philosophy of the Unconditioned," an essay written in 1829.[4] He was a representative of the Scottish school of philosophy, which had culminated in the eighteenth century moralist Thomas Reid, whose Works Hamilton edited (1846-63). The reference to Hegel is only a passing one, and Hamilton, while familiar with and to some extent influenced by Kant, never displayed any knowledge of Hegel. The first time his name appeared in print in English, as a "figure" contributing to the study of philosophy and deserving of some consideration, however small, was in a translation of W.G. Tennemann's History of Philosophy, originally written in 1812, abridged to a "manual" in 1829, brought up to date by a Professor Wendt, and translated by Rev. A. Johnson in 1832. Wendt's chief contribution was an undiscriminating list of recent German philosophers. Hegel appears twice: first, coupled with Krause, a very minor figure, as a lapsed Schellingian, and secondly, in Wendt's appended list, as "G.W.F. Hegel (a professor at Berlin) whose system is one of Absolute Idealism." In 1852 Johnson's translation of Tennemann's Manual was revised, enlarged and continued by J.R. Morell. In his preface Morell states that in the intervening 20 years "England has become familiar with the German mind." But he affords no evidence that this familiarity was anything but superficial, or that the English mind had progressed beyond Carlyle's uneasy feeling that something of great spiritual moment had been stirred up by the German mind. Morell does attempt an evaluation, while admitting that "it is scarcely possible to do common justice to such a complicated system as Hegel's in a compendium like the present." Although he does not do justice to Hegel, at least his writing is free of that religious indignation which disfigured so much contemporary British discussion of German philosophy. He was apparently not interested in Hegel's theological shortcomings, and his brief sketch of Left Hegelianism - in the shape of David Strauss' Biblical criticism and Feuerbach's anthropomorphism - exhibits none of the virulent hostility then widely felt towards foreign philosophy and the threat it allegedly posed to native piety. His benevolence toward Hegel

---

[4] This and some other early works were collected by Hamilton for his Discussions on Philosophy and Literature (London, 1853). In the Dawes Hicks Lecture on Philosophy to the British Academy for 1971, Anthony Quinton comments on Hamilton's inexplicable claim to have known several distinguished British Hegelians that Hamilton was notoriously loose about facts. (A. Quinton, Absolute Idealism, p. 20.)

himself may be attributable to his fundamental error of believing the Hegelian system to be one of subjective idealism.

One instalment of an abridged translation of Heinrich Heine's Series of Essays on German Literature and Men of Letters appeared in The Atheneaum, July 6, 1833. With his mocking irony, Heine derided Hegel as a mere lackey of the Prussian church and state. Whether, even with his literary reputation, Heine carried sufficient weight with the English reading public to offset the subsequent impression that Hegel was a satanic figure is doubtful.

The earliest British mention of Hegel which is both favourable and based on some first-hand (or at least accurate second-hand) knowledge is in a review of five books on aesthetics - one of them being Hegel's Vorlesungen über die Aesthetik - which appeared in No. 25 of the British and Foreign Review for 1842.[5] The author - G.H. Lewes - bemoans the unreflective, unphilosophical state of English art and criticism and recommends the careful reading of Hegel as an antidote. He notes that while the works of such German writers as Lessing, Winckelmann, Jean Paul, Schiller, Schelling and Novalis are talked about in England, "the masterly and comprehensive 'Lectures' of Hegel remain without even the most vague and general notice."[6] He quotes the biographer Gans with approval, to the effect that Hegel could have no successor, "for philosophy with him accomplished its circle."[7] Lewes' assessment is self-contradictory, however: first, he insists that the English would do well to study Hegel's philosophy of art; then he suggests that Hegel's particular artistic judgments are the chief benefit to the student and the philosophical part dispensable, whereas the point of his article is the deplorably unsystematic state of English art criticism. It makes interesting reading in the light of his later scorn for Hegel. However, Lewes was always ready to concede the value and readability of Hegel's lectures on art, history and religion, while dismissing the rest of his work as obscure and confused. In his view, the Aesthetik is a delightful and instructive gloss upon repellent first principles.

Lewes appropriated two Hegelian ideas: that of the spirit of the age, of which art is a principal manifestation; and that of the purely explanatory role of any philosophical activity, such as aesthetics. Art, religion and philosophy, he says, are different ways of approaching the same truth. The poet "makes you in love with the truth and virtue, which religion has ordained and philosophy proved."[8] In spite of the hint of a Hegelian formula here, it would be quite wrong to suggest that this article was the seed of British Hegelianism. Lewes was rare at that time in having a sympathetic interest in any aspect of Hegel's philosophy.[9]

The first issue of The Oxford Magazine, which appeared in May 1845, contains an anonymous article on the German poet, Ludwig Tieck, in the course of which the author praises German philosophy - in particular, Kant, Fichte, Schelling and Novalis - for its services to moral and religious truth. He is of the opinion that if faith is to replace calculation in English

---

[5] This unsigned article is not anonymous. The Dictionary of National Biography attributes it to G.H. Lewes, the English positivist writer. George Henry Lewes (1817-1878) had little formal education, but travelled in France and Germany a great deal. He possessed a wide knowledge of European literature, especially dramatic. After a brief career as an actor he became a journalist. He wrote articles and essays on physiology as well as on psychology and philosophy. Lewes also wrote some novels and a play. But his literary achievements are extremely minor in comparison with those of his second wife, George Eliot. Their relationship began through a mutual interest in Comte and positivism.
[6] British and Foreign Review, vol. XIII, p. 39.
[7] Ibid.
[8] Ibid., p. 26.
[9] In a footnote Lewes claims that "the Times has quoted Hegel," which says more about the editorial style of that newspaper than about the reading public's state of knowledge.

thought and action, then "the admission of the fundamental principle of the entire system of modern German thought is and must be an indispensable condition." The article is remarkable, not only for its uncommonly favourable estimate of the moral and religious effects of German philosophy, but also for a curious reference to the allegedly wider English acquaintance with German philosophical literature. "At the beginning of this century, long passages of Hegel appeared translated in the writings of an English philosopher and there was no danger of detection." If he was referring to Coleridge - and it is hard to imagine whom else - then he was surely mistaken. Coleridge has been detected quoting Kant and Schelling without acknowledgment, but not Hegel.

J.D. Morell - unrelated to J.R. Morell - published An Historical and Critical View of the Speculative Philosophy of Europe in the Nineteenth Century in 1846.[10] His criticism of Hegel is largely theological. He saw in the Hegelian system the zenith of rationalism, and in Left Hegelians such as Strauss and Baur the inevitable disintegration of that system of thought. Hegelianism "may charm the mind that loves to rationalize upon every religious doctrine," yet "it can assuredly give but little consolation to the heart that is yearning with earnest longings after holiness and immortality."[11] He clearly had a generally correct appreciation of the place of religion in Hegel's philosophy: "Religion, if not destroyed by the Hegelian philosophy, is absorbed in it and as religion forever disappears."[12] Morell makes some shrewd observations upon Hegel's philosophy, remarking that the unity of contradictories is not as counter to common sense as it might appear. "As knowledge advances, differences become more and more merged into higher principles." The unity of thought and being contains a "germ of truth," because the "Universal Being" is a purely rational conception, a necessary idea which "does not come to its full reality except in the human consciousness."[13] Complaining that Hegel's unity of thought and being destroyed God and human freedom, Morell - at this stage at least - did nothing to dispel the prevailing suspicion and hostility felt toward philosophical idealism.

In a course of lectures entitled On the Philosophical Tendencies of the Age, delivered two years later in Edinburgh and Glasgow, Morell seems to have become somewhat reconciled to Hegel and rationalistic philosophy. He now maintains that philosophy is the property of everyman, that it appeals to "the common reason of humanity at large," a phrase which recalls Hegel's aphorism about the philosopher and his ladder which he cannot pull up after himself. Perhaps the democratic spirit of 1848 elicited a positive response in Morell. By 1856 he was still more receptive to German philosophical idealism. In "Modern German Philosophy," his contribution to the first two issues of a short-lived journal called Manchester Papers, he notes a welcome change in the English attitude toward German metaphysical speculation. In his own words, "the suspicion has oozed out that there are really grains of gold and specks of diamonds amongst this immense mass of reputed rubbish."[14] He is still highly critical of what he regarded as Hegel's confusion of the "formal processes of thinking and the real process of things themselves. This part of his philosophical system, to say the least, comes very near to a play upon words."[15] However, Morell has clearly been impressed by some of the more striking features

---

[10] John Daniel Morell (1816-91) studied theology at Homerton and philosophy at the Universities of Glasgow and Bonn. He was an Independent minister at Gosport from 1842 to 1845. He was appointed an inspector of schools on the strength of his Historical and Critical View, which post he held from 1848 to 1876.
[11] J.D. Morell, An Historical and Critical View of the Speculative Philosophy of Europe in the Nineteenth Century, vol. II, p. 154.
[12] Ibid., p. 159. Quinton commends Morell for his acuity in perceiving the threat posed by Hegelianism to revealed religion, and says that his survey provided "a fairly reasonable account of the main outlines of Hegel's system." (A. Quinton, Absolute Idealism, p. 20.)
[13] J.D. Morell, Historical and Critical View, vol. II, p. 156.
[14] J.D. Morell, Manchester Papers, vol. I, p. 6.
[15] Ibid., p. 105. The accusation that he punned his way out of contradictions was to become a

of Hegel's philosophy of history, which he retails in a somewhat tendentious fashion. Hegel is now the philospher of Protestantism and representative of one of the very highest stages in the dialectic of freedom and authority - but not its culmination. This, we learn, is embodied in the Church of England. But even here the conflict has broken out afresh. Morell is confident, though, that a new synthesis of faith and reason, authority and freedom, will emerge. Morell's Philosophical Fragments were published in 1878 and a Manual of the History of Philosophy in 1884, which treats of the Left, Right and Centre Hegelians rather than of Hegel himself.

In the same year (1846) that J.D. Morell published his Historical and Critical View of the Speculative Philosophy of Europe in the Nineteenth Century, the second series of G.H. Lewes' Biographical History of Philosophy - "from Bacon to the present day" - appeared. It is written with a heavy bias in favour of British empiricism and takes the positivist line that metaphysics is simply bad logic. Hegel is dismissed as a verbal juggler and as not substantially different from Schelling. He added only a method - which is true to the extent that Hegel's method and his results are inseparable. Together, however, they constitute a philosophical system far removed from that of Schelling, and as a critic of Hegel's "method" Lewes hardly inspires confidence. He begins his treatment of Hegel's notion of an identity underlying all contradiction by calling it "the logical law of the identity of contraries."[16] Whereas contraries can exist side by side, contradictories cannot - which is the motive power of the Hegelian system. Lewes concedes that there are thoughts "to be grappled with" in Kant and Fichte; but "in Hegel the form is everything...his distinctions are only verbal."[17] Verbal quibbling, however, is a defect of metaphysics per se:

"Philosophy itself, in all its highest speculations, is but a more or less ingenious playing upon words. From Thales to Hegel, verbal distinctions have always formed the ground of philosophy and must ever do so as long as we are unable to penetrate the essence of things."[18]

Whether Lewes thought that there could come a time when we would be able to "penetrate the essence of things" is difficult to say. Certainly Hegel's was not, for Lewes, the way to such knowledge. As for Schelling, his identification of philosophy and religion is the closing of the metaphysical circle, the inevitable debacle of German philosophical idealism.

The 1857 edition of Lewes' Biographical History of Philosophy is even more positivist in tone. Here he makes the Comtean claim that he is writing the first post-philosophical history of philosophy, that he is writing as a representative of the coming scientific age, in which it will be universally recognized that truth can be attained only through the "method of verification" and only about co-existences and successions of natural phenomena. In 1867 his survey appeared, revised and expanded, as A History of Philosophy from Thales to Comte. His estimate of Hegel remained unchanged. The 1871 edition of the expanded version contains much additional material on Hegel. Lewes had read J.H. Stirling's Secret of Hegel, and although it confirmed his view that Hegel's position was totally untenable, it forced him to take Hegel seriously - insofar as he was able to take any metaphysician seriously. He quotes both Hegel and Stirling at length, and he has a few kind words to say about Hegel's philosophy of history and philosophy of religion. The burden of his criticism is still the positivist-empiricist contention that Hegel is futilely attempting to "coerce nature." Lewes' History of Philosophy, in all its various versions, went through several editions, spanning thirty-odd years of British intellectual life. It is difficult to assess its influence precisely, but it and the cast of mind it represented were a formidable obstacle to the acceptance of philosophical idealism.

---

refrain of twentieth century critiques of Hegel.
16 G.H. Lewes, Biographical History of Philosophy, vol. IV, pp. 206-08. Earlier in this segment he describes Kant's forms and categories as innate ideas antecedent to experience.
17 Ibid., p. 230.
18 Ibid., p. 219.

In 1848 German philosophy became a topical subject. Germany did not escape the revolutionary upheavals of that year, whereas Britain did. There were many quick to draw the conclusion that Britain should increase her vigilance against subversive notions being flung out from the Continental "vortex of infidel democracy." J.D. Morell's <u>On the Philosophical Tendencies of the Age</u> was unusual in its sanguinity about the democratic implications of full-blooded rationalism. Among much that was written to the opposite effect, Hegel is named only once as a disseminator of subversive ideas, in an anonymous article entitled "The German Mind," in <u>The English Review</u> for December 1848. It professes to discuss, among other things, Strauss' <u>Leben Jesu</u> and a book by Gervinus on the philosophy of Hegel, as well as the works of both Lessing and Goethe. In fact, it is a political tract attacking disestablishment and universal suffrage, ideas for which the German mind was held responsible. The following passage is redolent of the prevailing cultural insularity at that time, an insularity combined with a sense of duty to the lesser breeds which was later to find its outlet further afield:

> "...we regard her [Germany's] pseudo-philosophy and her false humanitarianism with Christian pity and regret.... False modesty must not stay us from reminding the fallen German race that our national intellect <u>is</u> clearer and more practical than theirs; and that <u>that</u> Christianity is to us a Divine reality which appears to them a fiction; <u>that</u> freedom a noble and glorious possession which they would sacrifice to democratic lawlessness!"[19]

The ultimate villain of the piece was Goethe, an intellectually self-indulgent man whose place in German life and letters was such that he could have prevented the subsequent "triumph of Teutonic lawlessness."

Two items were published in 1855 which show some originality in their treatment of Hegelian ideas. The first is a translation of Hegel's "Mind Subjective" by H. Sloman and J. Wallon, "revised by a graduate of Oxford, and to which are added some remarks by H.S."[20] Sloman's remarks on Hegel are noteworthy, principally for two things: their illustrating a mood of receptivity to philosophical idealism of all kinds; and their striking resemblance to F.H. Bradley's "bloodless categories" outburst against Hegelian panlogism in his <u>Principles of Logic</u>.

> "Can we believe that those rich varieties by which we are surrounded – life, the soul, love, virtue and others – that these are everywhere and always the result of that one trilogical form of proceeding – thesis, antithesis, synthesis?"[21]

As for the first resemblance, the following passage is not unlike what John Grote was saying at the time and what Bradley was to say some twenty years later:

> "We are not foreign to the world wherein we live. The same tide of existence that sustains it flows through us, and it is not strange that a strong sympathy should make our instinct often at once conform to what our slower reason afterwards shows us to be the truth, but in every case many faults are and must be committed; the greatest of all being, perhaps, the necessity of dividing or decomposing that which is essentially one – a whole."[22]

Sloman's position on knowledge of the Absolute is that of H.L. Mansel.[23] It was an irreligious presumption on Hegel's part to assert the unity of thought and being; the human mind, without

---

19 <u>The English Review</u>, vol. X, p. 388.
20 <u>The Subjective Logic of Hegel</u>, trans. Sloman and Wallon (London, 1855). This was the first work of Hegel's to be translated into English, in this case from a French version which appeared in 1854. J. Sibree's translation of Hegel's <u>Lectures on the Philosophy of History</u> appeared in 1857, with a short preface by the translator expressing approval of the work's "leading conceptions."
21 H. Sloman, <u>Logic of Hegel</u>, p. 95. Compare F.H. Bradley, <u>Principles of Logic</u>, 2nd ed. (Oxford, 1922), pp. 590-91.
22 H. Sloman, <u>Logic of Hegel</u>, p. 72. See ch. 7, p. 57.
23 See ch. 3, p. 32.

the aid of faith, is incapable of knowing God and grasping the whole truth of things.

The way to acquire philosophical knowledge is Schelling's way, the way of "spontaneous intuition." The adoption of the so-called Schellingian method "places us between the excessive modesty of Kant, on the one hand, and the lofty pretentiousness of Hegel on the other; and besides, Faith, in this method, preserves its full value."[24] Sloman concludes with an aphorism which serves to remove him a long way not only from Hegel but from the whole philosophical enterprise:

"Not truth alone, but Goodness is our final end and aim: the ideal of both is in us, not distinct but instinct; not as science, but as conscience!"[25]

With the exception of phrases, chapter headings and other snatches, Hegel was not available in English until the Sloman and Wallon translation of the "Lesser Logic." Apart from a few selections in Stirling's Secret of Hegel and in the work of some of the St. Louis Hegelians in America, there were no further Hegel translations of any significance until the British Hegelians took on the task in the 1870s and after.

The second noteworthy item from 1855 is one of the contributions to a collection of essays entitled Oxford Essays. In the eighth essay, T.C. Sandars examines Hegel's Philosophy of Right.[26] Although only an essay - and ostensibly a summary - it was the first serious study of Hegel's political philosophy in English. Sandars had grasped the meaning of the Hegelian idea of Recht, and expressed it in a manner which was both fresh and faithful to the original:

"Prescription is not a matter of merely positive law, arranged for the advantage of the community; but it is a matter of natural right. It is the expression of the necessity which the will is under of continually exhibiting itself as external."[27]

He praises Hegel's elevation of the universal conscience of the state over that of the individual, of objective over subjective right, while recognizing the reciprocal nature of the organic theory of the state.

"Freedom attains its highest objective expression, while at the same time the freedom of the subjective will works unimpeded, for the State is the highest method of carrying out and developing the individual."[28]

It is not merely an ideal; it is "the sovereignty which makes the worst state still a state, like the principle of life which makes the cripple alive."[29]

Sandars took Hegel's "deification" of the state literally, accepting it as the will of God "expressed in the present world."[30] This was a most unusual view to hold in mid-Victorian England. It was also an erroneous one, insofar as Hegel's "deification" of anything was intended to be purely metaphorical. God was, for Hegel, the Word made flesh, not a transcendent being who can intervene in the world at will. "The march of God in the world" was an immanent and rational process for Hegel. Sandars understood at least one aspect of this process - that Hegel did not intend an exact correlation between the historical development of right and the dialectic of its idea; he was not trying to force historical forms into a logical order, nor make the moments of reason wait upon history. His rendering of one of Hegel's shrewdest observations upon Kant's moral theory is particularly good:

"Well-being is not good without right, nor is right good without well-being. We must

---

[24] H. Sloman, Logic of Hegel, p. 96.
[25] Ibid.
[26] Thomas Collett Sandars (1825-94) was a fellow of Oriel College, Oxford, and reader of constitutional law and history to the Inns of Court, 1865-73. His edition of Justinian's Institutes appeared in 1853.
[27] T.C. Sandars, Oxford Essays, p. 223.
[28] Ibid., p. 243.
[29] Ibid.
[30] Ibid., p. 244.

not say, Fiat justitia, pereat mundus, for we require that the world should be preserved as well as justice done."[31]
This is a point which Bradley was to drive home with great force and elegance in Ethical Studies. Sandars' study contains other evidence of an unusually acute understanding of Hegel's political philosophy. For example, he recognized that British economic life was a good illustration of Hegel's "civil society," and that Hegel's account of economic interdependence and of the dialectic of economic want and gratification owed something to British political economy.

The following year (1856) the French Hegel enthusiast, Augusto Véra, published a work in English which loosely linked the imported and the home-grown British varieties of philosophical idealism.[32] He purported to see in a work such as Ferrier's Institutes (of which more in a moment) signs of a revival of British interest in metaphysics, in "true philosophy." What little he has to say about Hegel marks no critical advance upon native British commentary. There is a great deal of diatribe against the philosophy of common sense and the alleged British predilection for applying the criterion of practicality in philosophical questions. Apart from the occasional mechanical references to Hegel which continued to appear in historical surveys, there is nothing worthy of comment between the English publication of Véra's work and Stirling's Secret of Hegel (1865).

None of the first British attempts to come to grips with Hegel are as intrinsically interesting as that entirely home-grown philosophical idealism which has already been alluded to. J.F. Ferrier and John Grote were elaborating distinctive idealist philosophies of their own during the 1850s and 1860s.[33] Ferrier denied any Hegelian influence, saying: "I am no follower of Hegel. I cannot follow what I do not understand."[34] His not understanding Hegel did not, however, deter him from writing an article on Hegel for the Imperial Dictionary of Universal Biography.[35] His remarks on Hegel's thought concentrate on the difficulties of the notion of the Absolute and its identification with rational self-consciousness. He questions Kant's theory of knowledge and its preclusion of the Hegelian solution to the problem. One of Ferrier's remarks is worth quoting, because it shows that, in spite of his disclaimer, he understood at least one important feature of Hegel's philosophy:

"Schelling was of the opinion that the citadel of truth was to be carried by a

---

[31] Ibid., p. 230. Compare G.W.F. Hegel, Philosophy of Right, trans. T.M. Knox (Oxford, 1942), para. 130, p. 87.
[32] A. Véra, An Inquiry into Speculative and Experimental Science (London, 1856). Véra's translation of Hegel's Encyclopaedia into French appeared in 1863. His Introduction à la Philosophie de Hegel went through two editions (Paris, 1855 and 1864).
[33] James Frederick Ferrier (1808-1864), after two years' study at Edinburgh, went to Magdalen College, Oxford, where he was much influenced by Sir William Hamilton. He graduated in 1831, after which he studied German philosophy at Heidelberg in 1834. He was Professor of Civil History at Edinburgh University from 1842 to 1845 and Professor of Moral Philosophy and Political Economy at the University of St. Andrews from 1845 to 1864.
John Grote (1813-1866) was a younger brother of George Grote, the historian. An undergraduate at Trinity College, Cambridge, he was elected a fellow in 1837. He was ordained in 1844 and moved to the college living at Trumpington in 1847. He succeeded Whewell as Knightsbridge Professor of Moral Philosophy in 1855. The first volume of his chief work, Exploratio Philosophica, appeared in 1865, the second not until 1900.
[34] J.F. Ferrier, Scottish Philosophy: The Old and the New (Edinburgh, 1856), p. 22. Anthony Quinton retells J.H. Stirling's story, that he discovered Ferrier reading a work of Hegel's upside down because he couldn't make any sense out of it right way up (Absolute Idealism, p. 21).
[35] This was collected in his "Philosophical Remains," vol. III of The Philosophical Works of the Late James Frederick Ferrier (Edinburgh, 1888).

coup de main, by a genial 'intellectual intuition.' Hegel conceived that it was to be won only by slow sap and regular logical approaches."[36]

Ferrier's magnum opus, Institutes of Metaphysics, was first published in 1854. In the tradition of British empiricism, its starting point is the problem of knowledge. Its conclusion is that mind per se and matter per se are unknowable. "Minds together with what they apprehend are the only veritable existences."[37] He asserts the "indissoluble unity" of subject and object - which has a distinctly Hegelian ring about it. However, by that unity he does not mean what Hegel means. For Hegel, the unity of thought and being entails an identity of identity and non-identity; reason actualizes itself in all the diversity of the natural and historical worlds. Ferrier places rational self-consciousness in opposition to sense-perception and the human passions, thus seriously impairing the full unity of thought and being. For Ferrier, this unity was not merely a necessary condition of any knowledge at all, but also a limitation upon knowledge. For all his willingness to see in Hegel the hard but sure way to philosophical truth, Ferrier did not allow for an Absolute which is anything more than an abstract universal set over against concrete particulars. It is, in effect, the Kantian thing-in-itself on Ferrier's interpretation. The ultimate reality or unreality of the external world is, in Ferrier's system, an unanswerable question. There is an external world, but only in its relation to minds. Minds cannot penetrate beyond the knower-known relationship; they are confined to the act - or state - of knowing. Ferrier's "agnoiology," or theory of ignorance, was an attempt, reminiscent of Kant, to delimit the range of valid metaphysical speculation. In this respect it resembles Sir William Hamilton's philosophy of the "Conditioned."[38] Ferrier owed little to Kant, however. His work was an original attempt to work out a solution to problems posed by sensationalist and Scottish "common sense" philosophy.

Unlike Ferrier, Grote was quite unsystematic, and deliberately so. His work is remembered primarily for its idealist aperçus. He stressed the need for the mind to be "at home" in the world of its experience. That the mind is adequate to the expression of the whole of experience in all its complexity, that there is nothing that the mind cannot penetrate and there find a reflection of itself, is the central Hegelian theme. But, as Ferrier dimly perceived, Hegel was a systematic philosopher; his results were achieved by a long, logical, step-by-step process, not by "genial intuitions."

Grote expressly made a sort of rational intuitivism the foundation of his moral philosophy. Pronouncements about virtue and duty emanating from our intuitive faculty point us in the same direction as the principles of utility and the greatest happiness. The greatest happiness of the greatest number is itself an intuited ideal. Sidgwick's utilitarian synthesis, universalistic hedonism, was in part inspired by this idea of Grote's and by his teaching at Cambridge.[39] Behind Grote's rational intuitivism lay an (unargued) assumption - partly religious, partly epistemological - that the moral universe is harmonious:

> "The belief that law or order, as opposed to chaos and randomness, must apply...to the entire of being...seems to me to play the same part in...life or the moral universe as it does in the intellectual universe. No experience could give us this belief, but...intellectually we could not think for a moment without it."[40]

Grote's intuitional ethics were an integral part of the climate of Coleridgean idealism at Cambridge, which prevailed for several decades. This line of thought owed something to Kant, but nothing to Hegel.

---

[36] J.F. Ferrier, Works, vol. III, p. 560.
[37] Ibid, vol. I, p. 540.
[38] See ch. 3, pp. 32-33, for a very brief discussion of Hamiltonian philosophy.
[39] See ch. 6, pp. 52-53 and 55, for Sidgwick's contribution to utilitarianism.
[40] J. Grote, A Treatise on the Moral Ideals, ed. J.B. Mayor (London, 1876), p. 373. (Cited in J.B. Schneewind, Sidgwick's Ethics and Victorian Moral Philosophy, p. 120.)

CHAPTER 3

Religious Resistance to Hegel: From Coleridge to Personal Idealism

As McTaggart pointed out, not for the first time but more trenchantly than others had, Hegelianism is a dangerous ally for Christianity. Yet it came to be regarded as a possible defender of the faith by a number of British philosophers and theologians in the middle years of the nineteenth century. It made no frontal assault upon fundamental Christian dogmas such as the existence of a divine personality or the action of divine grace; but it claimed to explain them in purely conceptual terms. Whereas the Christian creed was traditionally expressed in word-pictures and visual imagery, Hegelianism claimed to be able to convey its essence - the reason implicit in Christianity - without literary or pictorial aids. This seemingly inoffensive claim of Hegelianism, to say the same thing as Christianity but in a different way, involved the further and more pretentious claim to understand the essence of Christianity directly, something of which the unphilosophical Christian was supposedly incapable. It claimed to understand Christianity better than it understood itself. Moreover, it claimed to comprehend Christianity not merely in the sense of understanding it, but also in the sense of including it within its system, thereby insinuating its spiritual superiority. A Christian apologist might reply that the supposed superiority of Hegelianism is based upon a merely intellectual and external grasp of Christian belief, but that true belief arises from an understanding which surpasses mere intellectual comprehension, and that in this sense the unphilosophical Christian knows more than the Hegelian philosopher. For the philosophically inclined Christian, Hegelianism can be deceptively attractive. An alliance with Hegelianism is expensive, however. It promises Christianity security against materialism and skepticism, but at the ruinous price of being decomposed and digested by a system of philosophy.

During the 1830s, 1840s and 1850s, the overwhelming majority of English divines and academics - who at Oxford and Cambridge were necessarily, if in certain cases only nominally, orthodox in their religious beliefs - were instinctively repelled by Hegelianism. Their knowledge of Hegel's thought was largely second-hand and extremely thin. Nevertheless, they were more truly guided by their instincts than were some of their more sophisticated successors by their enthusiasm for Hegelianism.[1]

The theological animus against German philosophical idealism was particularly violent in the 1830s and 1840s, coming to a head with the revolutions of 1848. It was tied into a defence of the British constitution - for which one could usually read the political establishment - and the Church of England. As some of the citations from the previous chapter suggest, the British reader might well have been made aware of something having gone seriously awry in German culture by a veritable spate of anti-Hegelian tracts in the 1840s. They originated in Germany, were written for a German audience, and were directed more against the so-called Left Hegelians than against orthodox Hegelianism. Virtually none of them were translated, but some of this onslaught on Hegel through his epigoni could have percolated into the English bien-pensant consciousness. In Shlomo Avineri's words:

---

[1] F.D. Maurice, an influential Broad Church theologian and exponent of Coleridgean religious thinking (and Grote's successor as Knightsbridge Professor of Moral Philosophy at Cambridge in 1866), was one of those generously - and uncritically - receptive to German philosophical idealism. In his historical survey, A Treatise of Moral and Metaphysical Philosophy (London, 1862), he refused to endorse the odium theologicum attached to Hegel in Britain. However, Hegelianism seems to have had as little to do with his thought as he with the course of Hegelianism in Britain.

"The vehemence of attacks from religious quarters on Hegel can perhaps be compared to the reaction in England to Darwin: few people have been so violently criticized for subverting religion and public order."[2]

Avineri describes well the various ironies involved in the attack on Hegel as an enemy of good order and religion. With rare exceptions - such as Jowett, who was in Germany at the time and understood German - this particular controversy had no particular impact on thoughtful Britons. However, it certainly did not facilitate the British reception of philosophical idealism. If it did anything, it must have merely strengthened the built-in resistance to such a strange and seemingly irreligious system of thought as Hegel's. For those few who could read German, the form and style of Hegelian philosophy were forbidding and, to many, repellent; and there was the hurdle of the native empirical tradition to get over, as well as the theological one.

What about the home-grown reaction to empiricism, associationist psychology and the total rejection of metaphysics? It has been claimed for Samuel Taylor Coleridge that he alone among British thinkers in the first half of the nineteenth century really understood what Kant was talking about. He was one of the very few English men of letters who read German. However, his understanding is said to have been the result of his having independently arrived at essentially the same position as Kant, chiefly through his study of the seventeenth century Cambridge Platonists.[3] Therefore, it is said, what he gained from Kant was merely supplementary, reinforcing his own distinctive statement of philosophical idealism. Wellek and, more recently, Orsini have questioned this assesssment, maintaining that Coleridge drew heavily upon Kant and Schelling in his struggle against atheism and hedonism, and indicating that, in his zeal to combat such grievous errors - or perhaps it was due to lack of comprehension - he failed to exercise sufficient discrimination in his borrowings.[4] In short, Coleridge did not "get inside" the Critical philosophy. For Coleridge, reason was akin to faith and opposed to the discursive understanding. Such a view does not do justice to the intricacies of Kant's solution to the problem of accounting for knowledge of both a physical and a moral world without splitting the human intellect and divorcing pure reason from sense experience. Reason came close with Coleridge to being the source of exalted feelings and spiritual expansion, notwithstanding his adoption of Kant's theory that the truth of religious beliefs is guaranteed by practical reason and everyman's moral experience. As Wellek suggests, Coleridge stood much closer to Schelling, the leader in Germany of the Christian reaction against the ambitious intellectual claims of philosophical idealism, than he did to Kant.[5] On all accounts, Coleridge did not bring Kant to England.

My own reading of Coleridge is that like the rest of that first group of Englishmen to come into contact with Kant - and Hegel - his intellectual frame of reference was to a great extent a theological creation. Coleridge did not enjoy the philosophical benefits of being part of a movement of ideas, of participating in the intense interchange of ideas and, in effect, professional industriousness of speculation which marks a period of intellectual development such as that which occurred in Germany between 1770 and 1820. Human reason was not its own arbiter, as it was for the German idealists. They belonged to a rationalist tradition which is not shy of pursuing a philosophical argument wherever it might lead; they observed no theological barriers to thought. All the German idealists had religious convictions of one sort or another. The original impulse of both Kant's and Hegel's thought was partly religious. In the case of Kant, it was a desire to find a place for human moral freedom and the Christian God in a world of causally determined phenomena; Hegel's mature philosophy originated in speculation about the nature of Judaism and Christianity. These men were not, however,

---

[2] S. Avineri, "Hegel revisited," Hegel: A Collection of Critical Essays, ed. A. MacIntyre (New York, 1972), p. 339.
[3] See J.H. Muirhead, Coleridge as Philosopher (London, 1930), passim.
[4] G.N.G. Orsini, Coleridge and German Idealism (Carbondale, Ill., 1969), esp. ch. 8 and 9.
[5] R. Wellek, Immanuel Kant in England, p. 116.

committed, as was Coleridge, to any sectarian dogma or religious establishment.

What distinguished Coleridge from his contemporaries in Britain was his philosophical receptivity to German idealism. He shared many of their theological but few of their philosophical presuppositions. He was an enthusiastic student of Neoplatonism from Plotinus to Cudworth. Although he had been an adherent of Hartley's associationist psychology at an early stage of his philosophical development, he came to detest the "common sense" philosophy because of its seeming indifference to the moral life and its rejection of intuitive knowledge which can put man in touch with the world of Platonic Ideas. Like Herder and other German Romantics, Coleridge was looking for a philosophical explanation of the productive energy of the creative mind, revealed especially in art and the aesthetic sense or imagination. This was a highly unusual intellectual pursuit in the first two or three decades of nineteenth century Britain. Most of his contemporaries contrived to accommodate conventional religious belief with a passive acceptance of pleasure-pain ethics and a large measure of philosophical materialism. Coleridge was fighting an indigenous philosophy which was largely indifferent to man's moral and spiritual nature with whatever weapon came to hand, although many of his weapons were drawn from an indigenous store. Kant's transcendentalism and his categorical imperative were grist to Coleridge's mill rather than the bearer of fresh insight into the perennial problem of how to make a coherent whole out of experience. He had an intuitive grasp of the central problem of philosophical idealism; but, as the following passage from "The Statesman's Manual" (1816) suggests, Coleridge's overall view of that philosophical tradition was rather poetic and fuzzy as to philosophical relationships among thinkers contributing to that tradition:

"Whether ideas are regulative only, according to Aristotle and Kant; or likewise constitutive and one with the power and life of nature, according to Plato and Plotinus...is the highest problem of philosophy and not part of its nomenclature."[6]

Hegel remained for Coleridge a baffling postscript to Schelling's absolute idealism. There are some intriguing marginalia in Coleridge's own copy of Hegel's Wissenschaft der Logik, which is held in the British museum.[7] They end on page 91 of volume I and he apparently read no further, because the remaining pages were still uncut at the beginning of the present century. His verdict on the first 91 pages of the Logik is somewhat perfunctory: "bewilderment throughout from confusion of Terms,"[8] and "proof of the neglect of sound Logic by the disciples of der neueste Philosophie and that the Ruckfall von Kant has avenged itself."[9] These two accusations of verbal conjuring and bad logic have reappeared again and again over the years as the substance of British reaction to Hegel.

Another familiar charge, that of Spinozism, is levelled at Hegel by Coleridge in the course of a discussion of "Determination." He seems to have thought that Hegel's theory of differentiation through negation was no advance upon Spinoza's theory of substance and its attributes, and that it made insufficient allowance for individual differences. The suspicion that Hegelianism posed a grave threat to individuality was a recurring one, and later in the century it was primarily responsible for provoking the revolt of the personal idealists. This suspicion is, in all probability, what lies behind Coleridge's remark that "it may explain a wave; but not a Leaf or an Insect."[10] The applicability of this enigmatic remark to Spinoza is doubtful enough; it is quite pointless to try in Hegel's case. One of Hegel's principal aims was to invest nature with a dynamic which would sublate or "lift" it into the realm of self-conscious mind. At the same time he set out to defeat monistic concepts of unity without

---

[6] S.T. Coleridge, Lay Sermons, ed. D. Coleridge (London, 1852), pp. 124-25.
[7] These have been published in A.D. Snyder, Coleridge on Logic and Learning (New Haven, 1929), pp. 162-65.
[8] From the facing pages of Coleridge's copy of Hegel's Wissenschaft der Logik.
[9] Coleridge's copy of Hegel's Logik, p. 54.
[10] Ibid. p. 65.

differentiation - the worst offender in this respect being Schelling's Absolute, with which Coleridge himself flirted. In his notebook of October 1818, Coleridge lumps Spinoza, Schelling and Hegel together as exponents of a totally unmediated unity of "Ens and Non-Ens."[11]

Coleridge's most persistent complaint is that Hegel's system is theologically unsound. He attached undue significance to the dialectical triad, interpreting it as an attempted literal translation of the Christian trinity and thereby paving the way for his own and others' serious misunderstanding of Hegel's purpose. Hegel regarded the Incarnation and the Atonement as the religious consciousness' imaginative rendering of rational truth, the continuous process of cancellation and preservation in all things. Hegel's assertion that Being is the unity of determinateness and indeterminateness met with Coleridge's approval because, he said, it concurs with the Platonist maxim that God is the "common measure of the Infinite and the Finite." "This," says Coleridge, "is the first sensible Remark that I have met with"[12] - and apparently the last, because he then severely reprimands Hegel for saying that the Kantian thing-in-itself is none other than that Absolute which men can know nothing about. Coleridge calls the thing-in-itself the rational "Idea in God," but adds that only God can realize unity-in-difference.

Coleridge is the most notable of those who struggled without success to understand Hegel's philosophy - not that Coleridge tried particularly hard. There are several relatively obscure figures whose struggles were more intense and whose approach to "der neueste Philosophie" was more earnest, if no more enthusiastic; but the fruits of their labours were on the whole no more promising. The "secret of Hegel" remained dark and seemingly impenetrable, save for occasional glimpses, until the 1870s. One of the first to penetrate the supposed mystery was Benjamin Jowett.[13] He published no work on Hegel and barely figures in the history of philosophy, but he has his own intrinsic interest as a transmitter of ideas. There were many more abortive attempts to understand - and more successful ones to discredit - Hegel's philosophy after Jowett began to quietly "spread the word." Jowett's role as a teacher of philosophical idealism will be discussed in a later chapter.[14] Here it will suffice to say something about Jowett as an intellectually sophisticated Christian who strove to assimilate Hegelianism and then totally rejected it.

In the summer of 1844 Jowett went on a reading tour of Germany with A.P. Stanley. In Dresden, Jowett sought out Erdmann, a disciple of Hegel who was attending a philological congress there. Like many students of philosophy in England, Jowett had heard of Hegel and his German reputation; but unlike most of his fellows he was prepared to undertake the arduous task of studying Hegel in the original. He and the future Archbishop Temple collaborated on a translation of Hegel's Wissenschaft der Logik, but abandoned the project in 1849.

His falling out with Hegel, like that of so many of the first Englishmen to come into

---

[11] The Notebooks of Samuel Taylor Coleridge, ed. K. Coburn (London, 1973), vol. III, entry 4445.
[12] Coleridge's copy of Hegel's Logik, p. 89.
[13] Benjamin Jowett (1817-93) went up to Balliol College, Oxford, in 1836 and remained a member of the college until his death. Elected a fellow while still an undergraduate, he then became a tutor (1842-70), was ordained in 1845 and was appointed Master of Balliol in 1870, which post he held for the rest of his life. He was appointed Regius Professor of Greek in 1855 and was Vice-Chancellor of the University, 1882-6. He became a controversial figure in the mid-century religious disputes because of his liberal views on Scriptural interpretation, as put forward in his Epistles of St. Paul and in the more widely read Essays and Reviews. His theological views were thought inconsistent with his Oxford professorship and there was considerable agitation against him. Throughout his career he was active in educational and university reform.
[14] See ch. 5, pp. 43, 44, 45-46 and 47.

contact with Hegel, was theologically motivated. On the other hand, like Coleridge he was philosophically receptive to many of the "leading conceptions" of German philosophical idealism. Unlike Coleridge, he put them to scholarly use. Whereas Coleridge's knowledge of Hegel was sketchy in the extreme, Jowett's was thorough, added to which he had a much better understanding of Hegel's overall purpose and his relationship to the idealist tradition in Western philosophy.

Jowett was not a Hegelian primarily for reasons of religious belief, the insurmountable barrier between Hegel and many nineteenth century English writers. These reasons became inextricably bound up with a growing distaste for the direction taken by German philosophy. In a letter to A.P. Stanley, dated August 20, 1846, he says:

> "The problem of...Truth idealized and yet in action, he does not seem to me to have solved; the Gospel of St. John does. Hegel seems to me not the perfect philosophy, but the perfect self-consciousness of philosophy."[15]

In another letter to Stanley (1847) Jowett complained that "the German theologues get more and more drawn into the whirlpool of philosophy, and all their various harmonies are but faint echoes of Schelling and Hegel."[16] He admired F.C. Baur, the doyen of the Tubingen school of theologians, for not allowing his Hegelianism to get in the way of his Biblical criticism.[17] In his contribution to Essays and Reviews (1860), "On the Interpretation of Scripture," there is no trace of Hegelianism, if one excepts the ideas of progressive revelation and of applying modern scientific and historical knowledge to Biblical criticism - which ideas are not directly attributable to Hegel, although he was one of those responsible for creating the German climate of opinion in which they were developed. A digression here upon Jowett's part in Essays and Reviews, a collection of articles questioning the literal interpretation of Scripture, may throw some light on the climate of opinion in mid-Victorian England.

Jowett's reputation rests upon his classical scholarship and his Mastership of Balliol. It is usually forgotten that he was also one of the "seven against Christ," the contributors to Essays and Reviews. This book has often been coupled with Darwin's Origin of Species (1859) as marking the great turning point in Victorian life, the beginning of an age of doubt. In fact, Essays and Reviews was written by sincere Christians with no desire to undermine the faith of their readers. Most of them were ordained, including Jowett, which gave a misleading appearance of official sanction to the heterodox views which they expressed - but which they by no means originated. Their timing upset an ecclesiastical hierarchy particularly sensitive to intimations of heresy. The Church of England was at that time under intellectual pressure both from within and without, and sober criticism soberly presented was not well received. Jowett's essay, "On the Interpretation of Scripture," was a model of sobriety and judiciousness. Drawing upon his studies in German Biblical criticism, Jowett proposed that the intellectual energy expended on making Biblical texts fit current problems and preconceptions be applied to discovering "not what Scripture may be made to mean, but what it does."[18] To do this required the critical tools of the philologist and the historian and the attitude of mind with which we approach a pagan text. We must make the effort to understand the minds of the Prophets and the Apostles and the circumstances in which they spoke and wrote. Above all, we must attend to the text without preconceptions. Only in this way can we hope to establish a fixed, certain and authoritative interpretation of Scripture. Scripture is, of course, sacred. It is divinely inspired. How can it, therefore, be susceptible to criticism? How can it be shaped in any way by historical accident? Jowett introduced the idea of progressive revelation to meet this problem. "The Word" corrects and expands itself. No one utterance in Scripture is sufficient

---

[15] E. Abbott and L. Campbell, The Life and Letters of Benjamin Jowett (London, 1897), vol. I, p. 92.
[16] Ibid., p. 142.
[17] See a letter to Stanley of 1848 in Ibid., p. 162.
[18] B. Jowett, Essays and Reviews (London, 1860), p. 240.

apart from the whole, but the meaning of Scripture is there, entirely within itself, as it is in "any other book written in an age and country of which little or no other literature survives and about which we know almost nothing, except what is derived from its pages."[19] This is what Jowett meant by saying: "Interpret the Scripture like any other book." These few words - which he italicized himself - appear innocent enough now; but in the middle of the nineteenth century, when for most people the Bible was not like any other book, these words were heresy.

That Jowett was discussing the interpretation of Scripture and not the evaluation of its content could easily be overlooked. He particularly distinguished between the interpretation and the adaptation and application of Scripture. Jowett's interpretative canon was actually rather puritanical and fundamentalist: no assistance from patristic or other commentary; no a priori notions about nature and origins. His avowed intention, however, was to ease the inevitable advent of full and untrammelled criticism of religious dogma and received truth, and to free the "moral power" of Scripture from theological accretion and disputation. He affirmed the religious quality of the search for truth. That the truth will be found in Scripture is, however, a question of faith. Jowett was concerned to elicit the true meaning of Scripture because he believed that it was, as no philosophical system could be, the absolute truth. He could never support the sort of claims made for human reason by Hegel.

Jowett was uneasy about the ideas of development and evolution because they threatened to undermine moral values by encouraging relativism. In his commentary on Plato's Republic, he earnestly endeavoured to reconcile his profoundest moral and religious beliefs with doubts raised by arguments drawn from the history of morals, arguments whose force he could not deny. As one might expect, he disapproved of many of Plato's political proposals, especially of those for the "guardian" class in the just society. But Jowett treated such ideas not as an expression of classical Greek culture or as a problem in Plato's thought, but as a dismaying mental aberration.[20] He defended the Christian scheme of values very much as if it were a timeless, immutable Platonic Idea. It is hard to resist the conclusion that Jowett was one of those who preferred philosophy to be a heritage or a legacy, a store of great thoughts, rather than a living force whose purpose is neither to reinforce religious belief nor to promote moral rectitude.[21] Jowett's alarm at the philosophical tendencies of his age was both Platonic and anti-Platonic: the new philosophy seemed to him sophistry, but his response frequently resembled that of Polemarchus in the Republic.

Towards Hegel, Jowett's attitude changed drastically, as Hegelianism acquired increasing prestige and authority in British universities. In his 1871 introduction to the Sophist, he says: "The system of Hegel frees the mind from the dominion of abstract ideas."[22] On the other hand, we must not become enslaved to Hegelianism, which has freed us to apply Hegelian criticism to itself as well as to other systems. In later editions of the same introduction, Jowett berates Hegel for the absence of a transcendent God or "beyond" in his philosophy. Some of his criticisms in his later notebooks - admittedly not published and therefore not to be read as his considered views - are bitterly anti-Hegelian. The Hegelian deduction of categories, he says, is defective because "any possible association by which he can pass from one abstraction to another is enough for him."[23] Then there is the rather intemperate remark that "Hegel did nothing at all for the elevation of German life."[24] Jowett's preference for poetry and religion and his distaste for systematic philosophy became increasingly pronounced

---

[19] Ibid., p. 382.
[20] The Republic of Plato, trans. B. Jowett, 3rd ed. (Oxford, 1908), vol. II, pp. 125-28.
[21] "Philosophy in late ages has been to a great extent a falling away from Plato." (B. Jowett, notebook No. 25, p. 38.)
[22] Dialogues of Plato, trans. B. Jowett, 4th ed. (Oxford, 1953), vol. III, p. 201.
[23] B. Jowett, notebook No. 25, p. 27.
[24] Ibid., p. 45.

in his last years.

H.L. Mansel is interesting for the use he made of Hamilton's interpretation of Kant's philosophy to combat the Hegelian unity of thought and being.[25] He was widely read as a theologian in mid-Victorian times and enjoyed a minor philosophical reputation. In what little he wrote about Hegel, Mansel used him as an awful warning to the "neophyte in Rationalism."[26] For Mansel, Hegel was merely the most extravagant of the German absolute idealists, the logical result of the philosophical pantheism initiated by Kant. This is a somewhat ironic outcome since, according to Mansel, it was Kant who had shown the limitations of consciousness and the inaccessibility to pure reason of absolute, unconditioned reality. But Kant had ignored the warnings of his own theoretical philosophy and, on the basis of his moral philosophy, made rash speculations about the nature of the absolute and unconditioned region beyond consciousness.

> "Kant proved, though he did not accept his own conclusions, that whatever is made known by consciousness must be relative: his successors admitted the conclusion, and consistently attempted to construct a philosophy of the absolute which should be above consciousness. Kant had proved it to be impossible to bring the object within the grasp of the subject: there remained the wilder attempt to expand the subject to the immensity of the object."[27]

Mansel saw quite correctly that in the philosophy of Hegel there is a strong suggestion that "man must himself be God."[28] In company with many twentieth century French commentators, Mansel held that Hegel's philosophy is one of unqualified atheism - or rather, a pantheism, which for Mansel amounted to the same thing.

His philosophical point of departure was Hamilton's philosophy of the "Conditioned." Hamilton's conversion of Kant's forms and categories into anti-metaphysical barriers afforded much-needed philosophical ammunition for the theological resistance to the "wilder attempts" of German philosophical idealism. The divergence of the Hamiltonians from Kant is clear, however. For Kant, the substantively non-existent may have a practical existence as well as a regulative function - not in the sense that it is morally useful, but that its existence is necessitated by the experience of the moral life. God, freedom and immortality are for Kant moral necessities; neither pure reason nor revelation can verify them.

Mansel's philosophically bolstered theological objections to German idealism represent the religiously motivated opposition to Hegel at its most cogent and discerning. They pivot on the contention that Hegel was guilty of the sin of intellectual pride. He presumed to show that thought is the measure of existence. In the Bampton Lectures for 1858, <u>The Limits of Religious Thought</u>, Mansel tried to show that thought cannot be the measure of existence, and that "...the contradictions which arise in the attempt to conceive the infinite have their origin, not in

---

[25] Henry Longueville Mansel (1820-71), an undergraduate at St. John's College, Oxford, from 1839 to 1843, was first a private tutor, then elected a "professor fellow" in 1864. He was ordained in 1845. He was a reader in moral and metaphysical philosophy at Magdalen College, and became University Professor of Ecclesiastical History, 1866-8. In the latter year he was appointed Dean of St. Paul's and left Oxford. A High Church Tory, his edition of Hamilton's <u>Lectures</u> (1859) was the occasion for a vitriolic dispute with J.S. Mill - see Mill's <u>Examination of Sir William Hamilton's Philosophy</u> (1865).

[26] Mansel's <u>Metaphysics</u> contains a six-page (hostile) survey of Hegel's ideas, and the footnotes suggest some direct acquaintance with Hegel's <u>Logik</u>.

[27] H.L. Mansel, "Lecture on the Philosophy of Kant" (delivered at Magdalen College, May 20, 1856), pp. 37-38. Compare George Santayana's <u>Egotism in German Philosophy</u> for a wide-ranging and provocative presentation of the theory that German philosophy, particularly since Kant, has been a persistent attempt to transfer the whole objective world to the domain of the subjective will.

[28] H.L. Mansel, "Lecture on Kant," p. 38.

the nature of that which we would conceive, but in the constitution of the mind conceiving...."[29] Substantive knowledge of the infinite is impossible. We do, however, have valid regulative ideas about the infinite, which knowledge is revealed to us only by the grace of God. Mansel's distinction between substantive and regulative is not Kant's. For the latter, regulative ideas are aids to speculation. It can be very fruitful to regard reality as if it were purposive or as if it were a plenum, although we cannot say that reality is really purposive or a true plenum. These notions have no substantive application to the world of space and time. Mansel uses "regulative" in the ordinary sense of rules and regulations. The God of our religion commands us and we act accordingly. The Christian religion tells us how to behave; it is not supposed to satisfy our intellects. The highest principles of thought are principles of action: "...they do not tell us what things are in themselves, but how we must conduct ourselves in relation to them."[30]

Mansel was a theologian rather than a philosopher, but his Bampton Lectures attracted considerable hostile criticism on the grounds that he had depreciated theology intellectually. We do, said his critics, have substantive knowledge of the infinite, of God. What Mansel was doing, in fact, was cordoning off an area of knowledge in which revealed religion - not theology - would be the arbiter. To accomplish this, he used philosophy against itself. Philosophy is self-limiting: when properly undertaken it delimits the area beyond which it is necessarily incompetent. It can discover the necessity of its own limitations. The Hegelian reply to such philosophical modesty is that it is false modesty - knowledge of the limit suppresses the limit. As a Christian theologian, Mansel started from a hard core of religious belief. But he attempted to beat the philosophical idealists at their own game. By using philosophical weapons to defend revealed religion, he could be accused of bringing the enemy into the sacred camp. However, there can be no doubt that Mansel's intention was to harness philosophy to the service of religion. Philosophy, he claimed, cannot make cognitively worthwhile pronouncements about the Absolute, nor can it establish a higher moral law, such as Kant's categorical imperative, by which one might judge Christian doctrine. Mansel attempted to subordinate philosophy to religion. As we shall see later, there were attempts to isolate them from each other and also attempts to find in philosophical idealism a substitute religion.

A.S. Pringle-Pattison was a pioneer of the movement which later developed into personal idealism.[31] His first appearance in print was as a collaborator with Bernard Bosanquet, D.G. Ritchie and others in the production of a kind of philosophical manifesto, dedicated to the memory of T.H. Green.[32] It was inspired by the confidence of a new generation of British philosophers in the tools made available to them by German philosophical idealism, and above all by Hegel. In his contribution, "Philosophy As Criticism of Categories," Pringle-Pattison - or Seth, as he then was - is already steering that middle course between Kant and Hegel which he held to, with considerable latitude, in all his subsequent work. He accepts the initial Hegelian assumption that we can have knowledge of reality, but with a Kantian caveat about the dangers of a priorism: "...the trustworthiness of knowledge is and must be an assumption. But

---

[29] H.L. Mansel, *The Limits of Religious Thought* (London, 1858), lecture II, p. 60.
[30] *Ibid.*, lecture V, p. 141. Compare J.H. Newman, *Grammar of Assent* (London, 1870), pp. 90-91: "...man is not a reasoning animal; he is a seeing, feeling, contemplating, acting animal.... Life is for action. If we insist on proofs for everything, we shall never come to action: to act you must assume, and that assumption is faith." These words were actually written in 1841.
[31] Andrew Seth (1856-1931) changed his name to Pringle-Pattison in 1898 as one of the conditions for inheriting a family estate. From 1878 to 1880 he studied in Germany, where he imbibed a good deal of Lotze. Perhaps for reasons of ancestry, he was a lifelong proponent of the Scottish "common sense" philosophy. He also contrived to be a neo-Kantian and a Hegelian. He was Professor of Logic and Metaphysics at the University of St. Andrews, 1887-91, and at Edinburgh, 1891-1919.
[32] *Essays in Philosophical Criticism*, ed. Haldane and Seth (London, 1883).

this does not mean that every reasoned conclusion is true."33 For Pringle-Pattison the chief value of the Hegelian unity of thought and being lay in its solution to the epistemological dualism of Kant's philosophy:

> "From the standpoint of a theory of knowledge, it will be found that the mind and the world are in a sense convertible terms. We may talk indifferently of the one or of the other; the content of our notion remains in both cases the same."34

From the moral and metaphysical standpoint, however, he became more and more dissatisfied with the Hegelian enterprise.

While T.H. Green thought the Cairds had been "overpowered by Hegel," Pringle-Pattison lumped Green together with Edward and John Caird as Hegelians who had not read their Kant well enough. They had reduced God to a bare geometric point, the abstract principle of unity which is the common centre of every rational experience. Kant had taken great pains to warn against the impropriety of hypostatizing such a purely regulative principle. In his Gifford Lectures (University of Aberdeen) for 1912-13, <u>The Idea of God in the Light of Recent Philosophy</u>, Pringle-Pattison takes Green, Caird and all the British Hegelians to task for their abuse of the principle of unity, "which recurs in their writings almost <u>ad nauseam</u>."35

The trouble, in Pringle-Pattison's view, began with Hegel himself. His "Spirit" or "concrete Idea" remains abstract,

> "...and unites God and man only by eviscerating the real content of both. Both disappear or are sublimated into it, but simply because it represents what is common to both, the notion of intelligence as such. They disappear not, indeed, in a pantheistic substance, but in a logical concept."36

Pringle-Pattison complained that Hegel, in his union of God and man in Spirit, had not been able, as he claimed, to successfully combine two different strands of thought, the one a logical hierarchy of universals, the other an historical development through particulars. What had happened was that the Hegelian Absolute had swallowed up "both God and man as real beings...leaving us with the logical Idea itself as the sole reality."37 Hegel's unity of God and man destroyed both: God became humanity or the human spirit or human civilization, and man became a generalized abstraction. In bringing God - the ideal, the Fichtean <u>Sollen</u> - down to earth, Hegel had overlooked the operation of transcendent ideals in human life and promoted the advent of a self-satisfied religion of humanity.

It was the "evisceration" of finite individual man which most agitated Pringle-Pattison. He maintained the "imperviousness" of the finite self in contradistinction to those British Hegelians, F.H. Bradley and Bernard Bosanquet in particular, who wrote in terms of the individual "merging" into the Absolute, and of his value lying entirely in his contribution to the whole. Bosanquet was Pringle-Pattison's principal target, because his monism was tempered by a certain "grudging" recognition of finite personality. He agreed with Bosanquet that reason is one and its unity the necessary ground of communicable human experience, that value judgments are objective, and that their objectivity is the sine qua non of the moral life. The universal inheres in every individual. Bosanquet went on to argue that the individual subject is dependent for his value upon his participation in the universal subject. For Bosanquet the fullest embodiment of the universal subject that we know is the state, the most highly organized and articulated form of political society. What Pringle-Pattison took strongest

---

33 A.S. Pringle-Pattison, "Philosophy as Criticism of Categories," <u>Essays in Philosophical Criticism</u>, p. 38.
34 <u>Ibid</u>., pp. 13-14.
35 A.S. Pringle-Pattison, <u>The Idea of God in the Light of Recent Philosophy</u> (New York, 1920), pp. 195-99.
36 A.S. Pringle-Pattison, <u>Hegelianism and Personality</u> (Edinburgh, 1887), p. 155.
37 <u>Ibid</u>., p. 191.

exception to was Bosanquet's "depreciation" of the finite self, his refusal to recognize the permanent value of the finite individual. The individual is the creative centre of experience. Universal reason lives in and through him: there can be no common shared experience but for his sharing it; there can be no objective morality but for his willing it. According to Pringle-Pattison, the monistic tendency in Bosanquet's thought led him "...to treat the individual, qua individual, almost as a negligible feature of the world, and in the issue, consequently...to treat the finite self as a transitory phenomenon."[38] The other half of philosophical idealism's organic theory of experience must be given its due. The universal realizes itself as much through individuals as they through it. Bosanquet had, in effect, destroyed individuality. The finite self was no longer a focalized unity or centre of experience, but a quality or adjective of the Absolute; and, having destroyed individuality, Bosanquet could not then assert the Absolute to be the only true individual.[39]

Bosanquet's crypto-Spinozism was not the only alternative to pluralism, to "a doctrine of ultimately self-subsistent, independent and unrelated reals." Pringle-Pattison felt the only satisfactory alternative to unmediated pluralism was a theory of membership, hints of which had appeared in Bosanquet's Gifford Lectures. The organic analogy which Bosanquet was so fond of deploying furnishes no grounds, according to Pringle-Pattison, for inferring the dissolution of finite individuals as centres of intrinsic value and independent development. The individual members of a state, for example, are self-conscious members, and their membership develops and expands their sense of selfhood. Bosanquet did not quarrel with the notion of whole and part deriving value from each other, but he denied that ultimate value resides in the individual self-consciousness, that the end of the process of Spirit's unfolding is a world of finite individuals. The value of the individual lay, for Bosanquet, in his contribution to the common store of value. It is a distinctive contribution, but the emphasis is on the contributing, not upon the contributor.

There were many like Pringle-Pattison who, in an age of doubt, took refuge in the consolations of philosophy. They had reasons of the heart for gladly, eagerly accepting the principle that the individual can realize himself only in something larger than himself, "through absorption in objective interests and in the currents of the universal life." But they also felt that there had to be something further. "Although the individual may not make himself his own End, the world of finite individuals may well constitute the End of the Absolute."[40] Pringle-Pattison's Absolute is, as one might expect, the Christian God, "who lives in the perpetual giving of himself, who shares the life of his finite creatures...."[41] Such an Absolute, realizing itself in everyday human experience, he considered the only one consistent with a unified view of the world. God, for Pringle-Pattison, was both "the fundamental structure of reality" and an infinitely suffering, infinitely sorrowing being. It is instructive in the present context to see what he had to see about the retrograde character of latter-day Hegelianism:

"The essential feature of the Christian conception of the world, in contrast to the Hellenic, may be said to be that it regards the person and the relation of persons to one another as the essence of reality, whereas Greek thought conceived of personality, however spiritual, as a restrictive characteristic of the finite - a transitory product of a life which as a whole is impersonal. Modern Absolutism seems, in this respect, to revert to the pre-Christian mode of conception and to repeat also the too exclusively intellectualistic attitude, which characterizes Greek thought in the main."[42]

---

[38] A.S. Pringle-Pattison, The Idea of God, p. 266.
[39] In Pringle-Pattison's homely metaphor, the individual is not a waterpipe through which the Absolute courses.
[40] Ibid., p. 294.
[41] Ibid., p. 401.
[42] Ibid., p. 291.

Pringle-Pattison's complaint about the excessive intellectualism of British Hegelianism had another dimension. He was one of those "back-to-Kanters" whose dissent from Hegel's ambitious claims for speculative reason drove them towards some form or other of dualism. The most important considerations in Pringle-Pattison's case were moral and religious. Like Kant, he was concerned to preserve God, freedom and immortality. The primacy of the moral will is a distinctive feature of his work.[43] He doggedly persisted in trying to make more room in the Hegelian system for individual moral action. This linked him informally with the personal idealists - Sturt, Schiller, Rashdall and others - which in turn placed him on the fringes of pragmatism. Pringle-Pattison frequently referred to himself as a "critical realist," one whose belief in the independent reality of what we know is conditioned by Kant's teaching as to what we can know.

The personal idealists were not, strictly speaking, Hegelians.[44] Although some of them regarded themselves as belonging to the "Oxford school" of philosophical idealism, their collective raison d'etre was a reaction against what they saw to be its increasingly dominant attitude: world-weary fatalism and a smug conviction that absolute idealism was the final philosophical word. The Hegelians were, as a group, excessively intellectualist and self-satisfied, and too remote from the "real world" of moral choice. There is a certain irony in this assessment, in view of the energetic reforming activities and social casework engaged in by many British Hegelians. However, their do-gooder politics - which, in fact, irritated some other, and philosophically important, Hegelians - were somewhat dirigiste, and they had a tendency to talk like the apostles of a new religion of the state. The personal idealists were not unjustified in detecting signs of hardening of the arteries in the Hegelian philosophical system, and in calling it static, especially in its theory of truth. There is indeed a constant danger that a coherence theory of truth will degenerate into a process of merely excluding or explaining away what is inconvenient. The personal idealists were expressing a feeling of unease that rapid advances in various departments of human knowledge were leaving idealism behind, as well as their own conviction - symptomatic of the restlessness of the age diagnosed by cultural historians - that the human vocation was active, not contemplative, and that experience was "kinetic and dynamic."

In order to counteract what Henry Sturt castigated in Idola Theatri as the "Passive Fallacy," the personal idealists drew a great deal upon William James and psychological theories of the primacy of the will. In their hands idealism became an assertion of personal freedom and individual initiative, rather than an explanation of the world and experience. In their anxiety to save personality from absorption in the Hegelian Absolute, the personal idealists adopted a stance oddly reminiscent of Marx's rejection of Hegelianism and academic philosophy in his Theses on Feuerbach - but without the revolutionary conclusion.

"Minerva's owl, said Hegel, cannot begin its flight till the shades of evening have begun to fall. But, I think, that owl has hooted long enough. Hegel's alleged necessity of thought is nonsense. It is the duty of philosophy, I maintain, to establish theoretical principles on such matters as politics, moral conduct and education, and these principles should be valuable for the guidance of practical men."[45]

In the case of at least one of them, the revolt was motivated in part by what amounted to personal animosity against F.H. Bradley, the pre-eminent metaphysician of the British Hegelians.[46] Personal idealism had American antecedents and its subsequent history in the form

---

[43] See especially The Idea of God, pp. 291-93.

[44] See Personal Idealism, ed. H.C. Sturt (London, 1902), and, for the clearest signs of pragmatism, F.C.S. Schiller's contribution.

[45] H.C. Sturt, The Principles of Understanding (Cambridge, 1915), p. vi.

[46] Bradley's work was "...inhuman, incompetent and impracticable intellectualism," said F.C.S. Schiller in "Axioms as Postulates," Personal Idealism, p. 127.

(or forms) of personalism was American and European, particularly French, rather than British. The British version easily slipped back into the loose-jointed pieties of a Christian idealism.[47]

The story of personal idealism is in part the story of resurgent religious resistance to the claims of Hegelianism, in part a good illustration of the fact that British Hegelianism was never as cohesive a movement of ideas or as monolithic a body of thought as its rapid rise to academic prominence and the extent of its brief penetration of British intellectual life has led some commentators then and later to believe. The most philosophically rigorous of the personal idealists, J.McT.E. McTaggart, was not a member of this "school" at all.[48] His personal idealism was neither motivated nor occasioned by a revolt against Hegelianism; he was never interested in Hegelian ethics, political philosophy or philosophy of religion. Other than to dismiss it along with spiritualism, he was never interested in Christianity or any sort of revealed religion. His interest in Hegel was limited to the formal logic of the dialectic, but Hegel arguably had no bearing whatsoever on the construction of McTaggart's own metaphysical system.

---

[47] See the later writings of Hastings Rashdall and C.C.J. Webb's <u>God and Personality</u> (London, 1919).
[48] See ch. 10 and 11, pp. 86-90 and 93-97.

CHAPTER 4

J.H. Stirling: Kant as the "Secret" of Hegel

As indicated at the beginning of the previous chapter, some British thinkers in the middle years of the nineteenth century considered employing weapons forged by German philosophical idealism to defend revealed religion. Its seriousness about "eternal verities" appealed to the Low Church religious sensibility, whose literary personification was Herr Teufelsdrockh in Thomas Carlyle's Sartor Resartus. As the previous chapter also indicated, however, German philosophical idealism in the shape of Hegelianism came to be regarded by some commentators as a weapon either too unwieldy or too dangerous to its employer. One of those whose passion for German speculative philosophy never dimmed was J.H. Stirling.[1] Throughout a long career stretching into the twentieth century, he promoted Hegelianism as the champion of faith in God and righteousness. For this, but more for other reasons to be discussed in this chapter, his continuing reputation as the initiator of British Hegelianism cannot stand.

"The Historic Pabulum," Stirling tells us in his frenzied Carlylese, "passing from the vessel of Hume, was received into that of Kant, and thence finally into that of Hegel; but from the vessels of the two latter the generations have not yet eaten."[2] It was Stirling's self-appointed task to feed the multitude. Unfortunately, digested in the "vessel" of Stirling, the "Historic Pabulum" emerged in a very unappetizing condition. His enthusiasm for the "German mysteries" was greater than his skill at untangling them. The Secret of Hegel is ludicrously metaphorical in places, convoluted and tediously repetitive. He would have done well to have followed Hegel's advice - and example - and kept his preliminary intellectual struggles to himself. If he had eliminated the minute record of his own tortured progress to comprehension, frequently disguised as helping the incredulous reader, Stirling's exposition could have been briefer and yet afforded ample scope for a more extensive commentary.

Stirling's part in stimulating an intelligent British interest in Hegel has been highly overrated.[3] The publication of The Secret of Hegel (1865) is conventionally regarded as the great watershed of Hegelian fortunes in Britain, the event marking the end of

---

[1] James Hutchison Stirling (1820-1909) received a medical degree from Edinburgh University in 1842. A competency on his father's death in 1851 allowed him to abandon his medical practice to study in France and Germany and devote the rest of his life to philosophy. He was the first Gifford Lecturer, 1888-90. The Gifford Lectures were to become a virtual preserve of the British Hegelians, and have continued to offer a forum for philosophical idealism long after Hegelianism ceased to be a force in British philosophy.
[2] J.H. Stirling, The Secret of Hegel, 2nd ed. (Edinburgh, 1898), p. 1.
[3] See especially J.H. Muirhead, "How Hegel came to England," Mind, vol. 36, October 1927, for the view that with Stirling's Secret of Hegel Hegel "arrived" in Britain. In spite of the illustrious names cited in praise of Stirling's work, we should not be misled about its nature. Even Green's endorsement is suspect because, as Jowett saw, Green exhibited a certain tendency to run Kant and Hegel together in somewhat the same way as Stirling did. Muirhead admits (p. 446) that Stirling failed to assimilate Hegel, and that his further attempts to establish Hegelianism upon the foundations of a firm grasp of the Critical philosophy were extremely badly done.
  The persistence of the belief that Stirling was the first to properly explain Hegel to the English-speaking world is illustrated by G.D. Stormer, "Hegel and the secret of James Hutchison Stirling," Idealistic Studies, January 1979, pp. 33-54.

apathetic ignorance or misinformed hostility and the beginning of informed criticism. However, there is considerable indirect evidence to suggest that the work of bringing Hegel's philosophy to the attention of a small but well-prepared and receptive audience was underway before Stirling publicly divulged the "secret." Nevertheless, Stirling was the first writer in English to attempt a comprehensive exposition of the whole Hegelian system "in origin, principle, form and matter." He was the first to attempt to see the Hegelian system whole, to explain its overall meaning and to put it in its philosophical context. As well as having only German commentaries to assist him - some of which are as opaque and closely wrought as the Logik itself, which, with some assistance from the Encyclopaedia, was Stirling's Hegelian text - Stirling had the added handicap of no formal philosophical training.

Stirling continually emphasizes Hegel's peculiar brand of rationalism. There is really no excuse for failing to grasp the so-called secret of Hegel.[4] It is the "concrete notion," the philosophical comprehension of everything as the working-out or rational explication of spirit. The form of the notion, the logical sequence which determines the course of spirit's development, Stirling maintains, was inherited from Kant; Hegel merely added the content. Stirling saw in the Kantian category of reciprocity the essence of Hegel's identity of identity and non-identity. He certainly did not deny Hegel's originality in putting flesh on the categories. He failed, however, to appreciate the full significance of what Hegel had done. Hegel did not simply put the finishing touches on the Kantian edifice. He boldly asserted the spirituality of the world and everything in it and made that most implausible point of view intellectually exciting. He gave it a rationale which is not divorced from the phenomena of consciousness and the natural world, nor from moral and political life. On the contrary, spirit achieves self-consciousness only in and through each of these.

Stirling did not grasp the full implication of the unity of thought and being. For him Hegelianism was no significant departure from Kantianism; the answer to Hegel's problem was set up for him by Kant and he had little more to do than dot the i's and cross the t's.[5] Although there is a continuous line of philosophical development traceable from Kant through Fichte and Schelling to Hegel, Stirling's view disregards Kant's distinctive purpose, which was not to establish the rationality of the universe, but to preserve an area of human experience free from causal determinism. He was a dualist, whereas Hegel was a monist.

In the conclusion to The Secret of Hegel, Stirling examines Hegel's philosophy of religion. He makes the cardinal error of regarding Hegel's system as a vindication of traditional Christianity, and of the doctrine of personal immortality in particular. Hegel was by no means anti-Christian; but, as Stirling himself is forced to admit, he "refined" many of the "crudities" of traditional religion, and this process of refinement and rationalization did not leave Christianity as it was. For one thing, he subordinated it to the philosopher performing the rational reconstruction. Philosophy must be superior to revealed religion in explanatory power at least. Hegelianism expresses conceptually the truth which Christianity can only express in imaginative terms. It has seen through the word-pictures to the pure unadulterated concept.

As for Hegel's political philosophy, Stirling interpreted the idea of an objective will as

---

[4] The old jape, "If Mr. Stirling knew the secret of Hegel, he managed to keep it to himself," was presumably aimed at the barbarities of his style; there is no reticence about the so-called secret.

[5] See J.H. Stirling, The Secret of Hegel, vol. I, esp. chapter 5, for the elaboration of Stirling's theory that Hegel's "concrete notion" lay complete within the Critical philosophy, and that he displayed ingratitude, even deliberate deceit, in covering his Kantian tracks. "The system of Hegel is contained all but ready formed in the system of Kant." (J.H. Stirling, The Secret of Hegel, p. 193.)

an attack upon the excessive subjectivity of laissez-faire political economy. The laissez-faire approach to political economy was particularly strong and self-confident when Stirling was writing. It often arrogated to itself the role of political philosophy proper. Nevertheless, it was highly proficient in its work of explaining economic life. Stirling seems to have looked upon political economy as merely poor political philosophy, whereas Hegel saw in it the explanation of bourgeois economic life and the means of introducing a subjective element into his theory of the rational state. Civil society is a necessary moment in the realization of the rational state, and is in itself implicitly rational. Stirling's lengthy attack upon political economy as such is, therefore, wide of the mark in an exposition of Hegel's political philosophy.

In a series of lectures on the philosophy of law delivered to the Juridical Society of Edinburgh in November 1871, Stirling explained Hegel's concrete universal in terms of free will.[6] The discussion is confined to the Hegelian sphere of "abstract right"; whereas, strictly speaking, law, the ostensible subject of these lectures, emerges only in the sphere of "ethical life." The aspect of Hegel's political thought which Stirling emphasized was the mediation of the subjective - here analyzed, in Kantian terms, as the heteronomous - will by the objective will. This stage too belongs to a higher sphere than that of abstract right. The exposition is much more lucid than that of The Secret of Hegel, but it is vitiated by Stirling's inability to adequately distinguish Hegel from Kant, an inability which continued to impede his understanding of Hegel. In this case, he tends to confuse the theoretical moment of the will's freedom from determination by natural impulse and selfish interest with that of the concrete realization of freedom in Sittlichkeit. The first moment occurs in the transition from particular welfare to abstract good; the stage of inward-looking self-certainty or purely formal conscience intervenes before Sittlichkeit or ethical life is achieved. Stirling had a tendency to identify the objective universal with duty for duty's sake, a maxim which, according to Hegel, is an abstract characterization of the good and leads to the most extreme forms of subjectivity, all of which may be advanced as the commands of conscience. Stirling speaks of Hegel's objective spirit as "the realization of free will...in actual outward fact. That actual outward fact is the world of Right, the rational system of observances, legal, moral and political...."[7] However, insufficient weight is given to specific determinations of the concept of freedom and to the historical necessity for societal actualization. About the reasoning from abstract right to a concrete and fully articulated "ethical life," and about the renewed activity of the dialectic of immediacy, particularity and individuality within the ethical order itself, Stirling says nothing, although it is only at the stage of Sittlichkeit that abstract right becomes embodied in law and subjectivity attains rational freedom. The cancelling and preserving of the subjective will in the objective ethical order is the chief distinguishing mark of Hegel's political philosophy, and it was in his own eyes the true fulfilment of what Kant had begun. Stirling evinced the continuity between Kant and Hegel at the expense of fundamental differences.

Stirling's was the first full-length study of Hegel to be published in English. But its success, measured in terms of a deeper and more imaginative understanding of Hegelianism, of scholarly criticism and new departures in philosophy, was negligible. Stirling did something to create a climate of opinion in which Hegel could be taken seriously, but he made no direct contribution to a sober appreciation and critical understanding of Hegelianism. His was an isolated attempt to divert the course of British philosophy - or to inject new life into it, depending on one's point of view. There was a further hiatus of ten years before the work of

---

[6] J.H. Stirling, Lectures in the Philosophy of Law (London, 1873). These lectures were first published in 1872 in the Journal of Jurisprudence and Scottish Law Magazine, and subsequently in book form together with Whewell and Hegel, and Hegel and W.E. Smith: A Vindication in a Physico-Mathematical Regard.
[7] J.H. Stirling, Lectures in the Philosophy of Law, p. 24.

assimilating Hegel got underway in a thorough and penetrating fashion.

Like the members of the St. Louis Philosophical Society in America - in particular, W.T. Harris and G.H. Howison - but without the advantage of their *esprit de corps*, Stirling was a zealous amateur for whom speculative philosophy or metaphysics offered a sort of religious consolation as well as an intellectual fortress in a world of materialism, skepticism and agnosticism, if not outright atheism. He ploughed a rather lonely furrow, not being part of the academically centred "Hegelian School" and, like Herbert Spencer, somewhat self-consciously not seeking popular acclaim. Unlike Spencer, his work was never popular, in spite of his long-standing reputation as the discoverer of Hegel. His genre, however, was one for which there was considerable demand from the Victorian reading public - serious-minded philosophical literature, designed partly to explain to the educated layman what was happening in the world of philosophy, partly to provide inspiration and reassurance to vaguely religious or agnostic people in the conduct of their everyday lives. Among the British Hegelians proper, only McTaggart took popularization seriously. He combined logical rigour and technical expertise with a lifelong commitment to the proposition that metaphysics is a matter of real concern to everyone and that the metaphysician is under some obligation to assist the common moral and religious consciousness in coming to terms with the cosmos. McTaggart came to doubt whether, as Stirling believed, Hegelianism could be of very much assistance in this regard.

CHAPTER 5

Hegel and Classical Scholarship at Oxford

Nothing was published between Stirling's Secret of Hegel and William Wallace's Logic of Hegel (1874) to further the cause of Hegelianism in Britain - with the possible exception of Stirling's Edinburgh lectures on the philosophy of law. During that time, however, the North British Review printed two articles by T.H. Green which were highly critical of "cultivated opinion."[1] The Anglo-Saxon mind, said Green, had not progressed beyond the sensationalism and subjective idealism of Locke and Berkeley, and had not grasped the import of Hume's skeptical conclusions. The first article, entitled "The philosophy of Aristotle," appeared in the September 1866 issue; the second, "Popular philosophy in its relation to life," appeared in that for March 1868.[2] Both assume the higher standpoint of the Critical philosophy and allude to the more unified Hegelian system. In the first, Aristotle is commended for implying ways of overcoming the Platonic dualism of the world and the Idea and then criticized for not pursuing these suggestions and for retaining a God who is an unmoved mover, a transcendent being and entirely passive contemplator. In this connection, Green cites the Hegelian dictum that God without the world would be no God at all - thought is nothing without its externalization.

The second essay is aimed particularly at the discrepancy between the political theory of utilitarianism and its theories of knowledge and moral judgment. Utilitarianism, says Green, is radically incoherent in that, while it bases itself on a sensationalist theory of knowledge and professes an egoistical morality, the political theory of utilitarianism assumes a common end superior to particular interests. Green argues that the greatest happiness of the greatest number is no more than an agglomeration of individual happinesses, but the greatest happiness principle is ostensibly a unifying principle and, as such, inconsistent with its atomistic construction. This internal conflict would not be irreconcilable if a unifying principle, adequate to the task of comprehending the final result in its development and in its totality, could be found. Such a solution to the problem of rationally and systematically explaining the apparent disintegration and disunity of civil society - the world of "getting on" - demands a fully self-conscious metaphysic which has "lived" everything it purports to explain; it cannot impose itself upon any aspect of experience.

In these early essays Green recommended that British moral and political philosophers pay more attention to theoretical considerations and to the work of the German philosophical idealists - which at that time had been out of fashion in Germany itself for almost a generation. The means to a fuller understanding of moral and political life lay close to hand. Not only were Kant and Hegel available - admittedly Hegel was not available in English except

---

[1] Thomas Hill Green (1836-1882), like Bradley and several other British Hegelians, was the son of an Evangelical clergyman. The peculiar significance of this background in the case of Green's philosophy has been well and thoroughly explained by Melvin Richter, The Politics of Conscience: T.H. Green and his Age (Cambridge, Mass., 1964), esp. ch. 1-4. He was Jowett's most distinguished student at Balliol. He was elected a fellow of Balliol in 1860 and became Whyte's Professor of Moral Philosophy in 1877, which post he held until his death. He served on the Taunton commission, investigating schools in the Midlands, 1865-6; he was from 1875 a reforming Liberal on Oxford City Council; and he was active in numerous voluntary associations (local and national) in aid of various kinds of social improvement, especially working-class education and temperance. In national politics he was a John Bright radical.
[2] Both are collected in T.H. Green, Works, ed. R.L. Nettleship (London, 1885-8), vol. III.

for a few badly translated excerpts - but Aristotle was readily accessible and familiar, if no longer the staple intellectual diet of the universities. Aristotle's idea of potentiality and actuality is one of the principal constituents in the Hegelian idea that the world is the unfolding of a single concept from bare abstraction to full concretion. Green was one of the first to make this affiliation clear to the English reader.[3]

In his biography of Benjamin Jowett, Sir Geoffrey Faber claims that he was the man responsible, more than any other, for the introduction of Hegel into England.[4] Although he never published any Hegelian translation or commentary, Jowett is supposed to have initiated British Hegelianism by word of mouth. There is clearly something in this, when one considers his length of tenure at Oxford, his influential position there and the distinguished academic careers of some of his students. He lectured on Hegel at Oxford and was tutor at Balliol to both Green and Edward Caird.

Jowett's fame was, first, as a teacher and an educational reformer, and second - but more lasting - as a classical scholar, especially as the translator of Plato's dialogues. He continually revised this work, and wrote introductions and analyses which were not superseded in some cases for decades. Jowett made use of Hegelian notions to illustrate Plato's theory of Ideas. There is an obvious danger in this of portraying Platonic philosophy as merely a stage in the development of Hegel's, as immature Hegelianism. Hegel himself maintained that earlier philosophies were partial expressions of the truth which his own system completed. This did not mean that these earlier systems were inadequate - they were necessary in their time, at their stage in the development of thought. But they are inadequate from the Hegelian vantage point afforded by their actualization. On the whole Jowett avoided the pitfall of anachronism in his explication of Plato. He repeatedly emphasized the fact that Plato was struggling, virtually at the beginning of philosophy, to clarify and refine the language of common sense and everyday experience in order to make it into a sharp, efficient philosophical tool. In I.M. Crombie's words, Plato was the "midwife's apprentice" - assisting, however, not merely at the birth of individual ideas, but at the birth of philosophy itself.[5] As Jowett points out, Plato was far from successful at his self-appointed task: he was often the victim of those verbal confusions and ambiguities, and metaphors taken literally, which he was trying to eradicate. But he did manage to expose many linguistic muddles masquerading as philosophical problems. More important than this, he saw philosophy as the discovery of the spiritual principle in the world and as the imposing of order upon the chaos of sense experience.

Plato's reaction against the crude inductivism in which he felt the thought of his day was floundering, and against the moral relativism which he regarded as the logical result, led him to advance an extremely bold doctrine: the theory of Ideas. These transcendent entities, known a priori, are timeless and immutable, unaffected by the flux of the sensible world, although the latter owes such shape and order as it possesses to the Ideas. Jowett felt that Plato's conception of a priori knowledge tended to confuse the process of acquiring knowledge with the contemplation of absolute knowledge. Nevertheless, he upheld the Platonic vision of a real world of Ideas. In entertaining such a vision, Plato was explained and partially justified by the continuing need felt for a comprehensive system of knowledge, a need which philosophers as disparate as Descartes and Hegel had attempted to satisfy.

"Nor can we deny that in ancient times knowledge must have stood still and the human mind been deprived of the very instruments of thought if philosophy had been strictly confined to the results of experience."[6]

---

[3] See especially T.H. Green, "The philosophy of Aristotle," Works, vol. III, pp. 75-80.
[4] G. Faber, Jowett (London, 1957), pp. 177-83.
[5] I.M. Crombie, Plato: The Midwife's Apprentice (London, 1964). "Plato was trying, for much of the time, to invent logical shape." (p. 26.)
[6] B. Jowett, Dialogues of Plato, vol. II, p. 80.

Jowett was very careful not to facilely attribute Hegelian anticipations to Plato. In his introductions to the *Parmenides* and the *Sophist* (particularly the latter) he carefully weighed the arguments for and against regarding Plato's criticism of the Eleatic doctrine of the impossibility of non-being as a foreshadowing of Hegel's doctrine of the identity of being and non-being. He also considered how far Plato's theory of determination through negation anticipated that of Hegel (and that of Spinoza). He concluded that Plato had given us hints of the concept of non-being functioning as the determination of being, but that he had not explained this function in Hegelian terms - he remained unaware of development through the opposition of being and non-being. The most extreme of the Eleatics had denied the possibility of both falsehood and a sensible world as species of non-being. According to Jowett, Plato introduced the Eleatics as an illustration of transcendental speculation which has lost all contact with common sense. Further, Plato's own thought exhibited a dialectical movement from abstraction and the transcendent to concreteness and the familiar, the *Laws* representing the conclusion and completion of this process. Jowett owed this notion to Hegel's view of the history of Greek philosophy. At one point he links the two philosophers together through "the spirit which places the divine above the human, the spiritual above the material, the one above the many, the mind before the body."[7] Jowett was fully aware that Hegel was not a transcendentalist, that for him the spiritual was present in the material, the one in the many. As a reflective Christian, however, Jowett could not accept the sheer immanence of the spiritual. On the other hand, he clearly could not on that account exclude Hegel from the idealist tradition. In spite of differences within that tradition, there is, he felt, the great connecting link of the repudiation of the isolation of ideas, one from another. "The Platonic unity of differences or opposites is the beginning of the modern view that all knowledge is of relations."[8] This Platonic unity, says Jowett, is the forerunner of "the Hegelian concrete or unity of abstractions."[9] It is not related, however, to the full Hegelian unity of thought and being, a theory of the nature of the world and experience which, in its sweepingly comprehensive monism, is much more audacious than Plato's theory of Ideas and which Jowett the theologian found repugnant.

Jowett's letters and unpublished notebooks make it clear that he came to regard Hegel as a man "drunk with metaphysics" and capable of a metaphysical fanaticism as pernicious as the more familiar religious kind. He had many harsh words for the new passion for metaphysics and the resultant neglect of "facts." Jowett was especially disappointed by Green, whom he had originally singled out to be the hammer of the philistine empiricists, such as Bain and Spencer. Unfortunately, as Jowett saw it, Green was infecting others with his own scholasticism. The revolt against the tyranny of empiricism had degenerated into "interminable disputes over abstractions." Among all the conventional strictures on Green's Hegelianism - excessive abstraction, immoral quietism, overweening intellectual pride - is the following shrewd comment:

"Like the true syncretist, he is unable to distinguish Kant and Hegel any more than the Neoplatonist was able to distinguish Plato from Aristotle. He is the servant of philosophy, not the master of it."[10]

In political theory, Jowett inclined toward a utilitarian rule of thumb. Although he considered utilitarianism inadequate to account for moral obligation, he maintained that "the most useful is the most holy" and was prepared to justify certain institutions by their social utility alone. Plato, he says, "did not intend to oppose the useful to some higher conception, such as the Platonic ideal, but to chance and caprice."[11] Generally speaking, he steered clear

---

[7] B. Jowett, *Dialogues of Plato*, vol. I, p. 263.
[8] B. Jowett, *Dialogues of Plato*, vol. III, p. 351.
[9] Ibid, p. 353.
[10] B. Jowett, notebook No. 25, entitled "Philosophy," dated August 9, 1881, p. 57.
[11] B. Jowett, *Dialogues of Plato*, vol. II, p. 212.

of the increasingly heated debate between atomist and organicist tendencies in political theory. The character of any human society, he says, is simply the balance of individual wills "limited by the condition of having to act in common." On the other hand, "we hesitate to say that the characters of nations are nothing more than the sum of the characters of the individuals who compose them; because there may be tendencies in individuals which react upon one another."[12]

Jowett argued that the search for an identity of individual and communal moral wills is indicative of a primitive type of morality which men revert to when under the influence of party or prejudice. He appears to have overlooked Hegel's injection of a subjective element into, and consequent radical alteration of, Plato's theory of the ideal state. Jowett attacked Hegel's political theory for the defects of a political theory which belonged to a period of human history when there were no individuals in the modern European sense, when there was not the same degree of individual self-consciousness. Moreover, he detected in Hegel's theory of the rational state an irrational appeal to the sort of collectivist sentiment cultivated by modern despots. In an unguarded moment he baldly stated that "political absolutism is the necessary result of philosophical idealism."[13]

On the model of his approach to the interpretation of Scripture, Jowett was at pains to distinguish - not always successfully - between Plato the Greek thinker of the fourth century B.C. and Plato the founder of that idealist tradition of which Hegel was the most notable modern representative. The Hegelian "succession of moments in the unity of the Idea" Jowett considered the nearest approach in modern philosophy to the universal science of Plato. Both philosophers "conceived the world as the correlation of abstractions...."

"There is, however, a difference between them: for whereas Hegel is thinking of all the minds of men as one mind, which develops the stages of the idea in different countries or at different times in the same country, with Plato these gradations are regarded only as an order of thought or ideas; the history of the human mind had not yet dawned upon him."[14]

Plato's system of knowledge was also a metaphysical system, an account of the world as it really is. The real was rational for him, as it was for Hegel. Plato's system, however, was a static hierarchy; Hegel's was an expanding movement from implicitness to explicitness. The nub of the Hegelian system is that it is developmental. The Hegelian notion of a rational spirit coming to be in the world by coming to know itself in the world is one of which Plato could not have conceived. Plato had no such conception in the back of his mind when he "confused" acquiring knowledge with the contemplation of absolute knowledge. He did not possess the idea of development, only that of change. Plato's Idea of the Good is both fully real and uninvolved in temporal change; it is eternally complete and explicit. Hegel's world spirit requires change, contingency and concrete particularity for its explication or realization.

Jowett was praised by many illustrious Oxford graduates as a great teacher and the one who made them aware of Hegelianism. By 1845 it would seem likely that Jowett was using examples drawn from German philosophical idealism in his teaching at Oxford, but the nature of his teaching is difficult to estimate. An examination of his notebooks in the Balliol library did not resolve the difficulty. His extant notes and jottings on Hegel consist of partial outlines

---

[12] B. Jowett, *Republic of Plato*, vol. II, p. 138.
[13] B. Jowett, notebook No. 1, p. 125. It might be of some minor historical interest to establish a date for Jowett's first notebook. If the date inscribed on No. 25 - 1881 - means anything, then perhaps No. 1 reflects in part the anti-Hegelian reaction which Jowett would have been exposed to when he was in Germany. On the other hand, it's more in keeping with the testiness of his later criticism of Hegel. At any rate, it anticipates the most common assessment of Hegelian political theory in the English-speaking world in the twentieth century.
[14] B. Jowett, *Dialogues of Plato*, vol. II, p. 159.

of the Hegelian system, subject headings which are frequently in the form of epigrammatic and enigmatic questions, and those obiter dicta which he considered the most valuable element in Hegel's own writings. His later notebooks contain a number of querulous remarks complaining of the abstraction of all metaphysics, especially Hegelian. Nevertheless, there is sufficient testimony that the teaching of Jowett at Balliol - with all his reservations about Hegel - made a significant contribution to the naturalization of Hegel. Furthermore, he taught other and more enthusiastic teachers of Hegelianism.

Edward Caird was one of those - a steady, persistent purveyor of Hegelianism for some forty years and the doyen of the British Hegelians in the 1890s.[15] By 1866, Caird was teaching more or less along Hegelian lines at Glasgow.[16] His Hegel, which was not published until 1883, is still a good short introduction to the study of Hegel's philosophy. His two full-length studies of Kant's philosophy were both written from a Hegelian standpoint.[17]

In spite of Jowett's, and Green's, teaching at Oxford, the university was extremely reluctant to give official recognition to Hegel. As for Cambridge, it was not until 1895 that the philosophy of Hegel was offered as a special subject in the moral sciences tripos. However, questions about various aspects of Kant's philosophy had been appearing periodically in the Cambridge examinations for almost forty years prior to that - which put Cambridge considerably in advance of Oxford, at least so far as official acknowledgment of German philosophy was concerned. One might detect in this the academic influence, both administrative and intellectual, of Henry Sidgwick.[18] His utilitarianism was subtle and broadly based, drawing upon the ethics of "right" and intuition, as well as that of "good" and consequences. The greatest happiness of the greatest number was a moral imperative for Sidgwick, as much as it was a natural good. In expounding this view he made direct use of Kantian arguments. In addition to the weight of his intellectual reputation, Sidgwick's activity in the cause of tripos reform was instrumental in expanding and enriching the moral sciences reading list at Cambridge. Cambridge's moral sciences tripos showed a broad interest in German philosophy long before Oxford's literae humaniores did. There is no doubt, however, that Oxford was the first to make significant and original contributions to Hegelian studies; and it continued to be the source of most of the best work in philosophical idealism.

It also appears certain that the dominance of Plato and Aristotle in literae humaniores, which lasted much longer than in the Cambridge moral sciences tripos, had a lot to do with the greater Oxford interest in Hegel. The "Greats" school at Oxford, in its application of classical scholarship to the study of ancient history and philosophy, made continual reference to modern philosophical developments and to the social and political problems of contemporary England.

> "The first condition of a right understanding of our institutions and ways of thinking and of a sane progress in politics and philosophy is the study of the growth of our civilization, both on the side of practice and on that of thought, from its

---

[15] Edward Caird (1835-1908) studied classics and philosophy at Balliol under Jowett. He was a classmate of T.H. Green, his close friend, with whom he shared an enthusiasm for working-class interests and improvement. He was briefly a fellow and tutor of Merton College before being appointed Professor of Moral Philosophy at Glasgow University, 1866-93, and then Master of Balliol to succeed Jowett, 1893-1907.

[16] Evidence for this, Edinburgh and Oxbridge recognition of German philosophy (discussed in the following two paragraphs) can be found in university calendars and degree examination papers from 1855 to 1905.

[17] See A Critical Account of the Philosophy of Kant (Glasgow, 1877) and The Critical Philosophy of Immanuel Kant (Glasgow, 1889). See also ch. 11 of the present work (pp. 92-93) for a discussion of Caird as a promoter of idealism as a sort of surrogate for religious belief.

[18] See ch. 6, pp. 52-53, for a discussion of Sidgwick's brand of utilitarianism.

roots in ancient Greek life and speculation."[19]

As we have seen from a discussion of his Platonic scholarship and because of his prominent position in the Oxford "Greats" school, Jowett was clearly a key figure in the transmission of Hegelian ideas. His progressive disenchantment with Hegel and with metaphysics as a course of undergraduate study led him to reduce but not eliminate the Hegelian ingredient in his commentaries upon Plato. The publication of Jowett's Dialogues of Plato in 1871 - a translation accompanied by lengthy introductions and analyses - was something of a philosophical as well as a philological and literary event, and it retained its authority through many editions.

William Wallace, another student of Jowett, translated the first part of Hegel's Encyclopaedia of the Philosophical Sciences as The Logic of Hegel, which was published in 1874.[20] It marks the beginning in earnest of British Hegelianism. It was with the stream of Hegel translations, Hegelian commentaries and Hegel-inspired philosophy, which flowed strongly from the mid-1870s through to World War I, that philosophical idealism came into its own as a school of British philosophy. The major source of that stream was Oxford, especially Merton and Balliol Colleges - Jowett and Green were Balliol men; Caird, after many years at Glasgow, returned to Balliol as Master on Jowett's death; Bradley was a fellow and Wallace a fellow and tutor of Merton.[21]

As Wallace pointed out in his "prolegomena" to The Logic of Hegel, Hegel had written his Logik (the "Greater Logic") almost sixty years before and many changes had occurred in intellectual life since then, the most significant of which were the spectacular success of natural science and the widespread assumption of the inductive method as the only sure way to reliable human knowledge. One by-product of these changes was a dismissive attitude toward speculative philosophy of all kinds. Positivism and empiricism and the self-denying philosophy of the unknowable had virtually swept metaphysics away by the time Wallace published his Logic of Hegel. Wallace's grasp of Hegel's meaning and purpose was unprecedented in English commentary upon German philosophy. His "prolegomena" offers an account of Hegel's unity of thought and being - its progressive self-development, the expansion and explication of logical categories from an abstract point in being - which does not confuse the logical dialectic with its manifestations in nature and human history. At the same time, the necessity of spirit's self-externalization in nature and human history is made evident. As Wallace says, Hegel's philosophy is the intellectual grasp of "what is" and is itself an actualization of the rational. Like Stirling before him, Wallace proclaimed the Hegelian enterprise: philosophy is both the real process of the world's creation and its culmination. Unlike Stirling, however, his presentation is notably clear and succinct.

"True philosophy must show that it has got hold of what it means to discuss: it has to construct its subject matter; and it constructs it by tracing every step and movement in its construction shown in actual history. The mind is what it has been made...,"[22]

At one point in his "prolegomena" Wallace attacks the prevailing political theory of individualism:

"The business of the political philosopher is not to trace the limits between

---

[19] D.G. Ritchie, Philosophical Studies, ed. R. Latta (London, 1905), p. 5 (from the biographical memoir by Latta).
[20] William Wallace (1844-97) came to Balliol College from the University of St. Andrews in 1864. He became a fellow of Merton College in 1867 and a tutor in 1868. He succeeded Green as Whyte's Professor of Moral Philosophy in 1882, which post he held until his death.
[21] The association of Merton with Hegel was maintained by H.H. Joachim and G.R.G. Mure, who recently retired as Warden of Merton.
[22] W. Wallace, The Logic of Hegel (Oxford, 1874), p. liv.

state interference and the liberty of particular citizens, nor to play the one off against the other so as to determine their several spheres, but to see how these two fragmentary aspects unite."[23]

This is a recurrent theme of British Hegelianism - the total interdependence of the state and its individual members, founded upon the unity of the individual and the collective mind. In the Gifford Lectures for 1895, Wallace put this in the context of the organic theory of society:

"That intelligence and reason, conscience and language, emerge only through social, collective or combined action is the point. Sociality is not mere juxtaposition, mere aggregation...."[24]

In another, more political essay Wallace is unreservedly Hegelian. The state is not only logically prior to the individual and the actualization of morality in the shape of legally enforceable rights, but it is also "the mortal God, and in this world it should be ubiquitous and omnipotent."[25] Such a strongly worded sentiment in favour of state power sounds an ominous note to those living in the latter half of the twentieth century, and it certainly suggests something other than Hegel's carefully articulated Rechtstaat. However, the doctrines of individualism and natural rights tended to provoke an exaggerated response from the British Hegelians. Under the calm surface of late Victorian and Edwardian political life a strong current of extremism was running, and Wallace's views reflected not only a passion for Hegelian philosophy, but also the Hegelians' intense dislike of the many current theories which "claimed too much for liberty." When the Great War broke out in 1914, the United Kingdom was deeply divided on a number of issues and large-scale violence threatened on the Irish and labour fronts, to such an extent that some commentators have said that a second English civil war was in the making.

Elsewhere Wallace expressed doubts about the state's capacity to fulfil the moral end for man. Like Green and Bosanquet, Wallace recognized that the social "organism" often appears to its member "organs" as a social "mechanism," an external and inhuman constraining force rather than the embodiment of their free rational wills. The social forms may become divorced from "the inner state of affairs" and the feeling of being coerced may be justified. When "the social form...comes to possess an authority of its own independent of what it represents," when "it asserts itself as a separate structure with a life and interests of its own," then it has become a "morbid growth."[26] Strictly speaking, the idealist theory of the state cannot accept a representational account of "social form," according to which it represents a rather mysterious "inner state of affairs." It is the necessary external reflection and embodiment of the "inner state of affairs"; there cannot be an inner state of affairs existing independently of the institutions of society. In the same essay, Wallace goes so far as to concede a right of ultimate judgment, even of rebellion, to individual conscience in matters which belong, according to Hegel, to the determination of objective mind. The state subsumes the claims of morality - and those of religion. Any conflict between the demands of the rational state and those of morality and religion can be resolved only by further social growth - that is to say, by expansion of the rational will, not by the state simply yielding to the morality of constituent individuals and groups.

Wallace is best known as an able translator and lucid expositor of Hegelianism. In addition to the Logic of Hegel, Wallace also translated the third part of the Encyclopaedia as Hegel's Philosophy of Mind (1894). He also wrote occasional essays, such as "The Relation of Fichte and Hegel to Socialism," which expounded Hegel's philosophy in a clear, concise fashion

---

[23] Ibid., p. clxiii.
[24] W. Wallace, "The Relation of Religion to Morality," Lectures and Essays on Natural Theology and Ethics, ed. E. Caird (London, 1898), p. 122.
[25] W. Wallace, "Our Natural Rights," Ibid., p. 263.
[26] W. Wallace, "The Legal, Social and Religious Sanctions of Morality," Ibid., p. 460.

and related it to topics of current British concern. He was, however, sometimes incautious in his restatements of Hegelian themes. One example is the following passage from his Gifford Lectures:

> "The rule for man is not to merely accept the given, but to mould and fashion it for himself. In him nothing merely is: it is to be: it has taken on it a new law, the law of becoming, as the law which governs him and the things he deals with."[27]

Here Wallace has taken the idea of an inwardly controlling pattern of logical development which permeates all things and projected it into the imperative. It then begins to look very much like the Promethean rule of man over his environment rather than an explanatory principle. The "law of becoming" is not quite the same thing as the Hegelian unfolding of Being. Wallace has here superimposed upon the Hegelian enclosed infinite the traditional open-ended one, the strictly endless infinite. The world, for Hegel, was not static or finished. But, while it may not have reached its end, the end is known and in that sense achieved. The end is full self-knowledge, the self-consciousness of the universe as spirit. The end is known because human reason is the vehicle of that self-consciousness.

For those reconstructions of Hegelianism which are both more original and more true to the spirit of Hegel, we must look to three of Wallace's contemporaries: F.H. Bradley, T.H. Green and Bernard Bosanquet. Before we do, something needs to be said about utilitarianism, the moral and political theory which dominated British intellectual life in mid-century and which had hardened into something like orthodoxy by the 1870s. The moral theory of self-realization and the idealist theory of the state were produced, in large measure, by way of reaction to utilitarianism, and opposition to that school of thought united the British Hegelians more than any other single factor.

---

[27] W. Wallace, "The Relation of Religion to Morality," *Ibid.*, p. 112.

CHAPTER 6

The Principle of Utility from Hume to Sidgwick

Hegelianism, as a movement in British thought, was impelled in great part by profound dissatisfaction with the utilitarian account of moral and political life. It owed its brief vigour as much to its fierce opposition to hedonism and utilitarianism as to the positive inspiration it drew from Hegel and German philosophical idealism. Utilitarianism or universalistic hedonism was the theoretical frame of reference for enlightened and progressive opinion during most of the Victorian age. Its classic formulation is usually taken to be John Stuart Mill's Utilitarianism, published in Fraser's magazine in 1863.[1] It is in this work that Mill committed that logical "howler" over which generations of critics have gloated, and because of which utilitarianism is held by many to be defective at its very core. Mill moved from the supposed fact that everyone desires only his own happiness to the alleged consequence that everyone should desire the happiness of all, the greatest collective happiness. Put like this, the mistake seems fairly obvious. In Mill's words, however, the notion has a certain initial plausibility:

> "No reason can be given why the general happiness is desirable, except that each person, so far as he believes it to be attainable, desires his own happiness. This, however, being a fact, we have not only all the proof which the case admits of, but all which it is possible to require, that happiness is a good: that each person's happiness is a good to that person, and the general happiness, therefore, a good to the aggregate of all persons."[2]

He immediately went on to establish that happiness is the only intrinsic good and the "sole criterion of morality."

There are, to be precise, two logical errors in Mill's statement. In the first place, it does not follow from each person's happiness being a good to that person that the general happiness is a good to the aggregate of all persons. No matter how one puts each person's private happiness together with everyone else's, the result is more likely to be a chaos of conflicting happinesses than a concerted general happiness; an aggregate of personal goods is not a common good.

Mill's second error is the celebrated is-ought slip. Now it is a commonplace of moral philosophy that one cannot derive an "ought" from an "is." That is, to proceed from a statement or statements about what is the case to statements about what ought to be, or be done, is to shift one's logical ground. Statements about what is and statements about what ought to be are of radically different logical types. If one attempts to ground the latter in the former, one commits a fundamental logical error. A non-moral "ought" - as in, "If you're going out to the theatre, you ought to get ready" or "It ought to rain tomorrow" - can follow from "is" statements without vitiating the argument; whereas the moral "ought" of obligation can only be derived from statements among which there is at least one which itself contains the moral "ought." Mill maintains that the only reason the general happiness is desirable is that each person desires his own happiness.

---

[1] It was first collected with On Liberty and Representative Government in 1910 for the Everyman's Library edition, and together with his System of Logic they constitute the best part of the "philosophy" if not the operating principles of reforming liberals in the nineteenth century.
[2] J.S. Mill, Utilitarianism (Everyman ed.), pp. 32-33.

> "The only proof capable of being given that an object is visible, is that people actually see it. The only proof that a sound is audible, is that people hear it: and so of the other sources of our experience. In like manner, I apprehend, the sole evidence it is possible to produce that anything is desirable, is that people do actually desire it."[3]

Here is that frequently imperceptible shift from "is" to "ought" at its most perceptible. The error is committed in the shortest possible space and with the least possible disguise.

It is so blatant that one feels that Mill may well have been aware of it, but had reasons for believing that he had not actually committed it. He may have been equating the fact that something is desired with its desirability. Desirability, or goodness, would then be the same thing as being desired; to say that something is desirable, or good, would be to say no more than that it is desired. This is the kind of tautology which G.E. Moore had in mind when exposing the so-called naturalistic fallacy. If "desirable" just meant "desired" it would cease to be an ethical word at all. Normally "desirable" means more than having a capacity for being desired. In this sense, it is quite unlike "visible" or "audible," and Mill's analogy breaks down - unless he was abandoning usage in favour of an entirely non-ethical meaning of "desirable," which is highly unlikely. Perhaps Mill did not intend to empty "desirable" of all ethical content whatsoever, but merely to detach it from the moral "ought." In that case, "desirable" would still be a synonym for "good," but goodness would be a pleasing quality like the warmth of the sun's rays on a winter day. This line of argument would have the net result of emptying "good" of any strictly moral imperative: what is good ought to be, but there is no duty incumbent upon anyone to further it. Again, it is highly unlikely that this was Mill's intention, since he commended the love of virtue for itself alone as a disposition valuable in the promotion of acts contributing to the general happiness - virtuous conduct is good as a means to the one intrinsic good, the general happiness. As a utilitarian, Mill could hardly maintain that virtue is an end entirely in itself.

It is in terms of a derivative theory of morality that one can partially justify Mill's logical carelessness. In a clearly definable sense, "ought" must be grounded in "is." Here is the second of a pair of antinomies: it is indisputably the case that "ought" <u>cannot</u> be derived from "is," and likewise that "ought" <u>must</u> be derived from "is"; and yet both are also untrue. The solution to these antinomies hinges upon the dual interpretation of "derived." In the first, one cannot derive "ought" from "is" in the analytical sense - in other words, there is no necessary relationship of implication - but one can in the looser sense that an "ought" is a natural desire that has been moralized. In the second, one must derive "ought" from "is," otherwise the "ought" is empty - one ought to do nothing. On the other hand, one must not do so, otherwise the moral quality of the thing that ought to be done is lost. The strictly moral properties of a desirable action are injected by the moral will; the fact that there is a desire to do it does not entail its morality. However, if it were not desired the moral will would be working in a vacuum.

As Hegel would say, the difficulty arises from taking each of the antinomies in isolation from the other. A synthesis of the two can be made in such a way that the truth of each is preserved. The synthesized truth is that what ought to be done satisfies human nature, and what makes it morally obligatory is the conscious decision to make it part of a rational plan of action. Every blind impulse, every unreflective desire is not automatically a moral obligation. However, a moral obligation created in defiance of natural good - and some moral codes have contained commandments contrary to human survival itself - must be unworkable. Furthermore, the content of the will is ultimately supplied by desire; the will imposes itself upon the desire - in the case of the moral will, from a moral motive. The moral will can be its own end, but to be an effective will it must be a will to do something good, and the handful of goods which are

---

[3] Ibid., p. 32.

intrinsically good are so largely because they are desired. Their goodness and their being desired are inseparable. Anything which is conducive to them ought to be done because it is desirable - in both senses of the word. If goodness - which is presumably something which ought to be for its own sake, if not the only end in itself - is detached from human desires, it surely loses all relevance to the moral life. The desirable must be capable of being desired, it must answer to some human need, as well as be desirable in the strictly ethical sense of the word. For the desirable to be good, it is not sufficient for it to be desired, but it is necessary.

Some moral philosophers have argued very convincingly that there are certain right actions whose rightness cannot be derived from goodness, that there are some things which one ought to do regardless of consequences, such as pay one's debts or tell the truth. Nevertheless, something must be done, some change in the actual state of affairs must be at least intended, and the moral will must place itself in the world of conflict and passion - either deliberately or heedless of the consequences. In the same way, the intrinsically good, whose goodness cannot be derived from some higher or more inclusive good, is a natural as well as an ethical object. It is a complex of needs and desires which have been moralized; a process of mediation is required before a desire can be desirable. The establishment of a connection between "is" and "ought" involves greater use of self-conscious reason than that revealed in Mill's apparently unwitting shift from desire to desirability. However, in making that shift, he implicitly affirmed an important ethical truth which has often been lost sight of: although that which is desired is not necessarily desirable, the desirable must be something which is capable of being actually, humanly desired.

Mill's "naturalism" places him, as a moral philosopher, closer to Hegel than those British Hegelians, notably Green, who were influenced in their ethics as much, if not more, by Kant as they were by Hegel. For Hegel, the natural heteronomous desires are not amoral, not something to be coerced into moral order by the good will. The pursuit of pleasure, for example, is implicitly moral, although not the height of moral endeavour. Contrary to hedonism, men do desire ends other than pleasure. Contrary to Kantianism, there is no loss of morality in the desiring of them - or of pleasure. There can be no morality without desire, not because morality must suppress desire or else die of inactivity, but because morality is rationalized desire. Hegel's concept of <u>Sittlichkeit</u> and Mill's version of the principle of utility both devote considerable attention to the morality of everyday life, including that of the marketplace. One frankly acknowledges the hedonistic motive; the other seeks to transform it into an ethical precept. While Hegel's is the more ambitious theory, tracing a rational continuity between family life and law, and between "getting and spending" and service of the state, both purport to unite unreflective need and self-conscious effort to realize the good.

Henry Sidgwick explicitly recognized Mill's logical error, and did not try to derive the desirability of something from the fact of anyone's actually desiring it: he saw clearly that to argue the entailment of a thing's desirability from its actually being desired was to confuse psychology with ethics.[4] He maintained that the utilitarian goal, the greatest

---

[4] H. Sidgwick, <u>The Methods of Ethics</u>, 7th ed. (London, 1907), bk. I, ch. 4 and bk. III, ch. 13.
Henry Sidgwick (1838-1900) was, like T.H. Green, a product of Thomas Arnold's Rugby. He went to Trinity College, Cambridge, in 1855, became a fellow in 1859, resigned in 1869 because of conscientious objection to the Thirty-nine Articles of the Church of England, and was reappointed when the law requiring subscription was changed. He was elected Knightsbridge Professor of Moral Philosophy in 1883. He lectured and wrote voluminously on a wide variety of topics, economic, political and literary as well as philosophical. He initiated an eccentric Cambridge tradition of serious philosophical interest in extra-sensory perception and psychical research, which has been continued, first by a student of his, McTaggart (of whom more later in ch. 10 and 11), and then by McTaggart's expositor, C.D. Broad.

happiness of the greatest number, was a fundamental moral intuition; whereas Mill believed that from their being desired it directly followed that any amount of happiness or combination of happinesses was desirable. Sidgwick regarded the utilitarian goal as ethically irreducible - it is an analytical truth that the supreme good is the general happiness.[5] One cannot, on the basis of human behaviour, prove the desirability of the general happiness and the superiority of universalistic over egoistic hedonism. The consistent egoist is irrefutable. He is also very unusual in that he has either successfully suppressed all his disinterested motives, or else he had none to begin with. Such a person will have to either conduct himself as if he were in a Hobbesian state of nature with other persons; or, given the existence of a moral sense in human beings, he must irrationally hope for better treatment from others than he metes out to them. The core of Sidgwick's argument is the construction of a universalistic ethic out of the alleged utilitarian intuition that individual welfare is inseparable from the general welfare. Psychological hedonism, the theory that each person desires only his own separate happiness, was an ethical red herring as far as Sidgwick was concerned.

For his defence of universalistic hedonism, Sidgwick drew upon intuitionist moral philosophers. From Bishop Butler's doctrine of the paramountcy of conscience and from Kant's theory of the self-legislating practical reason, he fashioned arguments in support of his belief that there is, in fact, a sense of moral obligation which prompts human beings to pursue the happiness of a widening circle of others. Sidgwick agreed with the intuitionists that people feel they are absolutely obliged in certain cases to act in a certain way, that they have moral duties which take precedence not only over their personal interests but even over some more general good; that there are, in short, moral rules which people obey without further consideration, without looking beyond the rule itself.[6] Sidgwick went on to assert that such rules, in spite of their being felt to be completely autonomous and categorical, can nevertheless be shown to be comprehended by the greatest happiness principle, and that conflicts between these categorical imperatives - which conflicts constitute one of the most demanding aspects of the moral life - are usually resolved by some such principle. The utilitarian end is a unifying, synthetic principle. It gathers together all the different duties and obligations, all the separate moral intuitions, under one head. It is their common ground, although not their common source, and it is itself an intuited moral truth:

"...the Intuitional method rigorously applied yields as its final result the doctrine of pure Universalistic Hedonism - which it is convenient to denote by the single word, Utilitarianism."[7]

Sidgwick's explanation of the connection between intuitionism and utilitarianism did not make the greatest happiness principle respectable in the eyes of the British Hegelians. Their quarrel was with the fundamental intuition itself, that the moral end for man was a net balance of pleasure. It was not redeemed by being a collective or social objective rather than one for separated individuals. Their critique of the greatest happiness principle is best exemplified in the work of F.H. Bradley, which will be discussed in the following chapter. Their objections to hedonism were an integral part of their campaign against the utilitarian view of man in society.

---

[5] "...if the duty of aiming at the general happiness is thus taken to include all other duties, as subordinate applications of it, we seem to be again led to the notion of Happiness as an ultimate end categorically prescribed - only it is now General Happiness and not the private happiness of any individual. And this is the view that I myself take of the Utilitarian principle." (H. Sidgwick, Methods of Ethics, p. 8.)
[6] This did not prevent Sidgwick from objecting, in almost Hegelian fashion, that Kant's conception of "humanity as an end in itself" was a sort of "paralogism," in that no principle of benevolence toward actual human beings with "empirical desires and aversions" could be deduced from it. (Ibid., p. 390.)
[7] Ibid., pp. 406-07. See also pp. 475-80.

Utilitarian political writings of the post-Napoleonic period were a defence of liberal-democratic gains against the general European reaction, in which campaign offence was the most effective form of defence for the English utilitarians because the Industrial Revolution and the attendant increase in power for the middle classes had advanced so much further in Britain than elsewhere in Europe.[8] Utilitarianism's belated success in inspiring many nineteenth century English legal and political reforms owed a great deal to its ideological links with laissez-faire political economy and its decidedly unrevolutionary opposition to those feudal remnants which both romantics and reactionaries were futilely trying to breathe new life into. With the co-optation of the industrial bourgeoisie by the British ruling class, utilitarianism became almost respectable. It had always been contemptuous of the natural rights of man, and its espousal of political democracy was one of cool calculation, not heartfelt commitment; but as a science of social reconstruction, it was inherently subversive of the closed corporations and hierarchical structure of traditional society. The method of utilitarianism's founder, Jeremy Bentham, was the method of enlightened despotism - the confidence in human malleability of a Condorcet wedded to the power of a Hobbesian sovereign.

James Mill proceeded, under Bentham's tutelage, on the assumption that society can be theoretically broken down into its individual components without residue or loss and that these individuals are independent, self-contained units. Furthermore, they are entirely and inevitably self-centred - each pursues only his own best interest. One's best interest is a favourable balance of pleasure over pain, which it is in the nature of the human being to seek. In his *Essay on Government* (1828) Mill says of human nature:

> "We must content ourselves with assuming certain results...for example, in general terms that the lot of every human being is determined by his pains and pleasures, and that his happiness corresponds with the degree in which his pleasures are great and his pains are small."[9]

Every human being, says Mill, "has an insatiable desire for the means to his own greatest happiness," the chief of which is the power to induce - or coerce - conformity of others' wills to the pursuit of his interest. This is a "law of nature," the result of which, in concatenation with other such laws, is that "the interest of the community, considered in the aggregate or in the democratical point of view, is that each individual should receive protection...."[10] It is, of course, one's interest to calculate the long-term and indirect consequences of one's actions, and the reactions of others, and to weigh pleasure against pleasure, pain against pain. The enlightened man recognizes that his pleasure frequently lies in that of others - there is a natural identity of interests. This natural harmony can be reinforced and enlarged by an artificial one, the manipulation by the government of the incentive of pleasure and, more effectively, the disincentive of pain. The good society on this view is a legal framework within which the individual can pursue undistracted his own particular happiness. His fellow members of society are no more to him than contributors - or hindrances - to his personal happiness.

The utilitarian account of society was an atomistic one. It derived much of its original impetus from the comparatively new science of political economy, which deliberately isolated the economic motive for the purpose of studying the exchange of material wealth, of land, labour, capital and their products. The theoretically untrammelled operation of the economic motive was taken by the early utilitarians to corroborate their theory that society is an

---

[8] The European dimension should be noted because, while utilitarianism was a primarily English-speaking phenomenon, it had deep roots in the Continental Enlightenment. Bentham drew at least as much from the philosophical materialism of Helvetius and the penology of Beccaria as he did from the associationist psychology of Hartley. Furthermore, he wrote for a European audience and was read much more widely in translation than in English.
[9] James Mill, *An Essay on Government*, ed. C.V. Shields (Indianapolis, 1955), p. 48.
[10] *Ibid.*, p. 65.

aggregation of self-centred pleasure-seekers. It was for them the mechanism and the activities of the free market writ large. The institutional side of social life - those slow historical accumulations which survive the generations - was regarded with intense suspicion as the shield of sinister interests. The role that society plays in shaping man as a moral being, and in presenting him with fresh moral demands and opportunities, was not recognized by Bentham and James Mill. In fact, they seem to have been singularly insensitive to the whole gregarious side of human nature. This cannot, in fairness, be said of either Sidgwick or John Stuart Mill; but they failed to take full account of the extent to which man is a creature of the society which he has himself created. J.S. Mill acknowledged the existence of "a deeply rooted conception which every individual even now has of himself as a social being, [which] tends to make him feel it one of his natural wants that there should be harmony between his feelings and aims and those of his fellow creatures...." "This conviction," says Mill, "is the ultimate sanction of the greatest happiness morality."[11] Mill never abandoned the atomistic view of society implicit in Benthamite utilitarianism, in spite of "this conviction" of social "harmony," and in spite of what Coleridge had taught him about the underlying rational meaning and purpose of many received opinions and ancient institutions. He continually reaffirmed the greatest happiness of the greatest number as the supreme good and refused to abandon psychological hedonism as the basis for utilitarian ethics. He talked of harmonizing individual feelings and aims, never of sharing a common interest which transcends any combination of individual interests.

Sidgwick had more sense of historical continuity than other utilitarians and tended increasingly to see some kind of moral fulfilment in the expansion of "the European polity." For Sidgwick the greatest happiness principle was primarily an explanatory device, a method of analyzing the moral life and of synthesizing moral rules. For both the Mills and Bentham, it had greater cutting edge, more practical employment. Although J.S. Mill belonged to a less revolutionary age than did his father and Bentham, he too looked upon the greatest happiness principle as the exposer of dangerous "fictions," the solvent of dogma and the scourge of antiquated laws and rotten institutions which impeded human progress. He was also confident that the enlightened man or "philosopher" could safely rationalize the common moral consciousness as enlarged self-love. Mill did not deny that conventional morality was indispensable to social cohesion; but it required rationalization, it needed to be examined in the light of the greatest happiness principle and trimmed accordingly. He was sure that the introduction of that principle into the moral life would simply confirm most of the established moral code and strengthen the existing sense of duty and social obligation. As has been noted many times before, Mill tried valiantly to combine two opposing philosophical traditions: the root-and-branch reform one of Bentham, and the conservative, historically minded one of Coleridge. He attempted to graft a sense of community and the notion of cumulative social growth onto the utilitarian trunk, the idea that society is no more than the aggregate of individuals who presently compose it and that nothing binds them together but enlightened self-interest. The attempt failed because it was a graft which could not take - the two ideas were incompatible.

It is interesting to compare Hume with the utilitarians on this matter - if only because coming to terms with Hume was seen by many of the British Hegelians, especially T.H. Green, as an essential propaedeutic to disposing of utilitarianism. Hume was a precursor of utilitarianism in his advocacy of the principle of utility. Yet in Hume's philosophy the principle of utility was invoked in support of natural sociability. Ordinary virtue was a useful means to the preservation of social harmony and stability. The utilitarians, on the other hand, regarded the social order as a means to promoting individual happiness, albeit the greatest amount of the greatest number. They conveyed no sense of society being anything other than the aggregate of individuals composing it, of its constituting any common bond among them. It is a common interest only insofar as it serves every particular individual interest;

---

[11] J.S. Mill, *Utilitarianism* (Everyman ed.), p. 31.

in other words, it is something different to each one. Morality is as much a matter of enlightened self-interest within society as it would be without - if such a condition were conceivable - the only difference being that one must in one's own interest be more considerate of the interests of others in an organized political society. One interpretation of Hume depicts him resisting the spread of this "personal convenience" view of society:

> "His 'utility' is based not exclusively or even primarily on the separate, calculating individual, but essentially on what he took to be general and objective social experience.... By derivation [from what was seen to be an organic relation between the market and society as a whole] the relationship between personal moral decision and the social process could also be seen as organic.... The emphasis on separate individual moral calculation had appeared long before Hume, and was an object of his conscious attack.... His whole enterprise can be seen as an attempt to restore the identity of social and personal virtues at a time when the tensions of change had forced and were forcing these apart."[12]

In the light of Raymond Williams' interpretation, one might discern an affinity between Hume's social and political thought and that of the British Hegelians. His appreciation for the social virtues places him closer to them than to his utilitarian successors. Strangely enough, both Bradley and Green evinced at least as much empiricism and Humean skepticism about theoretical preconceptions as did their supposedly inductivist utilitarian opponents. But then it was a common charge of their critics that the utilitarians were excessively abstract theorists of man and society. J.S. Mill himself, in the sixth book of his System of Logic, drew attention to Bentham's "geometrical method in politics" and its fundamental error of deducing social effects from one allegedly comprehensive premise about human nature.[13] The Benthamite premise is that men's actions are always determined by their private interests. One could argue for and against that premise, produce contradictory as well as confirmatory examples of human behaviour. The theoretical point of importance is that the utilitarians abstracted individuals from their social context, only to re-assemble society out of those same individuals, now stripped of prejudice and prescriptive right. The image of human nature which emerged from this procedure was a monstrosity. However, the utilitarians were less concerned to explain the real nature of man in society than they were to rid people of obscurantist political notions and replace them with the principle of utility. Mankind's "two sovereign masters, pain and pleasure...determine what we shall do." We can only "pretend to abjure their empire."[14] It was the pretensions of "principles adverse to that of utility" which Bentham was especially concerned to destroy. A lot of painful mistakes would continue to be made if legislators and administrators were not supplied with a clear utilitarian rationale for their actions. Such a rationale was the utilitarian science of morals, which is to say, of human behaviour.[15]

---

[12] Raymond Williams, "David Hume: Reasoning and Experience," The English Mind: Studies in the English Moralists Presented to Basil Willey, ed. H.S. Davies and G. Watson (Cambrige, 1964), p. 144.

[13] Macaulay is the critic usually credited with successfully identifying in the public mind the name of Jeremy Bentham and absurd abstraction from social reality.

[14] J. Bentham, Morals and Legislation, p. 125.

[15] "The only right ground of action, that can possibly subsist, is, after all, the consideration of utility, which if it is a right principle of action, and of approbation, in any one case, is so in every other. Other principles in abundance, that is, other motives, may be the reasons why such and such an act has been done: that is, the reasons or causes of its being done: but it is this alone that can be the reason why it might or ought to have been done." (Ibid, p. 146.)

CHAPTER 7

F.H. Bradley: The Organic Theory of Society

In the very first sentence of F.H. Bradley's first published work, The Presuppositions of Critical History (1874), that subtle combination of elements drawn from Hegel's and other idealist thought with apt and acute psychological insights and an elegant, cadenced prose style which distinguished all of Bradley's writing manifests itself:

"In the world the mind makes for the manifestation of itself, and where its life is the process of its own self-realization, there the action and the knowledge of it are children, the hours of whose bringings-forth are never the same, and whose births are divided. Alike in the life of mankind and in the development of the individual, the deed comes first and later the reflection; and it is with the question, "What have I done?", that we awake to facts accomplished and never intended and to existences we do not recognize, while we own them as the creation of ourselves."[1]

In spite of this Hegelian introduction to critical history, the critical part is itself strongly reminiscent of Hume on miracles. The historian, says Bradley, cannot accept testimony to the occurrence of an event for which there is no analogy in his present experience. If he is a critical historian, he possesses a coherent body of knowledge based upon the presupposition that, just as a natural event has a natural cause, so a historical event has a historical cause. Insofar as he can identify himself with the mind and the experience of the witness, the historian can accept his testimony; but his total experience is different and he is bound, as a critical historian, to apply the whole of his knowledge to his judgment of the acceptability of a piece of historical evidence. The critical historian does not passively receive facts; he exercises his judgment upon testimony. Every judgment is an inference, and every inference presupposes an already existing body of knowledge.[2] Bradley stresses the scientific element in the historian's knowledge - which is to say, the scientific knowledge available to him. It is scientific knowledge above all which makes of the historian's experience a criterion for judging the credibility of witnesses and the probability of historical events attested to. If there is nothing analogous in the historian's present experience, then the event as reported must be deemed improbable and rejected.

"The rule for the critical historian is always to keep on the side of safety. It is better to suspend the judgment and be wrong than to be right against reason and in the face of science."[3]

Natural science advances, and with its advance the presuppositions of critical history

---

[1] F.H. Bradley, Collected Essays (Oxford, 1935), p. 5.
Francis Herbert Bradley (1846-1924) was the son of a leading light of the Evangelical Clapham sect. While an undergraduate reading "classical moderations" and literae humaniores at University College, Oxford, from 1865 to 1869, he came briefly under the "spell" of T.H. Green. He became a fellow of Merton College in 1870 and remained there until his death. There were no teaching or lecturing duties attached to his fellowship, and he devoted himself to study and writing, being something of a recluse. Although he never exercised the sort of moral authority nor enjoyed the sort of community influence that Green did - nor could he in his circumstances - Bradley has been the British Hegelian most highly regarded by professional philosophers.
[2] This theory of judgment Bradley was to elaborate in his Principles of Logic (Oxford, 1883).
[3] CE, p. 64.

change. History is the history of the present - that is to say, of the present state of knowledge. In Bradley's presentation of this theory, the mind continually subsumes new matter until it discovers that its experience is divided, that it contains within itself two conflicting systems of knowledge. A synthesis will emerge in which the new system conquers the old while assimilating it. This dialectical growth of the mind must continue as the mind seeks to overcome its limitations and comprehend the totality of things, to discover in the universe and in itself the mutual reflection of unity and system.[4]

This was as close as Bradley ever came to professing the Hegelian unity of thought and being. His great metaphysical work, Appearance and Reality (1893), consigns all kinds of discursive thought, all manner of reflection, to varying degrees of unreality. Each distinct area of rationalized experience is adequate in and for itself; but viewed metaphysically - sub specie aeternitatis - they are all self-contradictory because they are all infected by relations. Bradley began his attack upon relational experience - in other words, experience as analyzed by thought or reflection into related elements - in his Principles of Logic (1883) and sustained it on an increasingly wide front thereafter.

A prevision of the Absolute, which for Bradley was the metaphysical totality of all appearances, may be experienced at the level of unself-conscious feeling. At this level, before thought has occurred, there is no distinction between subject and object. The subject is a mere "form" of consciousness inseparable from its content. To feel something is to be immediately, unreflectively aware of a "non-relational unity of many in one." Even at the pre-judgmental level of experience, "from the very first beginnings of soul-life, universals are used."[5] Between this level and that of the Absolute intervene countless levels of relational experience. The Absolute is supra-relational: it transcends relations while at the same time it is present only in relational experience; ultimate reality is contained entirely within its appearances. The Absolute resembles pre-relational experience in that it is a seamless whole, but it can only be reached through relational experience, through the various ways in which discursive thought separates and analyzes the modes of experience. We are never entirely separated from or unable to glimpse what Bradley calls the Absolute. Judgment and inference are thought processes which both separate and re-unite our experience. For Bradley, thought itself is driven to seek satisfaction - or rather, it is driven by dissatisfaction with its own partial "truths" - in comprehension beyond thought and its necessarily relational character.

The brunt of Bradley's attack on psychologism and the "school of experience" was that (logical) meaning and (psychological) "facts" or the alleged contents of the mind are two different things. His acerbic insistence on the difference was prompted by what he saw as bad

---

[4] See F.H. Bradley, "Presuppositions of Critical History," appendix E, Ibid., pp. 69-70. Unlike Jowett and other members of the English "clerisy" who drank from the spring of German Biblical criticism, particularly from the "vessel" of F.C. Baur, the Tubingen historian and theologian, Bradley's interest was entirely philosophical and without any ulterior theological motive. Indeed, Bradley's Presuppositions remained a unique English example of the "scientific" philosophy of history until the appearance of Michael Oakeshottt's Experience and Its Modes (1933) and R.G. Collingwood's The Idea of Nature (dating largely from 1934) and The Idea of History (dating largely from 1936). In his Autobiography (1939), Collingwood acknowledged a heavy debt to Bradley's work, as well as, of course, to the intervening and more extensive historicist writings of Dilthey and Croce.

[5] F.H. Bradley, The Principles of Logic, 2nd ed. (Oxford, 1922), p. 34. See also his "Association and Thought," CE, pp. 205-38; and for the unitary and the holistic quality of human thinking, A.N. Whitehead, Adventures of Ideas (Cambridge, 1933), esp. part 3: from Plato to Bradley, "the advance in psychology has added to our conscious discrimination, but it has not altered the fact that inevitably [bare intellectual] perception is clothed with emotion" (p. 299).

theory, an exercise in simple-minded reductionism which resulted in a unity where differences had been merely obliterated. His own theory purported to show that even animals are incapable of sense perception without judgment as to the meaning or significance of what is perceived, without connecting the perception and the perceiver's experience as a whole. Only human beings are capable of abstracting something called sense data from experience. "My impression is..." means that I have an idea, which means that I have made a judgment about the relation between something and something else. That something else is a collection of pre-existent experiences, which must be an integrating system of meanings and values. It could conceivably be a fully integrated, i.e. closed, system, in which case a new experience would be rejected – but that is a judgment. What it cannot be is a mere collection; otherwise each new arrival could not be inducted (as the empiricist might say), or made sense of at all; they would be meaningless "blips" on my perceptual screen. The relating of everything to everything else within a system of experience is not some arcane and mystical pursuit; it is the necessary accompaniment, from first to last, of all we feel, know and do. Analysis can arrest the flow of experience, but only to draw inferences which generate fresh relationships in the form of logical implications. This activity is "the development of an unbroken individual identity to a result which is its own and which meets its particular requirement."[6] There are unities within the unity of thought. But thought, no matter how unified, no matter how coherent, is not the whole of experience and essential distinctions must be maintained. There is no infallible model of how to think and reach the truth, and it is "the pleasure and the privilege of the emotions to take their revenge" upon those who would intellectualize our thought processes, either as the association of ideas or as the application of the rules of formal logic.

Because the Absolute is inaccessible to discursive thought, Bradley admits that its nature cannot be described. All that is known is that it must re-unite the separate but related elements of experience. Philosophy as a form of relational experience cannot be adequate to expression of the Absolute. Bradley's metaphysic gives the impression that thought is being forced beyond its limits, that a self-defeating self-transcendence is being attempted. As a coherent, self-consistent whole, Bradley's Absolute is modelled partially on Hegel's Vernunft, on human reason as the highest expression of world spirit. But it is more than coherent; it is all-inclusive as well, by which Bradley meant that it includes, and therefore transcends, philosophy. It looks back to a lost unity and is as much an emotional longing as an intellectual ideal.[7] Bradley was fond of saying that metaphysics is "the finding of bad reasons for what we believe upon instinct."

Bradley's mature work contains occasional oblique references to Hegel, Herbart and Lotze, but in his first full-length book, Ethical Studies, he quotes Hegel twice at length and cites a number of other passages from the Phenomenology of Mind and the Philosophy of Right. Most of these occur in "My Station and its Duties," a sustained and at times shrill attack upon individualism and the atomistic view of society. In this essay he affirms the derivation of the individual's moral sense from the society in which he has been born and educated and, furthermore, that he need not look beyond "the morality already existing ready to hand in laws, institutions, social usages, moral opinions and feelings."[8] Here is the content of the formula "my station and its duties." Only in the life of the community – which is the real moral idea, not a mere "ideal" – do individuals achieve self-realization. This view is advocated with great eloquence and passionate conviction, and although he came to regard Ethical Studies as excessively polemical in style and somewhat outdated in emphasis, Bradley never repudiated its main conclusions. It was a tract for the times, attacking the widespread notion that the

---

[6] F.H. Bradley, The Principles of Logic, Terminal Essay I, "On Inference," p. 618.
[7] Richard Wollheim, in his F.H. Bradley (1959), has speculated along Freudian lines on the (non-pejoratively speaking) infantile psychology of Bradley's metaphysical quest for wholeness in experience and its appeal to some subconscious human drive.
[8] F.H. Bradley, Ethical Studies, 2nd ed. (Oxford, 1927), p. 199.

individual is something substantial apart from society as well as the political theory associated with it, utilitarianism. It also attacked the "two undying and opposite one-sidenesses" of mechanical necessity and capricious liberty of the will in the name of "a philosophy which thinks what the vulgar believe...."[9] A person's freedom of choice is compatible with predictability precisely because he is not pre-determined, but has formed an habitual, reliable and predictable character for himself; his freedom is the obverse of his responsibility and moral imputability, which are impossible without a relatively "fixed" character.

Bradley's political theory is to be found in Ethical Studies, but the book is not primarily about political life. It is an inquiry into the nature of the moral end for man and it self-consciously treads the well-trodden path of Aristotle's Nicomachean Ethics.

"Is it not clear that, if you have any ethics, you must have an end which is above the Why? in the sense of What for?; and that if this is so, the question is now, as it was two thousand years ago, Granted that there is an end, what is this end?"[10]

With this kind of antecedent, Ethical Studies clearly has a great deal to say about the life of man in society. But it does not end with the notorious fifth essay, "My Station and its Duties." It does not identify the moral end for man with the life of the community, and the political part of Ethical Studies provides only a partial answer to the question: What for man is the ultimate end?

The short answer is self-realization, and Bradley gives it in the second essay entitled, "Why Should I be Moral?", devoting the rest of the book to enlarging upon this answer. The initial response is that it is an illegitimate question because it presupposes that morality is a means to an end. With great relish Bradley smites the philistines for suggesting that morality could be anything other than an end in itself. In defence of virtue against "those who do not love her for herself, against the base mechanical 'banausia' which meets us on all sides, with its 'what is the use' of goodness or beauty or truth, there is but one fitting answer from the friends of science, or art, or religion and virtue: 'We do not know and we do not care.'"[11] However, he does have logical grounds for rejecting the seemingly transparent question: Why should I be moral? As soon as one asks it, one has embarked upon a discussion of something else, not morality; one is discussing the something or other to which morality is a means. Within the limits of a discussion about morality, the question is strictly superfluous. It is a bit like asking: Why is a corpse dead? If the question is rephrased to ask, Is morality an end in itself? - if, in other words, the redundant "ought" is removed - then, says Bradley, the question is legitimate. The answer is not an unconditional yes, because the ultimate end is self-realization, of which morality is an integral part. When he speaks of morality being "included under" the end of self-realization, Bradley implies that morality is a, and not necessarily the only, means to the larger end. However, in a moral action the thing to be done and the doing of it are interchangeably end and means. It is quite correct, for example, to speak of an act of generosity as contributing to the self-esteem of a generous person without thereby detracting from the moral worth of the generous act itself. Conversely, the moral quality belongs as much to the agent, or self, as to the action and its consequences. To that extent, morality and self-realization can be identified. Thus morality remains an end in itself, although contained within the more comprehensive end of self-realization.

The pursuit of pleasure for pleasure's sake and the doing of duty for duty's sake are next examined, and both are rejected as maxims of conduct. Through neither can self-realization be achieved. Both suffer from the same defect of abstraction - the one an abstraction of an

---

[9] Ibid., p. 41.
[10] Ibid., p. 61.
[11] Ibid., p. 63.

endless series of pleasurable states of feeling from pleasure-producing activities, the other an abstraction of the pure, formal will to do good from all particular, concrete instances of the good will in action.

Hedonism, or pleasure for pleasure's sake, cannot offer a concrete goal in either its universalistic or its egoistic forms. Its objective is to amass the greatest net personal or social product in extent and intensity of pleasurable feeling. This is a futile pursuit, because states of pleasurable feeling are evanescent. It is also amoral, because the means are a matter of indifference to the end; one way is as good as another from the point of view of a consistent hedonism. Bradley was especially vehement in maintaining that the greatest happiness of the greatest number was not a pronouncement of the common moral sense. Utilitarianism was hopelessly entangled with hedonism or the pursuit of pleasure for pleasure's sake. Putting the pleasure of others before one's own and distinguishing between higher and lower pleasures did not mitigate the central and pervasive error of designating pleasure as the moral end for man. "If the alternative is presented to us of lower functions with less pains and greater pleasures or higher functions with greater pains and less pleasures, then we must choose the latter."[12] This was Mill's choice too. But in their anxiety to make happiness a tangible goal and a practical criterion, the utilitarians chose, for all its seeming solidity, the most illusory of goals, a balance of pleasure over pain. In addition, argued Bradley, they were flying in the face of the common moral consciousness. No one, not even the utilitarian moralist, adjusts his conduct with a view to maximizing pleasurable feeling. The moral individual conducts himself virtuously because it is expected of him by his fellows or because he cannot do otherwise - virtuous conduct has become a part of him - not because of the pleasure to be gained by such conduct. On the contrary, he often does so in spite of the pain it costs him. It would cause even greater pain if he were to act immorally; but the pleasurable satisfaction of being himself is not the moral end for such a person.

Just as the self as a collection of particular feelings is not the one to be realized, so neither is the self as an abstract universal, the pure form of the will. The formal will to do one's duty for duty's sake is, like hedonism, non-moral - in this case because it is open to the insertion of any content whatsoever: "The morality of pure duty turns out then to be either something like a hedonistic rule, or no rule at all, save the hypocritical maxim that before you do what you like you should call it duty...."[13] The categorical imperative ignores circumstances which determine the priority of duties in different situations.

Having eliminated both hedonism and Kantianism as ways to full self-realization, Bradley next arrived at the theory of "my station and its duties," which is intended to resolve the contradictions inherent in the pursuit of pleasure and in the good will. It is for some the locus classicus of the organic theory of society. It postulates a symbiotic interdependence of the social organism and its individual members. The collective moral being is superior to that of the individual only because it is the indispensable medium for self-realization. In Bradley's words:

"It is the self-realization of the whole body, because it is one and the same will which lives and acts in the life and action of each. It is the self-realization of each member, because each member cannot find the function which makes him himself apart from the whole to which he belongs; to be himself he must go beyond himself, to live his life he must live a life which is not merely his own but which, nonetheless, but on the contrary all the more, is intensely and emphatically his own individuality."[14]

The self to be realized is not the separate, particular self; it is the self which owes its

---

[12] Ibid., p. 91.
[13] Ibid., p. 156.
[14] Ibid., pp. 162-63.

ideals and aspirations, as well as its primary development and formation, to a community of selves. Full self-realization necessarily entails some self-sacrifice. The individual cannot "find himself" without accepting the laws, customs and morality - in short, the values - of the society in which he lives. This involves the suppression of what Bradley termed "the bad self" and the transformation of the unmoralized parts of one's character. The full assertion of certain personality traits, of all the talents (even of some considered entirely admirable in themselves), is inconsistent with the individual moral quality of society as a whole. This essay ends, however, with Bradley pointing out that its central contention is open to serious objections.

Full self-realization is thwarted by the opposition, on the one hand, between the "ought" in the individual and the objective world, and on the other hand, between the bad self and the general "ought." This conflict between the real as existent and the real as it is to be is crucial for Bradley's moral philosophy. His ethical, like his metaphysical, aim is satisfaction through harmony, the transmutation of all contradictions. In the process of reaching for this consummation, morality is superseded because it is found to be infected with an incurable self-contradiction, a contradiction without which morality would not be morality and because of which morality must transcend itself. It is essential to morality, in Bradley's view, that there be a ceaseless striving to realize what is not, to transform the "ought" into "is."

> "It is a demand for what cannot be.... Nothing is to be real (so far as willed) but the good; and yet the reality is not wholly good ["real" here meaning "existing"]. Neither in me nor in the world is what ought to be what is, and what is what ought to be; and the claim remains in the end a mere claim."[15]

The contradiction in morality is a contradiction in man. But man is above the contradiction in that he is aware of it and feels it as foreign to his real nature. If the contradiction is overcome and the tension between "is" and "ought" resolved, then there is an end to morality proper. "Morality issues in religion."[16] God is what ought to be, the realization of the moral ideal. But even God, who must exist in relation to the non-divine, is inferior to the Absolute. Only the totality of all things can overcome the limiting of each thing by what it is not, no matter how comprehensive in appearance it may be.

Morality, in addition to being self-contradictory, is partial. It does not comprehend goodness in all its aspects, "for every kind of human excellence - beauty, strength, and even luck, are all undeniably good."[17] Morality maintains that only the good will is good, that a man is to be judged solely on his inner will, on the intensity of his volitional identification with whatever seems best to him. "The doctrine that nothing is good but the Good Will is clearly untenable," says Bradley in a footnote to the sixth essay, "Ideal Morality," written shortly before his death and added to the second edition of Ethical Studies (1927).[18] No matter how good the will becomes, it cannot dissociate itself from its content, nor is it any worse for having non-moral contents. Goodness itself includes many qualities which have nothing as such to do with the good will or morality; yet they are all aspects of goodness and approved of.

While the content of the good will is acquired from many non-moral sources, and an instinctive or habitual goodness is not to be valued less than one which has to be continually and consciously willed, there is nothing which may not be moralized. It is, for example, a moral duty to amuse oneself; and it could conceivably be a moral issue as to whether one did it playing tennis or playing chess. Although the self to be realized is the good self in its widest sense, self-realization is a moral purpose. Bradley, like Green, could not - or would

---

[15] Ibid., p. 313.
[16] Ibid., p. 314.
[17] F.H. Bradley, Appearance and Reality, 2nd ed. (London, 1897), p. 387.
[18] ES, pp. 244-45.

not - contain <u>Moralität</u>. Self-realization "is not perfection simply, but perfection as carried out by a will."[19] In the seventh and final essay of <u>Ethical Studies</u>, "Selfishness and Self-Sacrifice," Bradley says that with self-conscious direction against the bad self, "good acts are now done as good...the good self is now morally good...."

"This higher will is known as the true will of the self, where law ceases to be external and becomes autonomy, and where goodness or the identity of the particular will with the universal is only another name for conscious self-realization."[20]

The political theory of "my station and its duties" - the theory that the moral end for man is realized in the existing state of society - is found wanting on two counts. First, it cannot keep pace with the bad self and the unremitting moral struggle to overcome it, to subordinate it to "the true will of the self." Secondly, it overlooks the fact that the social organism, no less than the physical, is susceptible to disease. The ideal of non-social perfection is introduced in recognition of two interconnected facts: the moral world, being in a state of historical development, cannot be self-consistent and all that it should be; and knowledge of other moralities in other communities results in some men professing a cosmopolitan morality. In aiming at a supra-societal ideal, "we are trying to realize ourself not as a member of any visible community."[21]

Nevertheless, "common social morality is the basis of human life," and it continues to sustain and direct "the ideals of a higher social perfection and of the theoretic life." There must inevitably be conflicts of duty, and occasionally the duty enjoined by social morality must defer to a higher;

"...but open and direct outrage on the standing moral institutions which make society and human life what it is, can be justified (I do not say condoned) only on the plea of overpowering moral necessity. And the individual should remember that the will for good, if weakened in one place, runs the greatest risk of being weakened in all."[22]

Any organized society is the repository of laws and customs, the moral code, the habits of mind, that distillation of moral and political experience, without assimilating which no individual can find his moral bearings. It is the embodiment, however imperfect, of a moral order without which no individual can challenge either himself or the conventional wisdom of his group; it is society that supplies the incentive and the materials for the individual's freedom of action as well as the standards for the exercise of political judgment by free moral agents. Bradley rested his case upon the "common moral consciousness" and the "vulgar notion of responsibility," neither of which have ever been noted for their tolerance of social protest or eccentric individual conduct. Yet Bradley was no enemy of freedom of artistic expression and philosophical inquiry. The feudal flourish of chivalry in his defence of "standing moral institutions" was his way of responding to the provocations of bad metaphysics - bad, in part, because unwitting - which masqueraded as social science. At times he seems to belabour the obvious, but as with his scathing attack on psychology which pretended to be logic, Bradley clearly enjoyed ridiculing his opponents, one result of which was that he argued himself into some extreme positions - this notwithstanding his oft-repeated assertion that the striking power of criticism lay not in its denials but in what it affirmed in place of what it denied. What Bradley affirmed above all was coherence, in both truth and reality. At the social and political "degree" of reality coherence consists in the individual member of the social organism recognizing in theory at least (but also in practice, if according to slightly different criteria) that his community is of greater value, because more inclusive, than he is. His individuality is borrowed from that of the society which has developed an identity for his generation, as it has for previous generations. Creating oneself through the act(s) of

---

[19] F.H. Bradley, <u>Appearance and Reality</u>, p. 366.
[20] <u>ES</u>, pp. 300-01.
[21] <u>Ibid</u>., p. 205.
[22] <u>Ibid</u>., p. 227.

character formation requires stability in the social environment and some expectation that models of conduct will not shift like tastes. Exceptional individual characters are important, but not as important as the shared social nature. Regardless of how assured or how magnanimous an individual's moral character may become, it would be a kind of ingratitude – as explained by Socrates in the <u>Crito</u>, when he refused to escape the Athenian sentence of death – to detach himself from the mores of that society with which, willy-nilly, he is identified. At best it would be a delusion of grandeur, at worst an expression of <u>hubris</u> threatening the whole social fabric. Bradley offers advice, attributed by Hegel to some unknown Pythagorean, to the effect that the best civic education is that acquired by living in a state whose laws, customs, institutions and usages are in a healthy condition. The good life is lived by the lights of those who best exemplify the moral tradition of such a state.

Bradley bore an even more implacable hatred than did Hegel toward the romantic self-indulgence of unrestrained individualism – unmediated claims for subjectivity, as against the objective moral order of organized society – which was the prevailing "one-sidedness" of the age. The principal focus of Bradley's animosity was J.S. Mill's <u>On Liberty</u>, in particular the chapter on individuality. He felt that the combination of a hard-headed felicific calculus with Mill's tenderness toward the individual conscience was morally debilitating. To allow the individual to pick his way through the rich and complex growth of received morality and tested institutions by the light of the greatest happiness principle was to promote moral disorientation and invite social disorder. Mill's presumption in favour of individual moral judgment evoked the same indignant response from Bradley as did the English Jacobins' assault upon the British constitution from Burke. There are parallels between Bradley's animus against utilitarianism and the ethics of individualism and Burke's against the radical reformers of his day. Indeed, Burke's enemy was the spiritual ancestor of Bradley's. Both men inveighed passionately and eloquently against the same "metaphysical abstraction," the unattached individual set in moral judgment over society.

CHAPTER 8

T.H. Green: The Pursuit of the Common Good

In the "general introduction" to his and T.H. Grose's edition of Hume's Treatise of Human Nature (1874), T.H. Green subjected Locke, Berkeley and, above all, Hume, the suicide of the "way of ideas," to a strenuous idealist critique. It was Kant's answer to Hume's skepticism which prepared the ground for the Hegelian system. The Treatise itself was an essential stage in philosophy's "progressive effort towards a fully articulated conception of the world as rational."[1] The crux of Green's argument is that the Kantian synthesis offers the only way out of the impasse of psychologism into which the empiricist tradition had worked itself. We are trapped in our perceptions of a putative external world unless we can establish some sort of relationship between the perception and what is perceived. We do not perceive any such relationship; it is supplied by our minds even as we perceive something. We know that the flash of white in the darkness is a headlight, a searchlight or a streetlight because of the way in which we have ordered our experience. The immediate raw data of white light is a highly intellectualized abstraction from the relatedness of our experience of it, and, as such, testimony in itself to the element of mental construction in even the simplest sensation.

The objectivity of what we experience is guaranteed, for Green, by what he calls "the eternal consciousness," which is reproduced in each individual consciousness. The natural history of human experience reveals a progress - never completed - toward a state of being which strongly resembles the timeless Platonic realm of Ideas. We know what we know to the degree that we participate in eternal consciousness. In virtue of our participation "in some inchoate measure in that consciousness which is also the real world of which it is conscious," we have an idea of perfection which directs our moral endeavours. As so directed, we are under the influence of "practical reason," striving to identify ourselves with a power for good in the world which is supernatural but not above and beyond us, not an external authority but something which commends itself to our rational faculty.

The rational ideal is a social ideal:
> "It is in fact only so far as we are members of a society, of which we can conceive the common good as our own, that the idea [of "some absolute and all-embracing end" which affords full satisfaction] has any practical hold on us at all, and this very membership implies confinement in our individual realization of the idea. Each is primarily to fulfil the duties of his station."[2]

Like Bradley, however, Green could not rest in the theory of "my station and its duties." The laws, customs and institutions of the existing social order are not morally complete. Green was more emphatic on this point than Bradley, insisting that the realization of the ideal is meaningful only in relation to personality. It is realized in individual human beings qua individuals, or nowhere; it cannot be realized in a supra-personal sphere or through any kind of self-immolation. Bradley was in complete agreement that the conception of the good life carries us beyond the norms and values of even the best organized political society, but he conceded less than Green to individual conscience in the development and actualization of the ideal.

The most interesting feature of Green's ethics from the standpoint of social and political

---

[1] T.H. Green, Works (London, 1885-8), vol. I, p. 4.
[2] T.H. Green, Prolegomena to Ethics, 5th ed. (Oxford, 1906), p. 209.

theory is his insistence that the reciprocal recognition of rights and duties in the light of a common interest, which characterizes the life of the citizens of a rational state, be extended to include the whole of humanity. Implicit in the development of the nation-state is the principle that all men are free. Bradley - following Hegel - attached more significance to the historical vicissitudes in the actualization of that principle than did Green. Green accepted the historical, developmental nature of the rational state, while embracing the Kantian kingdom of ends. The right of any man to be treated as an end and not as a means is not conditional upon his membership of polis or state. According to Green, it is a fact of the modern moral consciousness that the citizens of an organized political society have an idea of the wider application of the justice which obtains in their own class or community.[3] Bradley was more inclined to regard the historically created conditions of a community's justice as a necessary and inseparable element of that justice: remove the particular social conditions of a particular society's system of values and the remainder would be an abstraction, unable to subsist anywhere in the world. A universal code of rights presupposes a universal common interest in the reciprocity of rights and duties, a universal recognition that the exercise of rights requires the performance of duties in return. The principal drawback in the extension to the whole of humanity of the reciprocity obtaining in the rational state is that there is little experience, let alone habit, of community across the boundaries of nation-states. The extra-political extension of a principle so intimately connected with the state could be an empty gesture of charity, self-righteous and condescending, or, equally bad, a unilateral declaration of interdependence which was a futile sacrifice of solid moral achievement to an empty ideal.[4]

It is a Hegelian idea that the principle inherent in Christianity represents a spiritual advance on the principle inherent in the life of the ancient Greek polis. It is also a Hegelian idea that the modern nation-state comprehends both these principles. Green maintained that the state cannot contain the Christian principle, that it cannot satisfy the demand of all men to be free. The perfection of mankind, the realization of all human potentialities, necessarily involves a common good and a common effort as extensive as humanity itself. The common good transcends the limits of organized political society, even though it is a product of political development. Bradley argued, from the nature of the moral will as well as from the psychology of what he called the bad self, that the demands of the moral life exceed the capacity of any actual society to satisfy them. Green went further - as one of those evangelical humanitarians whom Bradley could not abide - saying that while the state affords the conditions of the good life, the moral life directs us to a higher form of community. Green insisted that self-perfection must subordinate itself to - or rather transform itself into - a pursuit of improved conditions and expanded opportunities for those whose capacity for self-perfection was frustrated by circumstances beyond their unaided control. The moral ideal is a social ideal; but it is logically prior to the state, no matter how much our sense of community may depend upon loyalty to established institutions. The legal person, in full possession of his rights and enjoying the other benefits of a well-organized political life, is comprehended by the person who seeks to improve his fellow man. Although political life is the necessary medium for the cultivation of humanitarian moral ideals, their pursuit is the ultimate justification of the rational state. To be moral is to be more than a good citizen, not forgetting that it is nothing less than that.

Green's political philosophy has been neatly encapsulated in the famous chapter heading

---

[3] Ibid., pp. 239-46.
[4] "And nations differ in value, and there is no organism to ensure that loss of one shall advantage the others." (F.H. Bradley, "The Limits of Individual and National Self-sacrifice," CE, p. 175.) This essay first appeared in Mind (1896). The same point might be made, mutatis mutandis, about the attempts of some of Green's followers to extend the fellowship of an Oxford college to embrace the whole population of a complex modern society.

from his <u>Lectures on the Principles of Political Obligation</u>: "Will, not Force, is the Basis of the State." It was aimed specifically at the definition of sovereignty which had been developed by John Austin and other "analytical jurists," and which had been incorporated into much utilitarian political theory. The habitual obedience which governments receive from the governed is primarily derived not from the government's coercive power and the subject's fear of it, as the Austinians would have us believe, but from "that impalpable congeries of the hopes and fears of a people, bound together by common interests and sympathy, which we call the general will."[5]

Social contract theorists were mistaken in postulating pre-social natural rights and morality which had been exchanged for legally defined rights protected by a legitimized political power. Rousseau corrected the error by recognizing the possibility of a common ego or general will, a disinterested sentiment of common good more powerful than any sovereign - indeed, the indispensable component in any political arrangement whatsoever. The general will, or recognition on the part of a group that it shares a community of interests, is presupposed by any political order, not the other way around. Furthermore, it is only through the political expression of the general will that morality itself can develop.

"It remains true that only through a recognition by certain men of a common interest, and through the expression of that recognition in certain regulations of their dealings with each other, could morality originate, or any meaning be gained for such terms as 'ought' and 'right' and their equivalents."[6]

Although the morality of reciprocating rights and duties is said to be that of "political subjection," it has nothing to do with subjection in the sense of oppression. The political subject has rights secured to him in return for the fulfilment of certain duties. He freely accepts this arrangement because he has made the common interest his interest. His civic actions are self-conscious attempts to realize the general will.

A state possesses a necessary reserve of coercive powers; but if the majority of its citizens are incapable of conceiving a common good, or of observing rules and regulations which further that good without compulsion or the threat of compulsion by the state power, then that state is no real state. If there were no collective conception of a common good, no mutual recognition of rights and duties among a group of people, then it could never constitute a state in the first place. The sovereign power in a state secures rights - and therefore powers - to its subjects, and without them they would have no moral life or self-development worthy of the name. But it cannot enforce morality, any more than it can create the common good presupposed by its sovereignty.

It has long been a criticism of Green's political theory that his treatment of what was for him the central problem of political obligation involves a bad case of is-ought confusion.[7] Obedience to one's real, i.e. the general, will is less a matter of reciprocating practical reason, of the principle that (in Rousseau's words) "no one but appropriates to himself this word <u>each</u> and thinks of himself in voting on behalf of all,"[8] than it is of the dictates of the social psyche. A particular state either has the requisite level of consciousness of common good, or it doesn't have what it takes.

"Whether or no any particular government has, on this ground, lost its claim and may be rightly resisted is a question...[which] seems generally, if not always, to answer itself. A government no longer serving the function described...brings forces into

---

[5] T.H. Green, <u>Lectures on the Principles of Political Obligation</u> (London, 1941), p. 98.
[6] <u>Ibid.</u>, p. 124.
[7] See, for example, L.T. Hobhouse, <u>The Metaphysical Theory of the State</u> (London, 1918), p. 121, and H.A. Prichard, "Green's Principles of Political Obligation," <u>Moral Obligation</u> (Oxford, 1949), esp. pp. 82-83.
[8] J.-J. Rousseau, <u>The Social Contract</u>, ed. L.G. Crocker (New York, 1967), p. 33.

play which are fatal to it."[9]

This formula can only provide ex post facto answers to questions about the legitimacy of a particular government or, for that matter, its policies. The same criticism applies to Green's treatment of what we would now call the human rights issue, the question of extending benefits to those who claim them as of right, but beyond what the majority may allege society can bear. There may be a right or rights which are not legally recognized, but which some conscientious citizen or group of citizens may assert, not so much against the state as for the fulfilment of its "ideal function," to realize "the true end of the state as the sustainer and harmonizer of social relations."

> "The reason that the assertion of an illegal right must be founded on reference to acknowledged social good is that, as we have seen, no exercise of a power, however abstractedly desirable for the promotion of human good it might be, can be claimed as a right unless there is some common consciousness of utility shared by the person making the claim and those on whom it is made. It is not a question whether or not it ought to be claimed as a right; it simply cannot be claimed except on this condition."[10]

Again, it might well be asked: How much is "some"? How much "common consciousness of utility" is needed to properly ground a claim as of right? And, one might further ask, where does that leave the "untaught and underfed denizen of the London yard with gin-shops on the right hand and on the left"?[11] A "common consciousness of utility" suggests a somewhat sophisticated, not to say calculating, sense of justice. The burden of the criticism, however, is that the legitimacy of a claim to a certain kind of treatment as of right does not depend upon a state of readiness in the common consciousness.

The coercive power of the state should, says Green, do more than merely abstain from intervention in the moral life (where it can, even with the purest intentions, only impede man's moral purpose); it should extend as well as secure those rights and powers whose exercise men require in their pursuit of perfection. In doing so, the state is only indirectly promoting moral development, although it may, in the process, directly interfere, in the interest of the common moral life, with the freedom of action of a certain class or classes of people. The state is the "society of societies," reconciling and sustaining "rights that arise out of the social relations of men."[12] Family and property are pre-political, but in return for certain restrictions the state guarantees, and may even increase, the scope and the autonomy of their roles in society. It is the state which established the family relationship and the possession of property as enforceable - and therefore actual - rights. In addition to enforcing and maintaining rights, the state can augment them. This can be seen clearly in the state's power to remove restrictions upon freedom of movement, of disposal of property and labour, and in its power to prevent interference with these freedoms. It is more difficult, however, to understand the state's capacity for increasing freedom as related to its power of restriction and constraint. Compulsory education, a controversial idea in Green's day, although it restricts the freedom of both children and parents, gives the child the added right of preparation for a fuller, more comfortable adult life, removing a major obstacle to self-realization and moral development. The state can also restrict freedom of contract and use of property, all in the name of the common good. An example of the first sort of restriction is legal recognition of the closed union shop. Such action contributes to the material welfare of the persons whose freedom is, in the first instance, curtailed - including employers, who have in many cases admitted the industrial peace and even the profitability of a measure of employee control over hiring and promotion practices. The critical and most awkward question for a theory such as Green's is, of course, whether state action or reinforcement of this sort contributes to the

---

[9] PPO, p. 62.
[10] Ibid., pp. 148-49.
[11] Ibid., p. 8 (My emphasis).
[12] Ibid., pp. 146-47.

moral welfare of those persons directly, or indirectly, involved.

If the state in any way regulates the individual citizen's liberty to do as he pleases, he has no counterclaim against this regulation unless he can, to the satisfaction of his fellow citizens, refer his claim to the common good. "It has been the social recognition, grounded on that reference, that has rendered certain of his powers rights."[13] There is no right against the state unless a discrepancy can be shown between the general will and the government of the state, the administrative expression of that will. Here the fundamental tension of Green's philosophy of man and the state has reappeared. Political action, for Green, was a continual moral struggle and reaffirmation of democratic virtue - not for him the easy acceptance of <u>Sittlichkeit</u> and the political leadership of the universal class, an "estate" of civil servants and academics. However, in spite of a career of volunteer community action which virtually drove him to an early grave, Green fell back on a curiously positivist approach to political power when a theoretical conflict arose between the imperatives of reform and the actual condition of the general will. As in his landmark Leicester address, "Liberal Legislation and Freedom of Contract," Green generally resolved the conflict by arguing that certain governmentally imposed reforms, far from decreasing personal freedom of choice, actually increased it by making possible a "growth of capacity" among whole classes of individuals previously incapable of exercising any but the most trivial freedom of choice. In other words, the problem tended to present itself to Green as one of convincing recalcitrant Liberals, if not rugged individualists and believers in the gospel according to Herbert Spencer, that affirmative social action requiring state revenue, state organization and state power did not "interfere with the spontaneous action of social interests."[14] That it rarely presented itself as a problem of political disobedience, resistance or rebellion had a lot to do with Green's practical experience as a reformer. He was quietly confident that God and history were on the side of social progress, and there were plenty of "forces" (to use his own term) in society and the economy, in religion and philosophy, which in Britain in the 1870s were promoting positive liberty as the natural successor to existing and rather shopworn conceptions of man and the state.

Like Bradley, Green was very diffident about his Hegelianism. For both, Hegel was one of the masters of those who know, but he was also far too ambitious. They both felt that he claimed too much for the discursive intellect, Bradley advancing the claims of feeling and emotion, Green those of religion and the external world. Green thought the dialectical method was an attempt, Hegel's assertions to the contrary notwithstanding, to construct the universe out of pure thought. He accepted the epistemological necessity of the Hegelian unity of thought and being, but preferred the Kantian approach to it. That is to say, he was a transcendentalist, when all is said and done, and maintained that Hegel's objective idealism "must all be done again."[15] Although "something like Hegel's idealism must be the result of the development of Kantian principles rightly understood," no man can fully comprehend the spirituality of the universe; although we are self-conscious participants in the eternal consciousness, we cannot "be God."[16] In a review of John Caird's <u>Introduction to the Philosophy of Religion</u> which appeared in <u>Academy</u> for July 10, 1880, Green expressed the view that Caird had been "too much overpowered by Hegel," and argued the need for caution in philosophizing about God and the totality of things.

> "The unifying principle of the world is indeed in us; it is our self. But, as in us, it is so conditioned by a particular animal nature that, while it yields that idea of the world as one which regulates all our knowledge, our actual knowledge remains a

---

[13] <u>Ibid</u>., p. 147.
[14] <u>Ibid</u>., p. 208.
[15] So says Edward Caird in his preface to <u>Essays in Philosophical Criticism</u> (London, 1883), p. 5.
[16] <u>Ibid</u>.

piecemeal process.... We never reach that totality of apprehension through which alone we could know the world as it is and God in it. This is the infirmity of our discursive understanding."[17]

The Hegelian unity of thought and being has here reverted to a Kantian regulative idea, no longer the ground and the result of all human experience.

There were two factors which impelled Green to withhold unqualified support from Hegelian metaphysics: first, his irreducible Kantianism, which was reinforced in later years by the German movement "back to Kant" and the seminal Critiques; second, his suspicion that Hegelianism was designed to supersede religious faith. Green felt that the Cairds, especially John, reproduced Hegelianism only too well, its vices as well as its virtues. The principal vice was the idea that human reason is equal to the grasp and penetration of the totality of things, the elimination of any distance between human self-consciousness and the eternal consciousness. The God of religion is comprehended by the Absolute of Hegelian philosophy. Green was not as reconciled - or as oblivious - as was Caird to the implications of this proposition for religion. For the less acute Hegelians, the "unifying principle of the world" and the God of religion were interchangeable. They clothed the unity of thought and being, a rational process and goal, with a religious aura, which had the side effect of destroying the Christian God's transcendence and converting Christian theology into a kind of pantheism. Perceiving the threat to religion in this procedure, Green retained a sphere of the unknowable beyond the reach of human reason. "Totality of apprehension" is beyond the reach of the human mind. We continually strive to approach perfect comprehension, but it will always remain unattainable. "To assume, because all reality requires thought to conceive it, that therefore thought is the condition of its existence, is indeed unwarrantable."[18] The Hegelian assumption is, in a sense, precisely this: we have significant knowledge because everything - including God - is a product of the _logos_ or world spirit. It is a distinguishing feature of Hegelianism that the external world is an externalization of the world spirit. Everything we experience is a manifestation of the spiritual principle whose supreme manifestation is philosophy, or fully rational thought. The only satisfactory explanation of our having knowledge of reality is that in acquiring it the mind is somehow recovering itself. An identity of subject and object is the necessary presupposition of our being able to think coherently about what we experience. There is, however, a universal and "inveterate supposition to the contrary" that the external world is another world. To exist is not to be conceived as existing. Green was not satisfied that Hegel's otherwise fruitful idea of self-externalization had not, while overcoming the dualism in Kant's theory of knowledge, contrived to reduce the natural and moral worlds to categories of his "subjective logic," and efforts to tame nature, human as well as physical, to moments in a theodicy of strictly metaphysical interest. He also felt, though less keenly than Bradley, that Hegelianism failed to do justice to the richness of human experience, conative and emotional, aesthetic and religious.

There is a long history of misunderstanding about the nature of Hegel's political philosophy arising out of the quietistic, contemplative tone of his oft-quoted dictum about the owl of Minerva in the preface to his _Philosophy of Right_. As a philosopher, Hegel was offering an explanation of political life, not a creed to live it by. Green was a lay preacher as well as a philosopher, and was trying to instil a civic religion in his readers and listeners. In

---

[17] T.H. Green, _Works_, vol. III, p. 145.
  John Caird (1820-1898), like his younger brother Edward, only more so, retained a close association with the University of Glasgow after undergraduate study there, and became a powerful shaping influence, helping to make it one of the academic founts of Hegelianism in Britain. His main interest was in the philosophy of religion, and after a brief spell as a minister he became Professor of Divinity at Glasgow, 1862-73, then Principal and Vice-Chancellor, 1873-98.
[18] _Ibid._

Hegelian language, he operated at least as much at the level of Sittlichkeit as he did at that of moral and political philosophy. He was trying to refurbish the mores of his society, and it would be no denigration of such activities to say that they made him a political subject but a philosophical object. As for Hegel, he was quite aware of continuing potential for divergence between what is the case and what ought to be. It is the philosopher's task to understand this gap and to give us insight into the teleology of its closure. He can, qua philosopher, only explain the potentialities in an existing, operative state of affairs; but "...once the realm of notions is revolutionized, actuality does not hold out."[19] For Green, the rationality of the real was a moral imperative and a demand for service and self-sacrifice which could not be denied. Like Rousseau, Green prized civic virtue above all else, but its field of action was not confined to the state. Charity, however, began at home, and the moral imperfections of British society in his day and age were, he felt, sufficiently grave to override the theoretical superiority of the vita contemplativa and the long-term, metaphysical truth that the real is rational.

> "It is no time to enjoy the pleasures of eye and ear, of search for knowledge, of friendly intercourse, of applauded speech or writing, while the mass of men whom we call our brethren, and whom we declare to be meant with us for eternal destinies, are left without the chance, which only the help of others can gain for them, of making themselves in act what in possibility we believe them to be."[20]

---

[19] Hegel, letter to Niethammer, October 28, 1808. See A.S. Brudner, "The significance of Hegel's prefatory lectures on the philosophy of law," Clio (Fall 1978), note 19, p. 48.
[20] PE, pp. 320-21.

CHAPTER 9

Bernard Bosanquet: The Idealist Theory of the State

As a political philosopher, Bernard Bosanquet belongs to the second generation of British Hegelians.[1] Although he was a contributor to Essays in Philosophical Criticism (1883), his fully developed theories of man and society did not appear until the late 1890s, some twenty years after the first blows for Hegel and the idealist theory of the state had been struck by Bradley and Green. He wrote when utilitarianism had lost all of its early radical thrust and become another stage in the history of philosophy. It was no longer a revolutionary plan of action; nor did it enjoy the intellectual dominion which it had in mid-century. The intellectual authority of philosophical idealism, on the other hand, was full and assured in the last two decades of the nineteenth century. Admittedly, it was still, in spite of the original and distinctively British work of men like Bradley and Green, regarded as something of an exotic growth. At that time, however, it was a serious contender for philosophical orthodoxy, if by no means the unquestioned truth of things. Pragmatism and the "new realism" were already beginning to challenge the recently acquired eminence of philosophical idealism. Nevertheless, the late Victorian and Edwardian ages were the years of idealism's widest appeal and greatest self-confidence, the years when synthesis and construction replaced much of the earlier analysis and criticism.

Bosanquet's The Principle of Individuality and Value and The Value and Destiny of the Individual (the Gifford Lectures for 1911 and 1912 respectively) represent British philosophical idealism in its fullness. In these lectures organicism is extended to describe the whole of experience, not just the political life. The experience of an individual is important not for its individuality but for its content, "the thing to be done, known and felt; in a word, the completeness of experience, his contribution to it and his participation in it."[2] His experience is part of a larger experience which goes before and after him; "and the more he realizes the continuity the less he cares about the separateness of the contribution to it. It is impossible to overrate the cooperative element in experience."[3] Although the universe is "from the highest point of view concerned with finite beings, a place of soul-making," the ultimate value of the individual experience lies in its special contribution to the whole of experience - "the value of the particularity is indirect and depends on what it helps to realize."[4]

---

[1] Bernard Bosanquet (1848-1923) was an undergraduate at Balliol, where he studied under Green. He became a fellow of University College, Oxford, in 1870. In 1881 he moved to London, an independent income freeing him from the need to perform regular teaching duties. He continued to write philosophy as well as engage in social work, for which the London of Mayhew afforded more than sufficient scope. He succeeded D.G. Ritchie as Professor of Logic and Metaphysics at the University of St. Andrews (1903-08). Like Green at Oxford, Bosanquet managed to combine a wide range of volunteer community work of both an organizational and a propagandist kind with teaching, lecturing and scholarship. He was one of the founding members of the London Ethical Society (1885), which was dedicated to both the teaching and the practical application of the "social gospel" of philosophical idealism. It attracted not only other Hegelians, such as Caird, Haldane, Muirhead and Wallace, but also the utilitarian Sidgwick and the Fabian socialist Graham Wallas. In 1897 it transformed itself into the School of Ethics and Social Philosophy, partly as an attempt by Bosanquet to counteract Fabian and positivist tendencies.
[2] B. Bosanquet, The Principle of Individuality and Value (London, 1912), p. 21.
[3] Ibid., p. 22.
[4] Ibid., pp. 26-27.

The individual person is, for Bosanquet, the finite consciousness of the particular self, and, as such, cannot be the ultimate good. True individuality is marked by completion and harmony, and is reserved for the totality of things. The universe is an individual in the fullest sense, and therefore the only true individual. It has overcome all contradictions without destroying differences or "negativity," as, after Hegel, Bosanquet preferred to call it. Differences are not fixed, as in the positivistic, atomistic view that everything is what it is and not something else, but dialectical, seeking unity in difference, the identity of identity and non-identity. The multiplicity of individual experiences making up the totality of experience, far from being a defect, is a contribution to the comprehensiveness of that totality, and "a certain completeness through incompleteness is attained."[5]

In the process of overcoming suffering and wrongdoing in their quest for completion, finite conscious beings undergo relative loss of self. Self-completion requires a harmony amidst the tension of pleasure and pain, good and evil. This sort of harmony between conflicting qualities can occur to some extent in the finite individual; but when the conflict ceases, when the bad self ceases to be an obstacle to goodness, with the power to prevent its realization, then morality and the finite self have been transcended. The harmony of total experience does not exclude - in fact, it demands - the presence of evil and suffering. Their presence is a function of its completeness. Although they have been transcended, they have not been obliterated. They persist in finitude and finite conscious beings, through whose struggles alone can completeness be attained.

The completion or fulfilment of finite individuals is a process of "negativity" and conflict, not of formal contradiction. In this process, which exhibits an underlying continuity between self-consciousness and "what is more than the self," both satisfaction and sacrifice "contribute of their nature to the complete experience."[6] If the Hegelian Absolute is to contain discord and unify differences qua differences, then it must include imperfect finite beings in all their imperfection. The tension and the disharmony which are features of the experience of the finite self seeking perfection afford a partial clue to the nature of the Absolute:

"...it is in the highest of our own experiences that we must seek for the clues to the fullest reality. And that we experience ourself most completely just when we are least aware of its finite selfness is a clue which must not be forgotten."[7]

Self-perfection is a matter of selfless self-seeking. This is Green's prescription for self-realization through service to mankind. Sacrifice and satisfaction are interdependent, and an element of discord is an essential truth of the self. "A soul which has never known pain, like a nation which has never known war, has no depth of being, and is not a personality at all."[8] This is a hard saying, but it was easier to say before the First World War. Bosanquet, like Bradley and McTaggart, was no militarist, nor an advocate of moral hygiene through punishment (although there are grounds for doubt about McTaggart on the latter score); but he, like they, assumed a Roman fortitude and patriotism in the face of claims of duty to valued institutions (although, once again, a partial exception must be made of McTaggart, who could never understand the high value placed by other British Hegelians on something as abstract as the state).

The single individual, the finite self-consciousness, is a "world of experience," limited but conscious of its limitations. In other words, the individual has the power to realize "the logic and spirit of the whole." The ultimate value - in other words the only value of which one can finally say there is no further end to be served - of any individual experience lies in the

---

[5] Ibid., p. 288.
[6] Ibid., p. 256.
[7] Ibid., p. 250.
[8] Ibid., p. 245.

whole of which it is a fragment. The criterion of ultimate value was, for Bosanquet, a logical one: the combined consistency and comprehensiveness of the totality of any experience. The same logic governs both the world of truth and existence and that of satisfaction and value. Value judgments are not simply isolated expressions of feeling, although they originate in feeling; as judgments, they are susceptible to rational, objective argument. They and the finite individuals who make them seek a wider and fuller unity. A particular state of consciousness always implies a unity of self-consciousness, and each unity is bound by mutual implication to all other unities, and to the full unity of thought and being.

> "When you have admitted the unity of the person with himself, it is impossible to stop short of his unity with others, with the world, and with the universe; and the perfection by which he is to be valued is his place in the perfection of these greater wholes. The principle that all value is value of individual experience is thus absolutely maintained; the difference is in what we call individual experience, and the point of departure in valuing it."[9]

For Bosanquet, organized political society was the most striking example and the best available model of an infinite (in the circular, Hegelian sense) whole of finite centres of experience which is at the same time a hierarchical standard of perfection. Not all good is social good.[10] But every society, great and small, involuntary as well as voluntary, partakes of that ultimate unity-in-difference which is the logical ground for evaluating the elements of experience.

> "The social life and experience is that of one mind in a number of bodies, whose consciousnesses, formally separate, are materially identical in very different degrees."[11]

The state exhibits a very high degree of perfection, as much because of its comprehension of differences, its inclusiveness, as because of its integrating power. As he himself was the first to admit, Bosanquet drew directly from Plato as well as from Hegel for the idea of the unity and individuality of the state. Furthermore, his version of the rationality of the real and the metaphysical necessity inherent in a system of values owed as least as much to Plato's Idea of the Good and to Kantian and Coleridgean conceptions of reason as it did to Aristotelian and Hegelian teleology; and, to complete this eclectic picture, he threw in a great deal of social psychology (as will be seen later in this chapter and in chapter 13).

From the insufficiency of the finite individual Bosanquet concluded that the world of distributive justice, of deserts apportioned according to merit, of claims and counterclaims, is as nothing beside "the great world of spiritual membership."[12] The individual who is conscious of being a member of a larger whole is content to identify his lot with that of the society of which he is a member. Its good is his good, its pain his pain. The result is that the best suffer most. The justice of this is that they are best equipped to sustain the suffering and to derive some lasting value from it. The comfort of the weak is fitting and just, not so much from their point of view as from that of society as a whole. They do not "deserve" the opportunity to "die to live." Those who do, because of their reasoned convictions about the universal order and their own place in it, are free from any illusions about their own personal importance.

---

[9] Ibid., pp. 315-16. Compare ch. 7, pp. 58-59, and the discussion of Bradley's logic of internal relations. Bradley continually urged his readers to consult Bosanquet's writings on the logic of philosophical idealism, especially his account of inference.

[10] Compare Bradley's "Ideal Morality," the sixth essay of *Ethical Studies*, for the view that even the "best lights" of the mores current in a society may be inadequate, and that there is a non-social as well as a social ideal of the good life. See ch. 7, pp. 62-63.

[11] *PIV*, p. 314.

[12] B. Bosanquet, *The Value and Destiny of the Individual* (London, 1913), p. 152.

Like D.G. Ritchie, Bosanquet made great play with the principle of natural selection in his social philosophy. However, in keeping with the Hegelian view of man and society, social change is seen as the outcome of a rational will, not of irrational forces. The spiritual world is "'elicited' from the primarily natural by the activity of the thinking will."

"We should note, further, that in eliciting this the will is by the same operation eliciting a definite and adapted shape of itself. Thus the creative process of volition is the process of moulding by natural selection as interpreted from the point of view of the soul which is being moulded. We are finding our self in the world as the world comes to life in our self."[13]

It is natural that we should shape ourselves as conative beings in constructing and reconstructing social structures. The clue to Bosanquet's connection between "soul-moulding" by natural selection and the strictly biological theory of natural selection could be said to lie in Hegel's "civil society," the world of industry and competition. In another one of his hard sayings, Bosanquet maintains that "society carries on the work of soul-formation by a severe and inevitable process."[14] The morally weak go to the wall - not necessarily of material destitution, but of spiritual impoverishment. This is natural selection in its social form, and according to the "social gospel" of British Hegelianism the state should do no more and no less than remove obstacles to and create opportunities for active self-perfection by individual selves.

In The Philosophical Theory of the State (1899) Bosanquet was already propounding the organic theory of self-assertion, the theory that the moral end and value of the finite individual is his contribution to something larger, something more comprehensive and coherent than himself. "It is in the difference which contributes to the whole that the self feels itself at home and possesses its individuality."[15] In this work Bosanquet lays considerable emphasis upon the classical Greek source of the idea that man aspires to a good which "is necessarily in some degree a good which extends beyond himself, or a common good."[16] The constant factor is the Platonic element in the classical tradition of political thought, whose principal legacy is the logical priority and ethical supremacy of the state. Man cannot be man without the polis. A.E. Taylor, an early Bradleyan who later became a Christian apologist, was highly critical of Bosanquet's Hegelianizing of that tradition.[17] In Taylor's view, Plato meant just what he said about studying the human soul writ large in the polis. His prime concern was the conduct and quality of the individual life, not the nature of the rational state. Bosanquet insists that the classical tradition is, above all, a political one and, indeed, that the modern nation-state is a much better illustration of classical political theory than the polis itself was. What was only implicit or dimly discerned in the Athenian city-state has now emerged into the full light of day.

Contrary to Taylor's contention, Bosanquet was in danger of Platonizing Hegel rather than Hegelianizing Plato. Bosanquet held the view that political theory was in a condition of reculer pour mieux sauter between Plato and Rousseau. The ideas of natural law and sovereignty, the political thought of Hobbes and Locke, the historical speculations of Vico and Montesquieu - all were mere preparation for the recovery of the philosophical theory of the state by Rousseau. This view of the history of political philosophy achieves unity at the expense of accuracy. Bosanquet tended to neglect the individualistic strain in modern political thought,

---

13 Ibid., p. 113. See ch. 10, pp. 82-84, for a discussion of Ritchie's use of the idea of natural selection.
14 Ibid., p. 89.
15 B. Bosanquet, The Philosophical Theory of the State, 4th ed. (London, 1923), p. 118.
16 Ibid., p. 114.
17 See A.E. Taylor, Plato: The Man and His Work, 3rd ed. (London, 1929), esp. the chapter on Plato's Republic, and his Gifford Lectures (1926-28), The Faith of a Moralist (London, 1930), series 1, pp. 241-43.

which reflected and was reflected in the ideology of natural rights, the expansion of economic life, and the growth of bourgeois society during the seventeenth and eighteenth centuries. Hegel was acutely aware of all these developments and regarded them as increasingly self-conscious manifestations of the subjective strand in the unfolding of the world spirit in human history. The average citizen of ancient Athens was, according to Hegel, in quite unself-conscious unity with civic law and custom. There was only the most rudimentary recognition of individual autonomy and initiative. Modern civil society structures and articulates the play of subjectivity, and its emergence has forever precluded the reproduction of the city-state. The modern state, with its multiform social, economic, professional and cultural life, is a higher form of human society than the polis. Its unity is a function of self-conscious individuality, so that the individual is not lost as an individual. His membership entitles him to a sphere of autonomy and sheer self-assertion, which finds its most characteristic outlet in the economic life of civil society. By giving the individual scope for self-assertion, civil society performs a moral function. It rationalizes the appetitive side of human nature without suppressing it, giving it a necessary place in society.

Bosanquet's political theory allows insufficient weight, by Hegelian standards, to civil society and the subjective element. The unity of his state is insufficiently mediated through the labour of the negative, through the fissiparous self-assertion of artisans, factory-owners, traders, and guilds and corporations of all kinds.[18] With Bosanquet, civil society is tightly reined in as an implicitly objective element in "the general life of the state."[19] There is no moment in Bosanquet's state of sheer subjectivity. It is a characteristic failing of British Hegelianism to employ the anaemic concept of reciprocity in place of the thrust and parry of the dialectic, and so it is in Bosanquet's treatment of subjectivity and objectivity in civil society. Bosanquet was well versed in social psychology and small-group theory, but his equipment in, for example, political economy was such that the "philosophical theory of the state" could not "draw blood" and penetrate the industrial society of his day. His state looks more like Plato's "republic" than Hegel's Rechtstaat, with economic life reduced to a realm of sheer physical necessity and emptied of all moral or rational significance.

One of the central notions of idealism, and one that continues to bear fruit in political theory and our attempts to render normative judgments about social conflicts, is its linking of the concept of liberty to the quality of life. Freedom from external constraint is shown to be cancelled but somehow completed by freedom from the rule of appetite. Internal control of one's irrational impulses and transient desires sets free capacities for living a larger and more satisfying life; political control over the freedom of certain classes or interests makes possible the wider enjoyment or prevents the destruction of certain values. Such a life is lived in common, and such values are shared with others. The ends pursued are such that they are not diminished by being shared.[20] In this freedom through the conquest of a "lower" and egocentric by a "higher" and social self lay the key to the "paradox of self-government," as Bosanquet termed it. Pursuing the common good, the good citizen obeys the commands of the state, because they come to him as the imperatives of his "real will" and express his true self. To be a good man and a good citizen can never be conflicting objectives. The selfish will

---

[18] "The family feeling and the individual interest are in the modern State let go, accented, intensified to their uttermost power...." (PTS, p. 261.) But Bosanquet nowhere affirms the autonomy of economic life; it is decorously likened to soul-formation, no longer recognizable as competition for material goods and power.

[19] Ibid., pp. 254-57.

[20] This is the language of St. Augustine. It is used deliberately, to point up the contention that those, like Bosanquet, who followed Green out into the world of social reform had a quasi-religious vocation. They were enjoined to practise, and preach to the privileged and the underprivileged, an ethic of self-sacrifice - not in a quest for grace but for worldly goods and satisfactions.

can find no lasting satisfaction in its partial and transitory objects, and is drawn to seek it in that of others and, by a necessary progression, to seek it in the common life of all. The larger and more stable objects of the general will, not his casual impulses and random passions, no matter how strong and insistent, are what give the individual the greatest and most genuine satisfaction. The "lower," less satisfying and less satisfactory self is disciplined and organized by life in society, above all by membership in a state, and it is directed towards "objects which have power to make a life worth living for the self that wills them." Thus the problem of political obligation is solved, for Bosanquet, by a combination of Rousseau's general will and Bradley's notion of what it is to be moral.

"Any system of institutions which represents to us, on the whole, the conditions essential to affirming such a will, in objects of action such as to constitute a tolerably complete life, has an imperative claim upon our loyalty and obedience as the embodiment of our liberty."[21]

Bosanquet had put forward the same theory about the nature of the will and the moral end for man, but without the political setting, in his Psychology of the Moral Self (1897). Here the moral self is described as "the realization of a certain nature which is the outcome of those (other) selves working together in society."[22] The individual cannot realize or "find" himself fully in isolation from the moral efforts of others. He requires a moral end larger than himself. The individual moral self must have a systematic, rational purpose in life. The wider the compass of that purpose, the fewer the loose ends and the greater the prospects for fulfilment. Such a purpose is not a mere ideal, but can be gleaned from everyday experience. Bosanquet illustrates the point by arguing that an ideal means something in the life of an individual only insofar as it is not something set over against the present social facts and then projected into the past or future. Insofar as it is unrealized, it involves "a mere rounding off or completion of the whole."[23] The realization of that ideal is to be found in actual social life or nowhere.

"That which constitutes the measure of morality seems to be the actual identification of the private self with the universal self, the actual surrender of the will to the greater will of the system to which we belong."[24]

While some British Hegelians conceived of an ideal society beyond the political sphere (or, in the case of McTaggart, beyond space and time), Bosanquet's good society was firmly political. As the acknowledged British spokesman for the idealist theory of the state, he bore the brunt of attacks upon it. These became increasingly virulent during the 1914-18 war with Germany. Bosanquet resolutely defended the theory throughout, and published a third edition of The Philosophical Theory of the State in 1920, unchanged except for some additional vindicatory remarks in the introduction. In 1917 he published a collection of essays under the title, Social and International Ideals. Two of them in particular, "The Wisdom of Naaman's Servants" and "The Function of the State in Promoting the Unity of Mankind," are noteworthy for their undiminished support for Hegel's theory of the rational will and skepticism about international political organizations. Those who blamed the war on the existence of sovereign nation-states and called for their dismantling and the creation of a world-state ignored the absence of the indispensable conditions for such a state. Another school of thought foresaw the imminent dissolution of the state in the evolution of political, economic and social relations, maintaining that the state, far from being "powerful but malignant, is an unreal creature of theory." Bosanquet reminds us of Bradley's saying that in times of stress the state does, "with the moral approval of all, what the explicit theory of scarcely one will morally justify."[25]

---

[21] Ibid., p. 139.
[22] B. Bosanquet, The Psychology of the Moral Self (London, 1897), p. 94.
[23] Ibid., p. 108.
[24] Ibid., p. 113.
[25] See ES, p. 166.

Contemporary events were providing further evidence of the hold of the idea of the state over men's minds, but that did not somehow warrant the abuse being heaped upon state institutions. The persistence of war did not detract from the rationality of the general will. The spirit of the state is "the same thing as conscience," and, like the individual, the state pursues moral order and the actualization of right. While the objectivity and universality of the state are superior to those of the individual conscience - being ground and goal for our highest moral endeavours - nevertheless the state too can commit moral errors:

"The simple fact is that the spirit of the community, brought to consciousness and practice in its executive organ, the State, is the great moral force of the world. Like every moral force, it can, when biased or perverted, make wrong its right."[26]

In such cases, the corrective normally consists in bringing the errant state back into line with its own immanent idea. An "enterprising" foreign policy is usually a sign that a state is trying to avoid its own better self, and diverting attention from internal defects by embarking upon foreign adventures. If, as many critics of sovereignty assert, the state is an invariably irresponsible agent, then, says Bosanquet, there is need for more, not less, power to the state - in the sense of organization, cohesion and collective effort to achieve greater equality of opportunity, enlightenment, and so on.

There is a question as to how far the best life can be promoted by force or threat of force. For the most part, Bosanquet follows Green in restricting the use of force to indirect improvement, to the "hindering of hindrances" to the good life. Voluntary is always preferable to enforced reform - unless the only alternative to enforced is no reform, or the resultant increase in the quality of life is of such an order that the disadvantages of coercion are outweighed. In itself, force "is not in pari materia with the expansion of mind and character in their spiritual medium."[27] It is an affront to the reason of the communal mind, which is the true ground of all social action. Force, however, is the distinctive feature of the state. Because of what Bosanquet calls "its ultimateness de facto" the state is the "flywheel" of our lives. All the mechanical and apparently automatic processes necessary to the functioning of a complex organization are driven by the power of the state. Without this "automatism," state power could not be the supreme creator of opportunities for self-realization. The exercise of coercive power on the part of the state is not interference of the state with the individual unless there is an abuse of power, in which case the state hinders itself.

There are no natural rights vis-a-vis the state. Whereas Ritchie sought to retain some sort of role for the ideology of natural rights within an idealist theory of the state, Bosanquet stuck closely to Green, maintaining that every right is relative to the common moral consciousness, to the actual state of the general will. Any unrecognized right must be shown to be "a requirement of the realization of capacities for good."[28] Society must be seen to be inconsistent with its end, with what it professes to be, before one can say that there exists any unrecognized right. In other words, it has to be recognized before it can be recognized; until the state has modified the law, the right does not exist qua right. The state must enforce it in order that it be a right. The state, in short, creates rights, and they can emerge only in the context of an organized political society. These rights are means to self-realization, but its value is in turn instrumental. Ultimate value resides not in individuals but in individuals-in-community.

A long-standing and well-worn criticism of the idealist ethic, and one that Bradley dealt with at some length, is that self-realization is not an ethical concept at all. For all their talk of the moral self, the good self and the bad self, the idealists provided no criterion for distinguishing between the crudest forms of self-assertion and whatever it was they meant by

---

[26] B. Bosanquet, Social and International Ideals (London, 1917), p. 307.
[27] PTS, p. 175.
[28] Ibid., p. 198.

self-realization. Talk of coherence and completeness is of little assistance, because these concepts, again, are non-moral. The moral philosophy of Bosanquet (and of Bradley, too, in some respects) lends itself to an interpretation which suggests that the problem of self-realization may not be what it has so often been said to be. The idealists, far from attempting to make egotism respectable by clothing it in the high-falutin language of religion and patriotism, were seeking a solution to the alienation and rootlessness experienced by members of the ever-expanding and amorphous middle class of industrialized mass society. The value, as distinct from the psychology, of the moral self lay, for Bosanquet, in its modes of experience. He was all for expanding the range of a person's experience.

> "True individuality, as we have said, is not in the minimization which forbids further subdivision, but in the maximization which includes the greatest possible being in an unviolable unity."[29]

Now this could concentrate more and more around a single personal focus, or it could spread a person so thin that he ceased to have a distinct identity and became a mere vehicle for organizing experiences. An apt analogy might be losing oneself in one's work - or in good works. The individual is not free to carve himself out of society: all his modes of self-realization, including the non-social ones - such as the intellectual pursuit of truth or the artistic pursuit of beauty - are determined by the social setting. One might elect to lead a totally disorganized life with no goal beyond momentary pleasure; but assuming that one seeks satisfaction and some stable object in life, then one must pursue a common good, if only as an adjunct.

The paradox at the heart of the idealist theory of the state is the implicit denial that the individual's will is his own, combined with the claim that he is most fully and freely an individual when he submits to the sovereignty of the general will. The finite individual, on this theory, is not a stable, "real" entity. The "facts" of individual moral life and action can only be explained adequately by placing what Bosanquet calls "the centre of gravity of the self" outside the circumscribed individual, and by adopting a perspective which sees the individual as an abstraction from the communal mind. As such, the individual is not an entity unto himself or herself, but is a fragment of the common moral consciousness which seeks to be reunited in a way which enriches both itself and the whole of which it is a part. This is a psychic drive whose energy is metaphysical, in the sense that it is a universal necessity which can in fact be denied but only at the cost of self-diremption and frustration. The individual wants - in both senses of the word - the moral support of the community; and he can begin to find it by reflecting on the resources of his own psyche, their origins and their ramifications.

The moral force of the common good was, for Bosanquet, a matter of "social logic." This notion he derived from Hegel's world spirit, the rational principle at work in the world. The state is one of the highest manifestations of this rationality. Notwithstanding the violence attending the birth and development of actual historical states, each one is a manifestation of "divine Reason," just as every human being, whatever his physical, intellectual or moral shortcomings, is still a human being. The rationality of the state is expressed in its members' self-consciousness as members. Most people will admit, on reflection, to some consciousness of common good. Having conceded that, they are then driven to either reconcile it with the role of the state - law enforcement, the regulation of everyday life, and so on - or use it to "contradict" the immoral and coercive character of the state. Either way, a dialectic of state and society, common good and particular interest, is set in motion.

Bosanquet, as we have seen, expected the state to endure, and that the dialectic would resolve itself as a unity-in-difference in which the institutions of organized political society are "the ideal substance which, as a universal structure, is the social, but in its

---

[29] Ibid., p. 170. See also the discussion of Jones and Muirhead in ch. 13, pp. 106-07.

differentiated cases is the individual mind."[30] The greater the unity of society, the greater the scope for distinctive individual contributions to the common good; and the greater the differentiation among such contributions, the greater the resultant unity.

---

[30] *Ibid.*, p. 277.

CHAPTER 10

Idealism, "Evolutionism" and Utilitarianism

The publication of Darwin's On the Origin of Species in 1859 and the sort of anthropological speculation to which it gave impetus lent fresh credence to the theory that the mind of man and all that it had produced were natural phenomena, explicable entirely in terms of material cause and effect. It gained persuasive - albeit invalid - support from the principle of natural selection. Darwin himself would not endorse this extension of his theory; and the foremost advocate of his work, T.H. Huxley, repudiated it.[1] Huxley argued that natural selection tells us nothing about our moral duties or the moral end for man, which hold true in spite of natural selection. In other words, the self-conscious mind - or, as the philosophical idealist might say, the self-positing world spirit - cannot be understood in entirely natural terms. Humanity is subject as well as object.

Whatever its natural history, self-consciousness presupposes order and continuity in human experience. This is not given; nor can it be created out of nothing. In Kantian language, synthetic a priori judgments are an indispensable part of our experience. We can perceive nothing without the transcendental unity of apperceptions. Human experience implies some persistent identity, an ongoing cognitive self. By the same token, there must be a moral self - the cognitive self from another point of view - without which we could not distinguish between impulse, conscious desire and morally purposive action. The moral self is the principle of order and continuity in the midst of various, frequently conflicting, wants and inclinations. As it is not a different self from the cognitive self, so the reason of moral judgments is not divorced from that of cognitive judgments, and unity and consistency are the chief characteristics of both the rational moral self and the rational cognitive self. The undivided reason demands that the moral and political world, no less than the natural world, be a world of experience and not a mere agglomeration or succession of sense data - even a bare succession of disconnected experiences is impossible in the absence of some ordering principle. The will for good is a rational will. It is therefore common to all human beings in virtue of their humanity and their human capacity for rationality. Its content varies from society to society, but its dictates are always objective, in the sense of intersubjective - they overrule purely subjective wants and inclinations - and its judgments are universal judgments.

For Hegel, rationality was immanent throughout nature and human history. He rehabilitated natural heteronomous desires, which Kant had set over against the rational good will. They are inherently rational, and require only to be mediated by the moral will for their rationality to be realized. In their turn, they provide the good will with its content, without which it would be a merely formal will, a will to do nothing in particular. The rational will is not simply a self-consistent will; its rationality depends upon what it wills and upon its realizing something. Self-realization requires putting oneself out into a world of other things and selves.

Putting the rational will to work in purposive moral action, and especially in social reform, was one of the primary goals of the majority party in British Hegelianism, which is to say, Green, Bosanquet and their followers. As did Kant, and in large part inspired by his example, these British Hegelians consciously directed their heaviest fire against naturalism in the moral sciences. It must be remembered, however, that the basic Hegelian principle is that

---

[1] See his Evolution and Ethics, the Romanes Lecture for 1893.

self-realization is a process of knowing as well as doing, and that what we realize (in both senses of the word) are manifestations of the universal reason at work in us as well as, and more so than, in other "things." The _logos_ is both the subject matter and the motive force of the process whereby everything comes to be, and the mind of man has a special role to play in that process. We must comprehend it - again in a double sense: to understand the necessity of what has happened and in what is temporary and contingent, and to round it off or complete it. This is what is meant by saying that man is subject as well as object, and it is important that the subjectivity in Hegel's idealist system of philosophy not be confused with the subjective idealism which plagued the British empiricist tradition. The Green-Bosanquet brand of idealism stressed the creative role of individual and, even more, collective moral endeavour, frequently in defiance of or in uneasy alliance with the historicist determinism of Hegel's world spirit.

Of those Hegelians who imbibed their idealism - both philosophical and practical - from T.H. Green, D.G. Ritchie was the most overtly political writer.[2] The problem to which most of his writing is devoted is the relationship of evolutionary ethics to the idealist theory of the state. The thesis of his popular _Darwinism and Politics_ (1891) is, first, that the biological theory of natural selection is applicable to the intellectual, moral and social development of man only if the supervention of human consciousness in natural history is accounted for by that theory, and second, that the theory "(in the form in which alone it can properly be applied to human society) lends no support to the political dogma of laissez-faire."[3] It is the power to reflect upon and evaluate social structures and mores, customs, laws and institutions which distinguishes human from other animal evolution. Man is not at the mercy of natural selection; he is capable of rational selection. Human history contains examples of societies deliberately embarking on a new policy or adopting an innovative technique, even in anticipation of changing circumstances. Such social adaptation is usually a matter of imitation - unconscious as well as conscious - of other human, often rival, societies. Human beings are not dependent upon heredity in a biological sense for the transmission of ideas, customs and sentiments. Their spread is achieved much more rapidly and securely by social inheritance, through language and institutional inculcation. The process of social "heredity" and social "variation" is less a blind instinctual struggle for existence between individuals and races than a competition of ideas and institutions. One idea or institution can supplant another without loss of life, although human betterment is impossible without a great deal of struggle. The struggle, according to Ritchie, is one against nature - primarily human nature - for which the so-called laws of nature cannot themselves dictate.

Like Green, Ritchie sought a moral role for the state and a theoretical justification for increasing governmental intervention to remedy social ills. Collective reform based on cooperative endeavour is not inconsistent with social evolution, which has nothing to do with the struggle for individual survival or, as Herbert Spencer insisted, with a progressive "restriction and limitation of state functions." On the contrary, state action for social purposes signifies an advanced stage of civilization. Furthermore, the individual person, possessing rights and liberties, will continue to benefit from state action; and maximization of heterogeneity, which Spencer extolled as the salutary design of evolution, is dependent upon increasing political articulation - to forestall, we might add over eighty years and many malign experiments in totalitarianism later, both political and non-political forces which contribute to a reversion to homogeneity. Whether one thinks of the state as an organism or as an aggregation, the individuals who compose it owe it such freedom of action as they have. The

---

[2] David George Ritchie was a fellow and tutor of Jesus College, Oxford, from 1881 until 1894, and of Balliol from 1882. In 1894 he was appointed Professor of Logic and Metaphysics at the University of St. Andrews, which post he held until his death in 1903. He was active in the London Ethical Society, and it was partly through the widely ramified membership of that society that he became a convert to Fabian socialism.
[3] D.G. Ritchie, _Darwinism and Politics_ (London, 1891), p. iii.

state is one of man's great triumphs in his struggle to escape from the struggle for mere survival, from the realm of sheer physical necessity. In Ritchie's words, this struggle has seen "a gradual diminution of waste...."

"In the lower organisms nature is reckless in her expenditure of life.... When we come to human beings in society, the State is the chief instrument by which waste is prevented. The mere struggle for existence between individuals means waste unchecked. The State, by its action, can in many cases consciously and deliberately diminish this fearful loss; in many cases by freeing the individual from the necessity of a perpetual struggle for the mere conditions of life, it can set free individuality and so make culture possible."[4]

The value, for Ritchie, of the idealist theory of the state was not entirely explanatory nor merely justificatory. It was also a program of political action. He was confident that the democratic extension of the franchise would increasingly bear out the theory that the state is the embodiment of the common good and that its action is the expression of the general will. He followed Green closely in regarding the idea that all are free in the modern state as an ideal yet to be realized, indirectly through legislation, directly through that self-culture for which legislation can establish the necessary conditions. He was more inclined than Green, however, to accept the necessity of direct state action for social improvement and less inclined to defer action out of regard for the autonomous moral will of the individual person. Jowett complained that Green's teaching turned his students into hair-splitting and quietistic metaphysicians. In Ritchie's case the effect was quite different, if no less disastrous from the standpoint of a conservative like Jowett. Ritchie proceeded, with few theoretical qualms, from the organicist conception of society to its alleged practical consequences of increased collectivism in public policy-making.

"The person with rights and duties is the product of a society...and for the purposes of practical ethics and politics, it is sufficient to recognize that personality is a conception meaningless apart from society."[5]

Ritchie claimed to have discovered a link between Green and Bentham in their conceptions of social welfare. Both emphasized the collective nature of social goals and both urged the desirability of collective action, using state power to achieve those goals. Although Ritchie preferred Green's conception of the greatest self-development of the greatest number to the utilitarian greatest happiness principle, he felt "we are safer with the Utilitarian method."[6] While it was "too narrowly conceived," the greatest happiness of the greatest number had more practical effect than the idea of self-development.[7] It possessed a further advantage in that it was a corrective against the complacency and quietism encouraged by the historical method in politics and by the success criterion implied in "theories which apply the conceptions of organism and evolution to society as if they were as adequate in politics as in biology."[8] As far as utilitarianism was concerned, Ritchie regarded Sidgwick's universalistic hedonism as an immense improvement upon the old individualistic or egoistic hedonism. Ritchie called them "Individualist" and "Evolutionist" utilitarianism. The latter's advantage lay in its recognition of the primacy of the general welfare. It also made room in its political perspective for a past and a future, recognizing the importance of the legacy of previous

---

[4] D.G. Ritchie, The Principles of State Interference (London, 1891), p. 50. This is a collection of four essays, two attacking the individualism of Spencer's The Man vs. The State, one on Mill's individualism and one on the political philosophy of Green. See, in addition, The Principles of State Interference, p. 148.
[5] D.G. Ritchie, Natural Rights (London, 1894), pp. 101-02 (Ritchie's emphasis).
[6] D.G. Ritchie, Darwin and Hegel (London, 1893), p. 28.
[7] As will be seen shortly, McTaggart was another self-styled Hegelian who used much the same argument in favour of combining philosophical idealism and political utilitarianism.
[8] Ibid.

generations and of the claims of posterity. Ritchie sought to combine a sense of organized political society's continuity and immanent moral purpose amidst the welter of transient demands and factional interests with the analytical egalitarianism of the felicific calculus.

In the essay which gave the collection its name, "Darwin and Hegel," Ritchie tried to incorporate the theory of natural selection into an idealist social theory. Darwin and Hegel could be reconciled without sacrifice on the part of either. There was no essential conflict; they were complementary. Ritchie's syncretic doctrine of "Idealist Evolutionism" could explain social advance in terms of rational, not natural, selection - in terms of reflection, foresight and voluntary change rather than blind and brutal natural processes - because, he said, Hegel and Darwin both recognized the operation of final causes in the Aristotelian sense. In the case of Darwin, the final cause was the survival of the species. In the case of Hegel, the final cause was the fulfilment of reason, especially in the rational state. For both, the end to be realized was a social or collective one. Like Green, Ritchie preferred the activist interpretation of the Hegelian dictum about the rationality of the real. The ideal is yet to be realized in social reform; "the process is not completed." Ritchie's easiness with naturalistic doctrines, such as utilitarianism, led him away from the Hegelian notion that development is not an open-ended process but a process of recovery in which we know enough to know the end by looking back over the history of the world, and in particular the history of self-conscious mind. The achievements of the modern state held, for Ritchie, the promise (but by no means the guarantee) of further progress toward human equality and enlightenment. Something like Kant's kingdom of ends was, if not inevitable, certainly the natural outcome of events as they were then unfolding - in a sense of "natural" to be explained shortly. In his zeal for a comprehensive synthesis, Ritchie also tried to enlist the idea of the social contract in support of his views. In spite of their mistakenly reversing the development of man as a political animal and finding the beginning in the end, contract theories did afford a glimpse of the rational ideal of free obedience to self-imposed laws. Although classical utilitarianism flatly and vehemently rejected the idea of a social contract, one may detect in Ritchie's attempt to graft natural rights as a political program onto a conception of society which was in part teleological and in part mechanistic the influence of Sidgwick's broadly based utilitarianism as well as Green's Kantianism.

In his best-known and most reprinted work, <u>Natural Rights</u>, Ritchie gathered together themes enunciated in his earlier essays on the relationship between Darwinian and Darwin-inspired theories of natural selection, on the one hand, and the idealist theory of the common good as propounded by Green, on the other. The tone is still strongly and sarcastically critical of Spencer and social Darwinism, but Ritchie's syncretic urge is as strong as ever. Now it is applied to the task of reconciling philosophical idealism with eugenics. In a lengthy, two-part discussion of the natural right to life, Ritchie subjects claims to parental control over child-bearing and rearing, and to what we might now call maternity benefits, to the argument that any such rights are subordinate to the state's right to enforce social hygiene. In short, the state has a "natural" right to determine the quantity and quality - both physical and mental - of its future citizens.

What does Ritchie mean by "natural"? The answer to that is the crux of the argument in <u>Natural Rights</u>, and it is to be found in chapter 5, "What Determines Rights?" In the previous chapter Ritchie makes great play of the distinction between <u>natura naturata</u> and <u>natura naturans</u>. The former is any and every particular phenomenon, "the totality of what exists." But "many phenomena turn out not to be realities (i.e. not to have worth), but to be 'shams'."[9] The correct way to view nature - including human nature - as a whole is teleologically. <u>Natura naturans</u> is an older and incomplete way of expressing the full Hegelian version of the idea that we are part of a scheme of things which in its totality is a process driven by a built-in

---

[9] D.G. Ritchie, <u>Natural Rights</u>, p. 76.

purpose or _telos_. Nature is an ideal, a potential seeking to be actualized; and the natural is not so much the normal or the original - and even less the "savage" or anti-societal - as it is the rational, which is to say, what human nature makes of the rest of nature and how it employs the instruments and achievements of its own evolution. Insofar as actual human societies are concerned, there is no equality of rights, but that is an unimportant "fact" by comparison with the potential of all human beings to be fully autonomous persons in virtue of their common humanity.

"The 'equality' of human beings as such, which alone is necessarily implied in an idealist system of ethics, would be more correctly expressed as their potential membership of a common society. It is only insofar as we can think of humanity as a possible society that we can regard human beings as equal moral units. They are persons potentially because they are potentially members of a society."[10]

Ritchie, like Green, conceived it as natural that human societies should evolve into a world society of all human beings. There is no guarantee that we will achieve that condition, given the human capacity for perverse and bloody-minded behaviour. But our knowing the rational necessity of the proposition that all are free, that all are persons, means that we know what is right, and what we could achieve, and puts us in a vastly different position vis-a-vis the existing state of affairs than are those whose highest expectations are dictated by the best that their society has been able to achieve, as opposed to what our "higher natures in advance of their surroundings" may prefigure.

Natural rights, for Ritchie, are social rights. They are not brought by individuals to society to be bargained against securities enforceable at law. Or rather, one should say, such an arrangement can have no moral validity; one cannot bargain with the sovereign good of society. "The good of a community gives us our only criterion for judging of what is right for individuals to do; but the good of a community is itself identical with the good of its members."[11] As it stands, the preceding statement is tautological - and perhaps deliberately so. There is no scope in it for particular goods, or for conflict between partial goods and the presumed good of the whole. Ritchie talks only of the (singular) good of the community's members. He shared the full-blown British Hegelian (Bradley out of Aristotle) assumption that we are born into a common good and that we never know any other good which is good without qualification.

In partial answer to the question, what determines rights?, Ritchie says that "...certain mutual claims which cannot be ignored without detriment to the well-being and, in the last resort, to the very being of a community may in an intelligible sense be called fundamental or natural rights."[12] One obvious upshot of this attempt to define natural rights is that we are faced with the further question: what determines well-being? Ritchie has no hesitation in saying that the general welfare is a utilitarian standard. We can make practical political use of the intuition that the common good of the earthly city is our highest rational good, "so that the details of a professedly Intuitionalist ethical code are filled up on Utilitarian principles."[13] Having become organicist, as well as universalistic with Sidgwick - having acquired an expanded view of before and after - the utilitarian ethic was now available to those who professed the common good as the highest good.[14] As for traditional, and still highly popular, theories of natural rights and the social contract, they are simply "an inaccurate, but possibly convenient, way of judging any given society from the point of view of a supposed

---

[10] Ibid., pp. 253-54.
[11] Ibid., p. 99.
[12] Ibid., p. 87.
[13] Ibid.
[14] "The conception of evolution or, more precisely, the theory of natural selection has at once corrected the errors and vindicated the truth of Utilitarian ethics and politics." (Ibid., p. 98.)

wider or higher society."[15] An example of Ritchie's use of the utilitarian criterion can be found in his treatment of property rights. An "inexpedient" property right, or a particular exercise of it, should be curtailed only "with the least amount of friction" and with "just compensation," because property rights have on the whole proven their utility.[16]

The truth of Ritchie's view that nature is normative was grounded in the evolution of public opinion. That there is an "underlying principle or immanent reason of the universe" is believed by "all except thoroughgoing pessimists or sceptics," who "practically do, whatever theories they may profess, whatever speculative doubts and difficulties they may feel."[17] Ritchie is fairly typical of the second generation of British Hegelians in availing himself of a wide range of theories drawn from social and natural science in order to give greater currency to the idealist theory of the state. There is little about the Hegelian unity of thought and being in his mature work, and arguments from the nature of reason and of our activities in pursuit of rational order in our experience are few and far between.

"As we understand nature better, and as we understand human nature better, we can secure adaptation and adjustment by bending nature in many ways to ourselves instead of bending ourselves in every respect to nature."[18]

All tendencies in science and society, he concludes, point in the direction of a collectivist solution to the "social question." He appeals to socialists to have patience and "reverence for the long toil of the human spirit." Although work is required to bring the "good elements" in regressive sentiments and institutions to the fore, and while ethically superior structures may be defeated by "inferior surroundings," nevertheless, the "Divine purpose...is gradually revealing itself in the education of the human race."[19] On the one hand, rights are only as good as the social consciousness out of which they emerge; on the other hand, there is an important educative role for new laws and institutions to play: "they must be such as prepare people to go beyond them in quiet and orderly fashion."[20] Social adaptation was not for Ritchie merely a matter of reacting to environmental changes. He possessed to a high degree the rationalist's confidence in human prospects for directing social change into just and orderly patterns of growth.

The remainder of this chapter will be taken up with an examination of that part of the work of J.McT.E. McTaggart in which he attempted to combine a form of utilitarian ethics with a metaphysic which was, at least initially, inspired by the Hegelian unity of thought and being.[21] McTaggart wrote extremely little that could be called moral or political philosophy, and what he did bears scant resemblance to that of any other British Hegelian - or of Hegel himself.

As C.D. Broad, McTaggart's first and most comprehensive expositor, has said, McTaggart's thought can be broken down into three distinct areas: commentary on Hegel's logic and what

---

15 Ibid., p. 102.
16 See Ibid., ch. 13.
17 Ibid., p. 76.
18 Ibid., p. 112.
19 Ibid., p. 286.
20 Ibid., p. 282.
21 John McTaggart Ellis McTaggart (1866-1925) was an undergraduate at Trinity College, Cambridge, where he studied moral sciences under Henry Sidgwick. He had already developed, even as a schoolboy, a precocious interest in Kant and a talent for speculative philosophy. He was elected a fellow of Trinity in 1891 and was college lecturer in moral sciences from 1897 to 1922. Like Bradley, he could not abide the generalized humanitarian sentiments and diffuse good works of other British Hegelians. As for his own views on current events and issues, there is no ready label, because "one of McTaggart's great intellectual virtues was that he chose his opinions à la carte." (P.T. Geach, Truth, Love and Immortality (London, 1979), p. 11.)

McTaggart called "Hegelian cosmology"; discussion of metaphysical propositions which are of interest not just to professional philosophers but to all human beings in their relations with what for McTaggart was the Real World; and, thirdly, McTaggart's own vision of that world worked out in a deductive ontology. The three areas of McTaggart's philosophizing are almost three distinct temporal phases. According to his most recent expositor, P.T. Geach, McTaggart "wrote Hegel out of his system" before turning to the philosophical method of Spinoza and Leibniz. McTaggart devoted himself in the middle period of his career to the semi-popular exposition of metaphysics, especially of questions relating to personal immortality, as well as to more formal teaching and his own philosophy. Although he continued to expound the importance of metaphysics to everyman, his latter years were primarily taken up with the laborious working and re-working of the argument of The Nature of Existence. McTaggart's thoughts on morals and politics are peripheral to his main concerns - which in itself makes him an exception to the general rule among British Hegelians - and they are to be found scattered through his earlier work on what he came to regard as Hegel's only permanent contribution to knowledge, the dialectic.

As will be discussed further in the next chapter on idealism as a substitute religion, McTaggart's vision of supreme good (in the Supreme Reality) is that of a society of perfect persons who perfectly and eternally know and love each other. That does not seem to have any bearing on the here and now, and McTaggart said as much. Nevertheless, his metaphysical personalism unavoidably coloured what he had to say about man and society. Geach thinks Hegelianism had virtually nothing to do with McTaggart's philosophical account of his vision of the universe. This is true, but McTaggart "knew" the nature of reality before he had dispensed with Hegelianism as the way to rationally persuade others of the truth of his vision, and his writings on Hegel exhibit a mixture of his own beliefs, Hegelian logic and utilitarian ethics, which, if hardly constituting a synthesis, does amount to more than just unconnected lines of thought. His comments on the moral and the political life were made in conscious opposition to other British Hegelians; but in discussing McTaggart on morals and politics, I will proceed on the assumption that, however eccentric, his mind was one and not two or more.

McTaggart's supreme good is a society consisting solely of incorruptible lovers, perfectly differentiated but transparent individuals; but, as will be seen in chapter 11, the supreme good will be realized whatever happens in or to the society we live in as mortal beings. It has no value in political theory or as a guide to political conduct. The perfect society is a perfect differentiation in unity, but this tells us nothing about temporal society.

> "Philosophy can afford us no guidance as to the next step to be taken at any time.... That must depend upon the particular circumstances which surround us at the moment - our needs, dangers, resources. It can only be decided empirically and it will just as often be a step which throws the unity into the background as it will be one which brings it forward into increased prominence."[22]

The modern state, the organized society of the present, "is the natural and inevitable introduction to the society of the future, but it is so only in the same way as everything else is." Anarchy, sin and hatred, as well as society, virtue and love, are all "necessary incidents in the movement towards the ideal." One cannot say that the state is organic as the Absolute is organic, any more than one can say that human love is perfect as love among the immortals of the Absolute is perfect.

> "Absolute Reality, according to Hegel, is eternal, and cannot be fully realized in any state of the world which is still subject to succession in time. Absolute Reality must see and be seen under the highest category only, and is not realized while any reality is unconscious of itself or appears to others under the form of matter. Absolute Reality, finally, is incompatible with pain or imperfection.
>
> "This is clearly not the society in which we live, and we are not entitled to

---

[22] J.McT.E. McTaggart, Studies in Hegelian Cosmology (Cambridge, 1901), p. 195.

argue that the society of the present is an organic unity because the ideal society is such a unity."[23]

However, we have lives to live in temporal society, and they must be lived as best we can, according to the best lights available to us as temporal beings.

To live in temporal society is to live in relationships upon which "overwhelming influence is exercised by considerations which we cannot suppose will have overwhelming influence in that ideal society in which all our aspirations would be satisfied."[24] Temporal society exhibits a continuous dialectical movement from differentiation to unity and back. At one stage differentiation will be the dominant tendency, even to the verge of anarchy; at the next there will be a swing to unity which threatens excessive homogeneity and uniformity. There is in this dialectical movement no "cunning of reason," no underlying progress towards an eventual state of perfect unity combined with perfect differentiation. The theoretical problem is how to define the relationship, here and now, between the individual and organized political society.

McTaggart's exaltation of the individual person, so evident in his vision of the Absolute, is reflected in his political theory.

> "Each of us is more than the society which unites us, because there is in each of us the longing for perfection which that society can never realize. The parts of a living body can find their end in that body, though it is imperfect and transitory. But a man can dream of perfection and, having once done so, he will find no end short of perfection. Here he has no abiding city."[25]

Here is a very clear expression of the connection between McTaggart's metaphysics and his view of man in society. The triumphs and disasters of man the political animal may have no bearing whatsoever upon the realization of the Absolute, but the nature of that perfection which will be realized in the Absolute is more like any one individual member of society than it is any society of individuals - short of the perfect society of the Absolute itself. McTaggart was the last one to argue analogically; but given the intensity of his personalist vision of the supreme good, it is hardly surprising to find him valuing one man's dream of perfection more highly than the collective compromises of political life. That the individual is to a large degree "determined in every direction by the society in which he lives" does not entail the state being the end for man, nor that it is in any way superior to the individual.[26] The existence of intrinsically determining relations between individuals and between the individual and "the unity in which he stands with the other individuals of the same system" does not entail any sort of subordination of the individual to society, temporal or eternal. Determining relations are compatible with a unity which is a mere means to the separate ends of its constituent related parts. Again, this sort of unity obtains only in the supreme good, where the constituent parts are literally immaterial, where the individual is a soul (in traditional, religiously inspired language) and all is spirit. However, the nature of perfection leaves us as free to say that society is nothing but a means to individual fulfilment as that the individual is an instrument of the common good.

> "...the highest realization of the State - that in which it is the universal which completely sums up the individuals which compose it - may be considered as being in the past or the future, but not in the present."[27]

From that it would be reasonable to infer that the perfection of differentiation in unity cannot be found in political life as we know it - from which it does not follow that the individual should defy or ignore the demands of the state. But the drift of McTaggart's Hegelian "cosmology" is clear: even the "highest realization of the State" (which is not a

---

[23] Ibid., p. 188.
[24] Ibid., p. 192.
[25] Ibid., p. 193.
[26] Ibid., p. 180.
[27] Ibid., p. 148.

practical political prospect) is so far removed from the individualism of the supreme good that it would be irrational to subordinate individuals to the state. It might be politic, it might help secure some temporal good - it would certainly have no effect, adverse or otherwise, on the supreme good - but such a policy could not rationally defend itself by trying to argue that the state is the good, the end, the fulfilment of the individual.

One of the features of British Hegelian political philosophy which McTaggart found quite intolerable was a propensity to invest Hegel's obiter dicta about the state being some sort of earthly God with evangelical seriousness, and to encourage the state to bask in the reflected glory of the Absolute. For those tempted to indulge in any form of state worship, McTaggart caustically remarks: "It would be as reasonable to worship a sewage pipe, which also possesses considerable value as a means."[28] As for the state's claim to exercise moral authority over the citizen, McTaggart has another aphorism: "A man is not a child, and the State is not God."[29] Men may have found their fulfilment, their perfection, in the polis; but the state is not the polis, nor is it the real or rational will of its citizens. The moral authority which society possessed in the ancient city-state has devolved upon the individual conscience. There are cases in which an individual may find himself "in the same childlike relation to the State as was possible in classical times," but on the whole "the development of individual conscience and responsibility has been too great for such an attitude."[30] The state can no longer be the unquestioned judge of right and wrong; it can now itself be judged and condemned by the individual on moral grounds. "It has still a claim to obedience, but not to unquestioning veneration."[31] In this part of his argument, McTaggart is attacking a straw man. He appears to have felt a dangerous imbalance in the political theory of philosophical idealism and the need to reassert the claims of the individual with the force of some exaggeration.

McTaggart's moral philosophy has the same curious relationship with his metaphysics as does his general theory of value. The supreme good could not be more remote, and yet it is right there, on the other side of a clear but impenetrable wall of glass. The Absolute has no logical connection with morality here and now. On the other hand, "if we care for virtue we can scarcely fail to be interested in the ultimate righteousness or iniquity of the universe...."[32] The Absolute, of course, is perfection, the complete development and realization of our ideals. That includes happiness, which "is also an element of perfection."[33] Happiness and moral development, or self-realization, cannot thwart one another as elements in the supreme good. For one thing, moral development is complete - by definition - and, for another, there cannot be morality without something evil, ugly, painful or simply incomplete to overcome.

When we look at the moral life of temporal man in temporal society, we can find no harmony among ethical principles. The great debate, when McTaggart began his philosophical career, was between the idealist ethic of self-realization and the utilitarian one of the greatest happiness of the greatest number. One might have thought that McTaggart, as a personal idealist, would have chosen self-realization as the most congenial ethical principle. But no, he found it too slippery a criterion to apply to hard cases; it could not meet the exacting demands of problems of moral choice. What McTaggart was looking for was something which worked as well as explained. The greatest happiness principle filled the bill, because "no one ever mistakes intense pain for intense pleasure, while ideals of perfection have been so different and incompatible that, whoever is right, many people must have mistaken great defects for great

---

[28] J.McT.E. McTaggart, Philosophical Studies, ed. S.V. Keeling (London, 1934), p. 109.
[29] SHC, p. 148.
[30] Ibid., p. 147.
[31] Ibid., p. 149. For the idealist theory of the state properly understood, the nexus of political obligation is neither obedience nor veneration.
[32] J.McT.E. McTaggart, Studies in the Hegelian Dialectic (Cambridge, 1896), p. 258.
[33] SHC, p. 122.

excellences."³⁴ To the contention that the employment of happiness as a moral criterion involves the addition and subtraction of intensive quantities, McTaggart's response was that no criterion, not even that of perfection, can dispense with the calculation of intensive quantities of itself.

> "How can we act rationally with regard to consequences, unless the different intensive quantities in different sets of consequences can be compared? Although the excess of A's intensity over B's is not a pleasure, it is, nevertheless, pleasure. Whatever has quantity must be homogeneous in respect of some quality, and it is only quantitative in respect of that homogeneous quality. If, therefore, pleasure has an intensive quantity, then each part of that quantity must be pleasure, including that part by which it is greater than another."³⁵

Scornful idealists such as Bradley, who charged the felicific calculus with futility and immoral casuistry, were nevertheless obliged to measure and compare the consequences of different courses of action. Let us suppose, McTaggart suggests, a man of limited means, with conflicting moral obligations making demands beyond those means:

> "Shall he send his sons to a second-rate school and pension his old nurse, or shall he send them to a first-rate school and let her go to the workhouse? Problems like these are the real ethical difficulties of life, and they are not to be solved by generalities - or even by contemplating the idea of the supreme good, in which there are neither school-bills nor workhouses, and whose perfections are in consequence irrelevant to the situation."³⁶

It is unlikely that the "laborious empirical calculation of consequences" which McTaggart's hypothetical father must undertake would involve the balancing of pleasures and pains, their intensity, duration, distribution and so on. It is quite likely that he would know intuitively what to do, or fall back on what Bradley called the common moral consciousness. In either case, what he might do and why, and how it might be rationalized theoretically, are two different things. McTaggart no doubt received the ethics of universalistic hedonism straight from Sidgwick; but the tenor of his remarks on the conduct of the moral life is oddly reminiscent of Bradley's <u>Ethical</u> <u>Studies</u>.

The upshot of what McTaggart has to say about ethics is that the supreme good can only offer a kind of religious consolation. The ideal of that perfect happiness which we will enjoy as members of the perfect society has to be transformed into the pleasure-pain principle in order to give us something to steer by in our everyday lives. Ideals of perfection, such as self-realization, have no practical moral bearing, and virtue is presumably left to its own devices. The observation with which this discussion of McTaggart's moral philosophy began now appears to mean that "to care for virtue," to have a moral sense, guarantees an interest - a vital interest for McTaggart - in the nature of the supreme good and the fate of human beings as the bearers of value. It does not mean that "the ultimate righteousness of the universe" can direct us into the paths of virtue. We have grounds for hope in the Absolute, but the most we can strive for is approximate happiness. A limited good is still good, though limited. "The beatific vision is good; and so is a bottle of champagne."³⁷

---

34 <u>Ibid.</u>, p. 117.
35 <u>Ibid.</u>, p. 116.
36 <u>Ibid.</u>, p. 105.
37 <u>Ibid.</u>, p. 193.

CHAPTER 11

Idealism as a Substitute Religion

   During the nineteenth century many in the educated classes of Britain turned increasingly from religion to philosophy as their source of spiritual inspiration and consolation. There was a tendency, in short, for philosophy to become a substitute religion. This tendency is associated particularly with the influence of Hegel and the development of a distinctively British version of philosophical idealism. Most philosophers, as well as other writers on philosophical subjects, at first resisted the claims of the Absolute, almost instinctively rejecting the idea that Hegelianism (or any other philosophy) could understand Christianity better than it understood itself. However, in spite of some later disenchantment, several British Hegelians made use of idealist metaphysics for quasi-religious purposes. Some tailored Hegelianism to suit a more or less orthodox Christianity; others, such as McTaggart, were carried by their speculation on the nature of the Absolute far beyond the confines of even the most unorthodox Christianity. Bradley's Absolute contained God, religion and personality as related and lesser degrees of reality. The Absolute was not, however, something he believed in instead of God or his immortal soul; he was driven to it as an inescapable metaphysical conclusion. Although he himself had no faith in anything supernatural, he respected the pronouncements of the common religious consciousness - as he did those of the common moral consciousness - and distrusted those thinkers who would presume to tell it what it was really trying to say.[1] This was in marked contrast to McTaggart, who sought to disabuse it of dogmatic errors and replace them with sound, rational belief in personal immortality.

   Green stands somewhere between the strict separation of religion and philosophical idealism and the collation of the two undertaken by Edward and John Caird.[2] There is a strong religious undercurrent in Green's Prolegomena to Ethics - for example, in his use of the term "eternal consciousness" to describe the metaphysical ground of his ethics and his epistemology. However, he rarely uses overtly religious language, and nowhere does he explicitly equate the eternal consciousness with the God of religion. Although, on the whole, he avoided the language of religious imagery in his philosophy, or anything to suggest that he might be using philosophical arguments to reinforce a religious creed, Green's "Lay Sermons" reveal an enthusiasm for social reform which was partly religious in inspiration.[3] The pursuit of self-perfection surpassed the limits of the political life; but the moral life was lived primarily in pursuit of the good of others, if only because of the still pressing "condition of England." Green did not say that political society and political virtue would ever become unnecessary. He did, however, look beyond the state to a world society in which the mutual regard and consciousness of common good which bind the members of the mature nation-state would bind the human race as a whole. Such a community would also be a form of communion for its members, their concern for each other's spiritual matching that for their material welfare.

   With the exception of Bosanquet, the British Hegelians were not content to tie man's

---

[1] See F.H. Bradley, "Concluding Remarks," ES, esp. pp. 314-24, and Bradley's diatribe against Matthew Arnold's "eternal not ourselves that makes for righteousness."
[2] See ch. 5, p. 46, and ch. 8, pp. 69-70, for earlier mentions of Edward and John Caird respectively.
[3] Practically every account of Green and his work makes reference to the character, Mr. Grey, in Mrs. Humphrey Ward's novel, Robert Elsmere (1888). The hero is racked by agonizing religious doubt until he hears one of Grey's charismatic sermons, most of which is lifted verbatim from Green's work.

destiny to that of the state. "Here," says McTaggart, "he has no abiding city." Even Bosanquet, however, displayed "une certaine ambiance réligieuse."[4] The Absolute was, for Bosanquet, no respecter of persons. Therefore it could not be God, unless it were a Spinozistic substance. Bosanquet talked about the ubiquity of the Absolute, its presence in varying degrees everywhere in the world. The strong whiff of pantheism repelled many, but it was Bosanquet's insistence that the value of the finite individual lay in his distinctive contribution to the world, his refusal to grant any ultimate value to personality, which most aroused the antipathy of Christian and personal idealists against Hegelianism.

The religious "ambience" of British Hegelianism is perhaps sufficiently explained by the fact that German philosophical idealism was a fascinating intellectual novelty which arrived at a time when many members of the educated classes were looking desperately for something to fill the spiritual void being created by the inability of the traditional faith to withstand rational criticism. It either ignored the challenge, condemned it, appealed to authority, or it sought the assistance of new ideas about man as a rational animal. Idealism was a self-confessed theodicy with far-reaching intellectual ambitions. The self-appointed task of "der neueste Philosophie" was set out by one of Hegel's first and most fluent translators, William Wallace:

"To explicate religion is...to show that religion is the truth, the complete reality, of the mind that lived in Art, that founded the state, and sought to be dutiful and upright; the truth, the crowning fruit of all scientific knowledge, of all human affections, of all secular consciousness. Its lesson ultimately is that there is nothing essentially common or unclean...."[5]

Edward Caird, whom we have already encountered as an assiduous and tireless spokesman for Hegelianism, found the key to the Hegelian system in self-consciousness as the unifying principle of experience. Just as the sun reveals both itself and the darkness, so self-consciousness is the light by which man knows both himself and all other things. This does not mean that the mind can know nature a priori, but rather that the fact of knowledge implies the unity of thought and being. Human reason discovers a rational principle in experiencing an external world. Hegel's unity of thought and being was, for Caird as for other Hegelians, the solution to the problem raised by Kant's version of idealism, which could be maintained "only if self-consciousness were found to be a principle adequate to the explanation of that which is the very opposite of self-consciousness - i.e., only if spirit could be shown to be the reason of nature, and mind to be the key to matter."[6]

The important feature of Caird's thought for us at this juncture is his identification of the unifying principle in experience with God. Green's eternal consciousness is the same unifying principle; but Green left its religious nature problematical. Caird also locked on the unity of thought and being as a principle designed to overcome the Kantian dualism of subject and object, experience and the thing-in-itself. But for Caird that principle may just as well be called God as self-consciousness.

"...in the consciousness of self is involved also the consciousness of the universal unity or centre which all knowledge implies, and in this sense the consciousness of self and the consciousness of God are essentially bound up with each other."[7]

This notion of self-consciousness and the consciousness of God being "bound up with each other" is, if anything, even more imprecise than Green's of our being "partakers in some inchoate measure" of the eternal consciousness. In the Gifford Lectures for 1890-92, Caird expressed

---

[4] Jean Pucelle, L'Idéalisme en Angleterre (Neuchatel, 1955), p. 16. "La philosophie anglaise n'a jamais été pleinement secularisée."
[5] W. Wallace, Introduction to Hegel's Philosophy of Mind (Oxford, 1894), p. xlvi.
[6] E. Caird, Hegel (Edinburgh, 1883), p. 132.
[7] E. Caird, The Critical Philosophy of Immanuel Kant (Glasgow, 1889), vol. I, pp. 215-16.

himself more forcefully, if no more clearly, on the matter of linking the unity of thought and being to the idea of God.

> "The idea of God, therefore - meaning by that, in the first instance, only the idea of an absolute principle of unity which binds in one 'all thinking things, all objects of thought,' which is at once the source of being to all things that are, and of knowing to all beings that know - is an essential principle of our intelligence, a principle which must manifest itself in the life of every rational creature."[8]

The question posed in this statement is whether Caird meant God or merely the idea of God. The parenthetical part of the statement, amplifying "the idea of God," suggests that he meant both, that he was talking about a creative "source of being" as well as a metaphysical principle. That would be consistent, as far as it goes, with the Hegelian *logos* or world spirit. But Caird apparently believed that Hegelianism was simply a higher form of the old faith and that the Hegelian principle was the God of religion in metaphysical guise.

Caird's religion comports easily with his Hegelianism. He shows no circumspection in concluding that the Absolute is God - in fact, it is less a conclusion than an assumption - and that the spirit of reason at work in the world is divine providence. There is a great deal in Hegel's writings to support such an identification. For example, Hegel makes very effective philosophical use of Christian revealed truths, such as the Incarnation and the Atonement. His philosophy is intended, however, to "see through" Christianity, not in the sense of exposing religious deceit but of understanding and making explicit the rational meaning of Christianity. In the sense of having been understood, Christianity has been "cancelled and preserved" by Hegelianism. Caird's identification of the Hegelian unity of thought and being with the Christian God is rather too facile.

Caird's religion of Hegelianism as a natural successor to Protestant Christianity - the Holy Spirit rightly understood - was one way in which idealism became converted into a substitute religion. Another, and intrinsically more interesting, way was that of McTaggart. In the following discussion of McTaggart's "religion," reference will be made exclusively to his Hegelian phase. I am not equipped to properly discuss McTaggart's *Nature of Existence* - which is a product of pre-Kantian pure reason, and which has been fully and fairly treated by C.D. Broad and P.T. Geach - and as already stated, McTaggart's faith was fixed before he abandoned Hegelianism as the method to establish its truth.

The Hegelian dialectic begins with the category of being and ends in the Absolute Idea. In between is a series of manifestations of the principle of the unity of thought and being. Of the whole dialectical process, says McTaggart, we can know absolutely only the beginning in the abstract idea and the end in the Absolute Idea. This knowledge assures us on general grounds that "everything *must* be rational, without showing us *how* particular things are rational."[9] Facts and events can only be known empirically, whereas we know the beginning and the end of the process a priori. Although the intermediate stages require sense perception to be known and something like intuitive judgment to be evaluated, they turn out in the end to be constituted by the highest category, the Absolute Idea. One cannot deduce the existence of the entire universe from pure thought, but one can discover the rationality of everything through pure thought. Hegel, says McTaggart, "endeavours to find the idea in everything, but not to reduce everything to a manifestation of the idea."[10] The highest category, the Absolute Idea, is present implicitly in all our thought and draws us on from the incomplete form of it which is explicitly before us at any one time to its full realization, its full explication. This is the motive force of the dialectic.

---

[8] E. Caird, *The Evolution of Religion* (Glasgow, 1893), vol. I, p. 68.
[9] *SHD*, p. 250.
[10] *Ibid.*, p. 29.

The universe as a whole is in fundamental agreement with the human mind. There is harmony of thought and being - the real is rational - but not identity.

"[Their relationship] may be expressed by saying that Thought is adequate to express Being, and Being adequate to embody Thought. On the one hand, no reality exists beyond the sphere of actual or possible knowledge, and no reality, when known as completely as possible, presents any contradiction or irrationality. On the other hand, there is no postulate which Thought demands in order to construct a harmonious and self-consistent system of knowledge, which is not realized in Being."[11]

The harmony of thought and being does not mean there is no immediacy - only contingency has vanished in Hegel's system, says McTaggart.

From the point of view of theory, reality is rational. From that of practice, it is righteous, "since the only view of reality which we can consider as completely rational, is shown to be one which involves our own complete self-realization."[12] If reality is righteous, if the completely perfect as well as the completely rational is eternally present, then the problem which all the idealists had to face presents itself: how to reconcile the perfection of reality with the existence of manifest imperfection. Imperfection is not a delusion; if it were, our being deluded would vitiate the perfection which permitted such a delusion to persist. Imperfection is the inability to see the whole universe immediately.

"...if we can attain to the point of looking at the whole universe <u>sub specie aeternitatis</u>, we shall see just the same subject-matter as in time; but it will appear perfect, because seen as a single concrete whole, and not as a succession of separated abstractions.

"...the whole drift of Hegel's system is as much against the ultimate reality of a succession of phenomena, as such, as it is in favour of the ultimate reality of individual persons, as such."[13]

The logical possibility of being able to stand outside time, like some neutral observer, and survey the whole thing, past, present and future, contradicts the possibility of "a succession of phenomena" past, present and future, because past, present and future are ascribable only from the standpoint of the present. The first possibility's reality precludes the second's. If time is unreal, it would seem that present experience is no longer a sound basis of knowledge. To solve the problem of how to reconcile the a priori arguments for the eternal presence of the Absolute with the equally sound a posteriori ones for the existence of change, McTaggart availed himself of Bradley's maxim that "what <u>may</u> be, if it also <u>must</u> be, assuredly <u>is</u>" - or, in Geach's even more Bradleyan wording, "when everything that is impossible has been excluded, whatever remains, however improbable it may seem, must be true."[14]

The supreme good, or the Absolute in its practical aspect, is so remote from our everyday experience that it would seem to be irrelevant to the moral life. The moral life is lived on a level far distant from that of the Absolute. Imperfection is its daily lot, and in non-philosophical parlance such a life is real. But its end - or reality, in the sense of its realization or fulfilment - is, like that of every stage in the dialectical process, the supreme good of the Absolute. The Absolute is both realized and to be realized, both implicit and in the process of becoming explicit.

Whereas Hegel found the Absolute in the presently unfolding life of the world spirit - in art, religion and philosophy, and in the rational state - McTaggart found it in a timeless heaven of immortal souls which he was nevertheless convinced would inevitably occur at some point in time. Perfection is not simply the Absolute, or the world seen <u>sub specie aeternitatis</u>

---

[11] Ibid., p. 119.
[12] Ibid., p. 120.
[13] Ibid., pp. 177-78.
[14] P.T. Geach, <u>Truth, Love and Immortality</u>, p. 18.

(if we could but do so), but also the necessary outcome of the temporal process. The seeming contradiction here McTaggart neatly eliminated by the proof of the unreality of time. However, he offered no reason why the temporary delusion of a temporal process might not last forever. Forever is a long time, but it is nothing to the Absolute. The supreme good, or absolute perfection, will come to be in spite of humanity if necessary. Hegel conceived of the history of the human spirit and all its works as the way of the Absolute Idea. McTaggart was not historically minded and the purely deductive derivation of his Absolute in no way impaired its reality as far as he was concerned.[15] In sketching the world's "progress," through past pain and despair and unimaginable future horrors to the perfect society, McTaggart displays a breathtakingly optimistic fatalism.

"The ideal is so enormously distant that the most perfect knowledge of the end we are aiming at helps us very little in the choice of the road by which we may get there. Fortunately it is an ideal which is not only the absolutely good, but the absolutely real, and we can take no road that does not lead to it."[16]

McTaggart's Absolute is not indifferent to persons in the here and now. Its realization will see "a complete development of our ideals, and a complete satisfaction of them when developed."[17]

"Every conscious being...will express all his individuality in one end, which will truly and adequately express it. The fulfilment of such an end as this would give satisfaction, not partial and temporary, but complete and eternal."[18]

The Absolute is a supra-organic society of selves or persons existing in a state of mutual love - not love of truth, or virtue, or beauty, nor sexual desire, but "passionate, all-absorbing, all-consuming love."[19] It is a city of God without God, a timeless communion of immortal souls. McTaggart defended his improbable Real World, the everlasting community of immortal Platonic lovers, partially on the grounds that it was the only truly adequate interpretation of Hegel's statements about the Absolute and the only conclusion consistent with the whole dialectical process. The whole drift of Hegelian metaphysics, he claimed, is in the direction of an Absolute which, infinite as a whole, nevertheless consists entirely of finite individuals - and these individuals, though finite, are perfect.

Bradley, Bosanquet and their epigoni were profoundly mistaken in arguing from the incurable contradictoriness of relations to the inevitable imperfection, the ultimate unreality, of the individual self. There is, says McTaggart, "no reason to hold that a finite person is necessarily an imperfect person."[20] The perfection of a person's knowledge, volition and emotion is a function of, but not constituted by, his relations with others; it does not lie in his self-sufficiency. Self-determination is the corollary of more intimate and complex relations with external reality.

"There can be only one meaning in calling a thing imperfect without qualification - that it does not realize the ideal inherent in its nature. Now what necessary imperfection in the realization of my nature is brought about by the mere fact that I am not the universe? What postulate or aspiration is involved in personality which is incompatible with external relations on the part of the person?"[21]

---

[15] McTaggart was the most mercilessly metaphysical of the British Hegelians, and he looked upon Hegel's moral and political philosophy, and his philosophies of history and religion, not as the explication of the Absolute Idea, but as misleading glosses on the only permanently valuable part of Hegelianism, the dialectic of categories.
[16] SHC, p. 196.
[17] Ibid., p. 122.
[18] Ibid., p. 96.
[19] Ibid., p. 260. Compare G.E. Moore's ideal, described in ch. 13, pp. 103-04.
[20] Ibid., p. 80.
[21] Ibid.

External relations do not destroy the harmony of the related object, nor is the harmony of the perfect society impaired by its being made up of externally related individuals.

The lodestar of McTaggart's life was the proof that the world was really people loving one another. One of the chief obstacles to achieving that proof was the account of the self given by Bradley and Bosanquet. In an essay entitled "The Individualism of Value," McTaggart explained his divergence from other idealists over the question of the social character of the supreme good. Too many idealists had failed to recognize the individualism of value, partly through "the assumption that the value to be found in a whole must have as much unity as the whole itself has," and partly through an over-emphasis upon the relation as distinct from the related objects in any particular good. Some had even argued that the relation had intrinsic value. But the British Hegelian argument - which McTaggart tentatively accepted[22] - is the organicist one that the whole formed by the relation and the related objects has value in itself: the whole is greater than the sum of its parts. From there it was concluded that the whole universe enjoys the highest intrinsic value. McTaggart repudiated that position, arguing, first, that value must be confined to consciousness, and second, that the universe, or any number of conscious beings, is not itself a conscious being:

"If A loves B, what is good is not the relation between them, but the state of A in being one of the terms of that relation...a state of A and a state of B cannot (as ends) have a different value together than the sum of the values they would have had separately. For A and B are not a conscious being, but an aggregate of conscious beings....

"[The only value of an individual sacrifice lies in the possibility of its being] a means to the creation, in other individuals, of value exceeding that which was lost in the self-sacrifice."[23]

McTaggart's views on morality have already been discussed in the previous chapter. All morality contributes to happiness as well as self-development. The supreme good is the perfect combination of development and happiness. But as we have seen, only happiness is a practical ethical standard and the felicific calculus a guide. The supreme good might just as well not exist as far as the moral life is concerned. We must, sub specie temporis, pass moral judgments and strive to realize goodness in ourselves and in society. But perfection is coming to be regardless of our efforts, whether they are crowned with success or not. The Absolute is remote and human moral effort ineffectual.

"Fortunately, the attainment of the good does not ultimately depend upon action.... If the nature of reality was hostile or indifferent to the good, nothing but the most meagre and transitory gains could ever be made by creatures so weak and insignificant as we should be in such a universe. But if, as Hegel teaches us, that which we recognize as the supreme good is also the supreme reality, then it must inevitably realize itself in the temporal process, and no mistake of ours can hinder the advance and the eventual attainment.

"For this is one of the most profound and important consequences of all metaphysical idealism. Virtue, and the science which deals with it, imply the possibility of sin, they imply action, and they imply time. And they share, therefore, the inadequacy of matter and the physical sciences."[24]

It followed for McTaggart, with rigorous deductive logic, that reality must be denied to everything except what can be proved without reference to experience. This doctrine was not, contrary to a widespread belief, the common property of philosophical idealists. Bradley's Absolute was timeless, but Green's eternal consciousness, like Hegel's Geist, was necessarily incarnate as nature and human history. The necessity in this process of incarnation was a bit

---

[22] See SHC, pp. 80-96.
[23] J.McT.E. McTaggart, Philosophical Studies, pp. 107-09.
[24] SHC, p. 127.

like the Christian doctrine of predestination: human freedom lay in carrying out divine providence in all too human ways - and for Hegel the greatest freedom lay in knowing that, as it were, from the inside out. McTaggart alone believed that the Absolute would realize itself in time, but not over time - perhaps we should say, all in good time. The reality of the Absolute was entirely indifferent to the temporal process, to the history of nature and of man. Knowledge of the reality of perfection may develop in human minds, but the truth of the matter was completely independent of change of any kind.

McTaggart's Absolute, his personalist vision of supreme good and reality, was an article of religious faith as much as a philosophical conclusion.[25] It had a certain practical value too. It gave consolation - and thereby some happiness - by assuring human beings of the ultimate righteousness of the universe. Although the Absolute can afford no explanation of, or guidance for, the moral and political life, it can supply comfort, reconciliation and justification.

> "...such conclusions as to the ultimate nature of things as we have seen can be reached by Hegel's philosophy have obviously a very intimate connection with the problems which may be classed as religious.... Any system of philosophy which gives any reasons for deciding such questions, in one way rather than another, will have a practical interest, even if it should fail to provide us with counsel as to the organization of society, or with explanations in detail of the phenomena of science."[26]

The practical value of "such conclusions" lies in their support for a loose collection of quasi-religious beliefs which McTaggart considered fundamental to human happiness - not in the sense of a balance of pleasure over pain, but in that of being at peace with the universe or Absolute Reality. To those who ask, "What is the use of philosophy?", McTaggart answers, first in the manner of Bradley, that it is an impertinent question to ask about the search for truth, and second, in a more personal manner, that its use "lies not in being deeper than science, but in being truer than theology - not in its bearing on action, but in its bearing on religion. It does not give us guidance. It gives us hope."[27] McTaggart maintained throughout his philosophical career that his theodicy without God was the only correct interpretation of Hegelianism. Those Hegelians who sought to apply the Hegelian dialectic to religion, to history, to morality and the state forgot that such phenomena all contain empirical elements and are open to contingency and unpredictable change. In no religious creed, in no moral code, in no form of political life, can we find the key to the Absolute Idea.

---

[25] Geach refers to McTaggart's "mystical experiences that gave him an utterly satisfying and unshakeable conviction that he had penetrated through appearances and divined the secret of the universe." (P.T. Geach, _Truth, Love and Immortality_, p. 15.)
[26] _SHD_, p. 236.
[27] _SHC_, p. 196.

CHAPTER 12

R.B. Haldane: Hegelianism With "Dirty Hands"

The strengths and the weaknesses of British Hegelianism as a school for life are nowhere better exemplified than in the career of R.B. Haldane.[1] Earnest and energetic in an eminently Victorian fashion, yet cosmopolitan in his tastes and interests, he came as close as anyone to being Edwardian England's philosopher-king. A.J. Balfour, Conservative Prime Minister from 1902 to 1906, and more (some have argued) a philosopher in his own right, made much less impact on either the philosophical or the political world. He was skeptical and fastidious and for him "politics was little more than a serious game."[2] By contrast, Haldane struggled throughout his political career to infuse the administration of imperial affairs - the War Office, the Lord Chancellorship, public education policy, whatever it might be - with moral purpose. His mastery of the details of high office, his high moral tone and his (sometimes devious) efforts to convert the fractious Liberal Party to his vision of social reform brought him both rewards and punishments.

In spite of his radical reforms, several high-ranking professional soldiers expressed their regret at his departure from the War Office. In 1912 Asquith asked him to be Lord Chancellor and he was created Viscount Haldane of Cloan. Although he was an active, and at times combative, member of the Liberal Party for many years (and laterally of the Labour Party), Haldane owed much of his political reputation to his discharging his ministerial duties in the manner of those illustrious servants of the Prussian state during the Napoleonic era upon whom Hegel supposedly modelled the administrative class of his Philosophy of Right. Even after his political star had fallen and philosophical idealism had fallen out of fashion, he was sought out by distinguished men of letters and science such as Einstein. On the debit side, his admiration for German culture and society made him the target for a press campaign of extreme vilification during World War I.[3] He was driven from office in 1915 in spite of testimonials from such a patriotically unimpeachable source as Field Marshal Haig, only to re-emerge as Lord Chancellor in the first Labour government of 1924.

While many intellectuals were driven by the war's devastations to despair of liberal democracy, and others of any sort of political action whatsoever, Haldane retained his

---

[1] Richard Burdon Haldane (1856-1928), like Seth (Pringle-Pattison), was one of a number of Scottish philosophers who took the cure for religious doubt at the University of Gottingen under Lotze. He returned to the University of Edinburgh in 1875, studied Hegel and then law, also finding time to translate Schopenhauer. He was called to the English bar in 1879. He eventually became Lord Chancellor (1912-15 and 1924), but he is best known as a reforming Secretary of State for War (1905-1912) - "the greatest England has ever had," according to Earl Haig. He was Liberal MP for East Lothian from 1885 to 1912. He joined the Labour Party in 1921 after gradual disenchantment with the Liberal Party, especially over its neglect of educational policy.
[2] George Dangerfield, The Strange Death of Liberal England, 1910-1914 (New York, 1961), p. 13.
[3] When the British government began negotiations for entry into the EEC in the early 1960s, the media credited one of its diplomats with extraordinary powers of persuasion because he knew enough German to rapidly reduce complex German proposals to what he called "Hegelian fruit salad" or "Kantian kitsch." Haldane conversed unaided in German with the Emperor and Chancellor of Germany when on his so-called secret mission to Berlin in 1912 to try to slow the Anglo-German arms race.

enthusiasm for both new theories and old values and his willingness to use the coercive powers of the state in defence of liberalism. He was one of the founders of Liberal Imperialism and he continued to believe in the civilizing mission of the Imperial government. For Haldane this mission was a universal one, for the improvement of metropolitan subjects as well as far-flung colonials. He was a Home Ruler, an advocate of woman suffrage as early as his first election in 1885, and a tireless worker for universal higher education. He was also the chief architect of the British Expeditionary Force and the Imperial General Staff, an advocate of the use of force against Ulster at the time of the Curragh Mutiny (although he trimmed his sails rather awkwardly on that one), and a strong anti-Boer, maintaining that the non-Boer Uitlanders were oppressed by the Boers and supporting Milner's draconian measures against them.

Haldane looked beyond the Empire and the English-speaking world to the establishment of, first, a European Sittlichkeit, and eventually a set of mores which would be the indispensable underpinning of an international legal order. In his capacity as Lord Chancellor, he was invited to address the American Bar Association in Montreal in September 1913. His address, entitled "The Higher Nationality: A Study in Law and Ethics," brings to bear upon a thorough knowledge and practical experience of the law a Hegelian conception of society and the state. The explanation of social conduct lies, Haldane says, not in legal sanction nor in private conscience, but in Sittlichkeit. Custom or the done thing is the cement of social cohesion. It is also - and here Haldane is at one with Green, Bradley and Bosanquet - the ground and condition of the civil rights and civic institutions whose possession and enjoyment provide scope and opportunity for moral improvement and self-realization.

"It is the instinctive sense of what to do and what not to do in daily life and behaviour that is the source of liberty and ease. And it is this instinctive sense of obligation that is the chief foundation of society. Its reality takes objective shape and displays itself in family life and in our other civic and social institutions."[4]

Haldane supported this view with a Hegelian theory of knowledge - that is to say, one which holds that "behind knowledge we cannot go; there is no standard of truth save in its own process."[5] We start with knowledge, not with a theory of knowledge. We are from the beginning immersed in a common intelligence, and "we cannot reach the intelligence of our fellow-men except by recognizing our very inmost selves as in them too."[6] If we were not part of the universal reason, we could not distinguish ourselves as individual selves. We would be reduced to solipsism if we did not "recognize that even our own knowledge is dependent for its possibility on being not so limited [limited, that is, by 'what the bodily self suggests to us']...." "[The mind] can recognize itself as identically present in other selves, and discourse not merely about a world but about a universe."[7] Although the distinguished Hegelian scholar, J.N. Findlay, has said that the British Hegelians' universe is less a concrete universal than it is a most un-Hegelian abstraction, Haldane - at least in his earlier, pre-World War I work - addressed himself to actual modes of human experience. According to T.M. Knox, "the writer in English who really was a Hegelian is Lord Haldane."[8] His Gifford Lectures for 1902-04, The Pathway to Reality, were in part a conscious attempt to demystify Hegelianism. "The world as it seems" has different aspects - life as well as mechanism, morality as well as art, religion as well as morality - all of which are adequate in themselves.

"And if Philosophy gives us back what Science threatens to take away and

---

[4] R.B. Haldane, Selected Addresses and Essays (London, 1928), p. 69.
[5] Haldane's preface to Hegel's Science of Logic, trans. Johnston and Struthers (London, 1929), p. 14.
[6] R.B. Haldane, Human Experience: A Study of its Structure (New York, 1926), p. 185.
[7] Ibid., pp. 193-94.
[8] T.M. Knox, "A Plea for Hegel," New Studies in Hegel's Philosophy, ed. W.E. Steinkraus (New York, 1971), p. 16.

restores to plain people their faith in the reality of each of these phases of the world as it seems, then Philosophy will have gone a long way to justify her existence."[9]

In spite of the suggestion that philosophy was being thrown into a holy crusade against science and irreligion, Haldane was a rationalist and orthodox Hegelian, a philosopher for whom philosophy is its own justification.

Haldane may have been most at home in the rarefied atmosphere of speculation, both political and metaphysical. Nevertheless, he acquired considerable skill in the parliamentary arena and risked the hostility of both his party and the electorate by defending some controversial public figures and by identifying himself with some unpopular causes. Although he never refused to dirty his hands, he developed a Platonic persona, seeming to assume the responsibilities of public office not for any satisfaction he might derive, but rather to ensure that the worse did not govern the better. He had a philosophical vocation, but he never withdrew from "the life of action generally, power, politics, success, wealth and ambition," essentially because he felt obliged to bring light into the cave of unknowing.

"What is the good of our reading to us who are in public life if we cannot use it in the effort, with all the strength we possess, to guide the current of opinion among our constituents."[10]

However much his approach to political education may strike us today as a species of upper-class condescension and paternalism, it is clear that his, as it were, extra-curricular activities in the field of public instruction cost him much leisure time - and Haldane was a very convivial sort of person who enjoyed the pleasures of society. Adult education was a lifelong passion and remained for him the key to improving the lot of the British working class. From 1881 he was an intermittent lecturer at the Working Men's College, he ventured to speak against the theories of Marx and Lasalle at the Soho Radical Club, and he was a consistent advocate of the expansion of a system of secular universities serving their respective communities. It was, he claimed, the Liberal Party's failure to vigorously pursue a democratic policy of higher education which more than anything else persuaded him to abandon it for the Labour Party.[11] From a Marxist or social-revolutionary point of view it is all too clear why Haldane of Cloan, Lord High Chancellor and confidant of kings, should be so zealous in the cause of adult education. He personifies the smooth transition from classical liberalism to welfare state politics. Indeed, Haldane's letters contain several references to the need for a "moderating conservatism" and "a steady effort to avert revolution." He might well be used as the prototype for all those who would domesticate the masses, training them to take up the command posts of liberal-democratic society. He believed in encouraging advances in working class power and responsibility, and he sought to influence their direction; but he never thought he could do that from afar, only through close cooperation on shared terms.

The problems attendant on trying to be a practising Hegelian are painfully apparent in Haldane's self-appointed role as conscience of the Liberal Party. The Liberals had become the embodiment of British respectability, and their leader, Herbert Asquith, was (in Dangerfield's words) "the Humour of Moderation." Unfortunately for the Liberal Party, there were highly immoderate forces surfacing and a general impatience with respectability. Haldane himself was anything but immoderate and was quite respectable, but he believed for rather recondite philosophical reasons that existing British institutions were the necessary expression of a necessary stage in the necessary unfolding of the world spirit. This was not a fatalistic

---

[9] R.B. Haldane, The Pathway to Reality (London, 1903-4), vol. I, p. 119.
[10] Letter to Mrs. Humphrey Ward from Germany, summer of 1890. See F. Maurice, The Life of Viscount Haldane of Cloan (London, 1937), vol. I, p. 55.
[11] In 1892, during the fourth and final Gladstone administration, Haldane advocated some reforming move which would gain the confidence of the "labour party" in the Commons.

doctrine. On the contrary, it compelled him to support any movement to expand the range of opportunities for relatively deprived groups and classes. His basic position, however, was not conducive to the structural changes demanded by many of those protesting social and political injustice. He looked upon improved conditions and enriched lives for individual members of society as a contribution to the self-realization of the individual writ large, the state. The ambivalence of Haldane's position - one could dub it conservative liberalism, democratic elitism or Hegelian socialism - is well revealed in a letter he wrote to a Liberal colleague in 1889:

> "To my dying day, I think, I shall maintain the proposition, based on the analogy of my own mind, that a democracy has not got, as is assumed in practice, a body of definite opinion for the expression of which in Parliament it seeks delegates, but that it is an assembly of human beings earnestly seeking guidance from those of whose sympathies it is sure."[12]

A democratic society is an embryonic political assembly on this view. Its potential for enlightened self-government has to be parentally nurtured and then cultivated by astute statesmen and patient public servants.

Although Haldane was not a product of Oxford University, and therefore not exposed to classical Greek studies to the extent that other British Hegelians were, the roots of his political philosophy clearly lie in the polis, even if it was plucked from Hegel's Philosophie des Rechts (which his biographer tells us Haldane kept by his bedside and read more than a dozen times). Haldane was one of many Victorians who wished to hellenize British public life to counteract the native philistinism. One of the leading motives with him, as with others, was to head off a general condition of middling prosperity coupled with mediocrity and complacency. The goal of life was the good life, pretty much along the lines to be found in Aristotle's Ethics. When Haldane broke with the Liberal Party in 1920, he made it clear that his departure was caused primarily by disappointment with Liberal failure in "soul culture."

> "Fifty years ago Matthew Arnold warned the Liberal Party of the certainty of the coming of the trouble which has actually wrecked it today. He asked in so many words whether material prosperity would permanently reconcile men to living in places like St. Helen's."[13]

---

[12] Ibid., vol. I, pp. 49-50.
[13] Ibid., vol. II, p. 75.

CHAPTER 13

The Decline of British Hegelianism

British Hegelianism, like the British Empire, was mortally wounded by the First World War; unlike the Empire, Hegelianism did not linger long. Philosophical idealism continued to show vital signs in the philosophies of art and of history, but British Hegelianism rapidly became a memory with very few defenders outside some Oxford colleges and the Scottish universities. It is still regarded as something of a period piece.

There is some justification for its being so regarded. It owed its brief ascendancy as much to its association with social reform tendencies in late Victorian and Edwardian times and the quasi-religious quest for metaphysical consolation as it did to intrinsic philosophical merit. Representative figures such as Green, Ritchie and Haldane entered into the world of political action at some risk to their philosophical credentials. There was the double danger of being seen as merely irrelevant or, alternatively, expedient. Theirs was not primarily a political doctrine, however, and such political impact as it had was largely the indirect result of its role in the political education of some leading members of the British ruling class. The greatest threat to the reputation of British Hegelianism was its own philosophical inadequacy. Radical departures from received truth in many fields of intellectual endeavour - particularly in social science, the philosophy of natural science and mathematical logic - in the years immediately preceding World War I, combined with the demoralizing effects of the war itself, drove British Hegelianism into a philosophical backwater. Bosanquet and the Haldane brothers tried especially hard to assimilate the new ideas. In spite of their efforts, British Hegelianism failed badly to convince the new wave of philosophers that it had much of continuing interest to say. Its lasting claim to fame was as a whipping boy - the most favoured example of how not to philosophize.

Without wishing to liken the British to the Roman Empire, it could nevertheless be said that the Hegelians were Stoics in a climate of opinion whose prevailing wind was Epicurean. They were no enemies of individual creative freedom and social experiment, but their generally Platonic attitude to art, their missionary zeal for civic uplift through mass education, and the classical republican _gravitas_ with which they treated the pressing social problems of the day served to isolate them from advanced and fashionable thinking. It is tempting to suggest that they were the ants of the fable, whose prosaic efforts to put the societal house in order before the winter storms of uncivil disturbance and discontent were somehow less engaging than the grasshoppers' displays of intellectual virtuosity and art for art's sake.

Something of the quality of that form of life which has become a stereotype of the Edwardian age has been captured by J.M. Keynes, who is one of those who took the peace and security of the Edwardian order for granted. Writing in 1938, he remarked: "One cannot live today secure in the undisturbed individualism which was the extraordinary achievement of the early Edwardian days."[1] Keynes was a prominent member of the intellectual circle whose Socrates was G.E. Moore. "We were," says Keynes, "living in the specious present, nor had we begun to play the game of consequences. We existed in the world of Plato's dialogues; we had not reached the _Republic,_ let alone the _Laws._"[2] They were the archetype of ivory-tower intellectuals, so otherworldly that they quite ignored "not only social action, but the life of action generally,

---

[1] J.M. Keynes, "My Early Beliefs," _Two Memoirs_ (London, 1949), p. 95.
[2] Ibid.

power, politics, success, wealth, ambition, with the economic motive and the economic criterion less prominent in our philosophy than with St. Francis of Assisi, who at least made collections for the birds...."[3] Keynes vividly evokes the mood of Platonic contemplation of that small group, which included, in addition to Moore and Keynes, Bertrand Russell, Lytton Strachey, Leonard Woolf and G. Lowes Dickinson.

Although they were a small, isolated group disdaining influence and oblivious of practical affairs, they represented an intellectual attitude which was peculiarly in keeping with the seeming timelessness of Edwardian life - an illusion produced by historical hindsight perhaps - and which has continued, with the assistance of the eminence attained by many of the group's members, to exercise a powerful attraction for the intelligentsia. It would be an extremely difficult and hazardous operation to make detailed connections between the highly intellectualized life of the Moore circle and Edwardian life as a whole, but one can sense an affinity even if one cannot trace any exact causal relations. There is a quality of suspended animation, of Arcadian calm, about both. The Moore circle's intellectual idyll owed much to a social, political, and economic stability of whose origins and conditions they were blissfully ignorant or which they chose to ignore. This indifference to their political and socio-economic environment did not survive the war. One has only to look at the subsequent career of Keynes. Nevertheless, the social concern and political involvement of Keynes, as of Russell, never completely lost its cloistered, academic air.

The source of the Moore circle's splendid isolation is to be found in Moore's philosophy. Although Keynes talks of the group's adherence to "Moore's religion," he hastens to add that they did not accept all that Moore offered. For one thing, they "discarded his morals," which included a good deal of "Sidgwick and the Benthamite calculus and the general rules of correct behaviour."[4] But Moore's *Principia Ethica* (1903) - the point of departure for much of the moral philosophy of the English-speaking world in the twentieth century - was their bible, in particular the last chapter, entitled "The Ideal." Keynes summarizes their "religion" as follows:

"Nothing mattered except states of mind, our own and other people's of course, but chiefly our own. These states of mind were not associated with action or achievement or with consequences. They consisted in timeless, passionate states of contemplation and communion, largely unattached to 'before' and 'after'.... The appropriate subjects of passionate contemplation and communion were a beloved person, beauty and truth, and one's prime objects in life were love, the creation and enjoyment of aesthetic experience and the pursuit of knowledge.

"Our religion closely followed the English puritan tradition of being chiefly concerned with the salvation of our own souls. The divine resided within a closed circle. There was not a very intimate connection between 'being good' and 'doing good'...."[5]

The tendency of those who fell under Moore's spell to divorce being good from doing good, to neglect rightness as an attribute of actions in their enthusiasm for goodness as an attribute of states of mind, protected them from "the game of consequences" and made them impervious to Benthamism. Their "escape from Bentham," as Keynes calls it, was outdone by that from philosophical idealism, by which they were untouched - apart from Bertrand Russell's brief flirtation with it.[6] All the two schools of thought had in common was their abhorrence (with

---

[3] *Ibid.*, pp. 95-96.
[4] *Ibid.*, p. 82.
[5] *Ibid.*, pp. 83-84.
[6] Russell was briefly converted by McTaggart, the British Hegelian with the least appreciation of Hegel's historicism and social philosophy. McTaggart's ideal bears, in certain respects, a striking resemblance to that of the Moore circle - it is characterized by the same timelessness and emphasis upon personal love. It is a curious and perhaps significant fact that McTaggart,

the notable exception of McTaggart) of the felicific calculus and the definition of goodness as a surplus of pleasure over pain.

Moore maintained that good was just good, no more definable than yellow, and any attempt to define it he called "the naturalistic fallacy." To be intrinsically good, a thing must have no quality beyond that of bare goodness. Moore's attempt to strip goodness of all but purely ethical meanings was subverted by his own definition of "the ideal." The supremely good he almost casually defined as consisting of the contemplation of and communion with beauty, truth and a beloved person. Each is an intrinsic good and an inseparable part of the ideal, although a type of love for which the adjective "Platonic" should be reserved seems to occupy a special place in this trinity: "...the love of love is far the most valuable good we know...."[7]

Moore's account of virtue in chapter 5 of Principia Ethica, "Ethics in Relation to Conduct," is an essentially utilitarian one, in which virtue is merely a means to the supreme good. Virtue is a disposition to perform duties, which are on a par with interests; an action performed out of a sense of duty and an "interested" action are both judged entirely on their results. The only ethical distinction between them is the utility of sanctioning duties, "since they are actions which there is a temptation to omit."[8] With this, Moore disposed of intuitional ethics and the problem of the moral will.

Moore dismissed "metaphysical ethics" - the ethics, for him, of both Kant and the idealists - as examples in supernatural guise of the naturalistic fallacy.[9] Moore's own description of the ideal commits a supernaturalistic fallacy as much - or as little - as do idealist theories. He was driven to identify goodness with something other than goodness and to try and show that there is some sort of rational, i.e. non-accidental, relationship between the quality of goodness and what we attribute it to. At the same time, he strove to detach (free ?) it from dependence on whatever it is which it qualifies, so that it would not be qualified in its turn. None of the "metaphysical" moralists advanced an ideal to match Moore's in its otherworldliness and remoteness from life in the terrestrial city. Moore's ethic was more suitable for anchorites than for active members of society. He acknowledged the social utility of conventional morality but took organized political society for granted, or implied that it was superfluous. The good life according to Moore could be lived in no society larger and more diversified than a kind of pantisocracy. Keynes remarked, revealingly, that Moore's fundamental intuitions "furnish a justification of experience wholly independent of outside events."[10]

Although Moore's socially detached ethics never attracted much attention from the British

---

Moore, Keynes and Russell were Cambridge men and those who applied Hegel to moral, social and political problems all Oxford men.

[7] G.E. Moore, Principia Ethica (Cambridge, 1962), p. 204. Bradley never reacted to Moore's moral philosophy in print, but it must surely have been an earlier example of the thinking of Moore and his circle which prompted the memorable phrase in Ethical Studies, "star-gazing virgins with souls above their spheres." Moore's ethic, with its utilitarian notion of virtue and its beatific vision of a timeless supreme good, would have been in Bradley's eyes the worst possible combination of hard-headedness and high-mindedness, the elevation and rarefication of his ideal serving only to encourage casuistry in a creed already prone to minute calculation and the cost-benefit analysis of moral action.

[8] G.E. Moore, Principia Ethica, p. 170.

[9] In an essay entitled "The Refutation of Idealism" and collected in his Philosophical Studies (London, 1922), Moore claimed to have destroyed the common and sacred ground of all philosophical idealism, the doctrine that to be is to be perceived. That doctrine has very little to do with an objective idealism such as Hegel's. Unfortunately its refutation is still used, and regarded as sufficient, to dispose of Hegelianism and idealism of all kinds.

[10] J.M. Keynes, "My Early Beliefs," p. 95.

Hegelians - perhaps because of that same social detachment - it presented a more potent threat to Hegelian moral and political philosophy than the old enemy, utilitarianism, ever had. The individualism preached and practised by Moore and his companions outdid that of any of the utilitarians. The latter at least had a social theory, and one which was closely integrated with their moral theory. The Moore circle did not recognize society at large as having moral significance at all. Following that lead, the most influential British moral philosophers of the twentieth century have put forward completely asocial theories of morality. No matter how far they have travelled from the rarefied ideal of Moore, they all, like Moore, treat ethics in abstraction from social and political theory. They have been preoccupied with the classification and analysis of moral judgments. They have examined the logic of moral judgments, or even the metaphysical presuppositions implicit in making moral judgments, but never their full social context. Since World War II, British moral philosophers have shown, partially under the influence of existentialist writings, a special concern for the autonomy of individual moral judgment - for the individual's moral freedom and independence from external causation - which is reminiscent of both Kant and the "imperviousness" of human personality insisted on by Pringle-Pattison and the personal idealists. As with Kant, the individual is depicted freely obeying the moral law in defiance of social pressures. Morality is treated as something which has its centre of gravity within the individual conscience.

The idealist tradition, with which Hegel is identified, places the moral centre of gravity outside the individual in the social whole, in the social complex of laws, customs and mores. It is a fundamental tenet of philosophical idealism that no philosophy can be coherent which does not attempt to explain all the facts of experience; certainly a theory of values cannot neglect a set or range of value judgments and expect to be taken as adequate. The moral philosophy of G.E. Moore ignored altogether an important area of the human experience of values and evaluational conflicts: the political life, and the life of man generally in modern commercial and industrial society. It was unattached to any social or political theory. Although the moral life and the political life can be distinguished, each involving judgments which are in no way dependent for their validity upon those of the other, a moral theory which disregards the social conditions of the moral life is deficient. In this respect, as well as in matters of metaphysics and epistemology, there was no real point of contact between Moore and the main stream of British Hegelianism (the most notable exception being Bradley, who was at least regarded as a worthy opponent by Russell). On the other hand, Moore's philosophy did not lack for that high moral tone and suggestion that knowledge (of the prescribed kind) was in itself virtue, which can be readily detected in some of the more widely read works of British Hegelianism and which partially accounts for their rather dated appeal. Although philosophical idealism satisfied many people's spiritual yearnings, its social and political theory also spoke to and for its generation. It was in harmony with the great changes occurring under the surface of Edwardian life - changes which have continued more or less in the same direction. It was a philosophy conscious, as we have seen with Bosanquet, of its peculiar fitness to explain the predominantly urban, heavily industrial and increasingly democratic state which was developing and asserting itself during the late Victorian and Edwardian years. This view of itself was not entirely justified, if only because idealism frequently stressed the identity of social interests at the expense of the subjective element's role in society. However, it stands in marked contrast to the social detachment of most British philosophy since Moore.

The Great War and its effect on Haldane's political career have been noted in the previous chapter. It had equally damaging consequences for British Hegelianism. This was due in part to a wholly unwarranted association with Prussian militarism. The proposition that Hegel's philosophy was one of the motive forces of the Reich was ludicrous; yet it emerged again, with even less justification, in literature about the Nazi regime (although not in the Nazis' own justificatory writings); and there are still learned debates about whether or not Hegel was a proto-fascist or in some way connected, however remotely, with totalitarian political doctrines. In 1918, L.T. Hobhouse, a distinguished sociologist, philosopher and one of the "New Liberals," directly linked Hegel's political philosophy with German war guilt in his attack on what he called the "metaphysical theory of the state."11 Apart from such crude but effective discrediting tactics, British Hegelianism was damaged by the widespread loss of faith induced by the war experience - faith in God, in church, in state and in civilization itself.

Generally speaking, the Hegelian faith was a faith in human reason and in the rationality of human institutions - which meant having faith in the real world. The logos or meaning of things was in all things, so there was no point in looking beyond things as they were, or wishing they were different, in order to satisfy human aspirations for freedom and justice. "To live in Main Street is, if one lives in the right spirit, to inhabit the holy city." This may be something to chew on for the moralist who thinks that liberal-capitalist society is beyond redemption, but it is difficult to discover the Hegelian "cunning of reason" in some of the starker horrors perpetrated by twentieth century man.

As we have seen, those British Hegelians who were not orthodox believers tended to be at least looking for some kind of metaphysical consolation in Hegel's philosophy, if not a substitute religion. One of the best illustrations of this cast of mind - and of its persistence well after the war and the displacement of idealism by more positivist and empiricist philosophies - can be found in J.S. Haldane, brother of R.B. Haldane and a distinguished natural scientist. He first appeared in print as a contributor to Essays in Philosophical Criticism (1883), along with his brother, Bosanquet, Ritchie, Seth, and a number of other (mostly minor) figures loosely associated with British Hegelianism. He became an expert on respiratory physiology, while retaining his faith in the intelligible principle of the universe, which he called "Supreme Active Reality."

> "The conclusion forced upon me in the course of a life devoted to natural science is that the universe as it is assumed to be in physical science is only an idealized world, while the real universe is the spiritual universe, in which spiritual values count for everything."12

It is our actual everyday experience, he argued, which guarantees the spiritual unity of life, because we cannot perceive anything or consciously direct our behaviour in any way without encountering shared values and shared interests. We strive to create them, but we cannot do anything in their absence, so, to put it very simply, there is something there, and it is not outside us or above us or beyond us.

In political philosophy the British Hegelians had to combat personalism, anarchism, internationalism and other varieties of doctrine directed against the state and some or all of its works. They chose, by and large, to fight on the ground that the state, for all its imperfections, was the only vehicle for realizing the common good, and that "every moral good is a common good."13 They confronted the problem of political obligation, as they did the problem of knowledge, as a problem in philosophical psychology. Bosanquet's treatment of the

---

[11] L.T. Hobhouse, The Metaphysical Theory of the State: A Criticism (London, 1918). Another wartime production which found Hegelianism guilty by association with German political and military excess was George Santayana's Egotism in German Philosophy (London, 1916). This hostile account of Hegel's notion of objective mind creates a caricature out of elements drawn from Fichte and Nietzsche, as well as from Hegel himself. "The existent did not really concern him, but only 'knowledge,' that is, a circle of present and objectless ideas.... Egotism could hardly receive a more radical expression than this: to declare the ego infinite because it can never find anything that is beyond its range" (p. 75). Santayana maintained that German philosophical idealism, by attempting to bring the world within the ego, had made the external world philosophically insignificant and idealism a philosophy obsessed with externals. The world thus conceived was the plaything of individual and national egos.
[12] J.S. Haldane, The Sciences and Philosophy (London, 1929), p. 273. This was first delivered as the Gifford Lectures (University of Glasgow) for 1927-28.
[13] Henry Jones, The Principles of Citizenship (London, 1919), p. 70.

general will can be taken as their paradigm. Their point of departure was the phenomena of individual volition. That society is "precipitate with instincts, habits and dispositions which, from the first, are not merely individual, but point beyond individual and exclusive interests to an interest in the whole," is explained on the analogy of an individual person referring "a particular object to a <u>whole of interest</u>, which in turn is overshadowed and penetrated in normal cases by the sense of the individual's <u>interest as a whole</u>."[14] The problem of reconciling man to organized society, or justifying the ways of the state, was particularly acute during and after World War I, because many writers in many fields were arguing very forcefully and effectively for a sharp division between the rationality of individuals or small groups of people and the atavistic irrationality of mass society. Although they drew different conclusions, Graham Wallas and Vilfredo Pareto are prime examples of how potent the case for collective unreason could be, and several of the British Hegelians felt compelled to take Wallas' <u>Human Nature in Politics</u> into account. They had to show that the seemingly inexplicable mass of inherited customs and folkways was "instinct" with a moral purpose in which the individual pursuing a coherent form of life for himself could be at home, and furthermore, that the state was both the chief agent of this process and chief bulwark against any relapse into barbarism.

Individuality was a process of comprehension in both senses of the word for Bosanquet and all those lesser Hegelian lights who more or less followed his lead: Henry Jones, J.H. Muirhead, H.J.W. Hetherington, J.S. Mackenzie, Ernest Barker, A.D. Lindsay and E.J. Urwick. The crux of their psychology of the general will was the individual self seen as the focus of collective moral energy. There is no such thing as the individual standing over against society or the state. He or she occupies a place in the social order - a "station" with "duties" - which may or may not change but which either way affords the only point from which to "focalize and assimilate" his or her world. "Man is measured by his world," says Jones, and "he helps the world at the level on which he finds it, and he finds in its needs his fulcrum for raising it."[15] It was an activist point of view, and it required a morally active state. Just as the individual member of a society must put himself out into the world and make as much of it a part of himself as he can, so the state must seek to comprehend and identify with - make a part of its moral life - more and different experiences of life.

"The sovereignty of states, like the liberty of individuals, depends not upon their privacy but upon their comprehension; not upon being free from the world but on finding the world to be bone of their bone and flesh of their flesh."[16]

As a political theory, the ethic of "comprehension" has distinctly aggressive overtones. What might have been defensive in the heat of battle - "a state that does not advance goes back," said A.C. Bradley in addressing the ethics of international conflict - can appear, when hostilities have ceased, to be nothing so much as a version of what was being fought against. However, the advance referred to is spiritual, and the comprehensive state is not a closed, totalitarian state but one that contributes to the "total work of humanity." The state is our "nearest" obligation and our only school of civility, but "insofar as the State is the guardian of the right on the part of its citizens to be put in full possession of themselves, its highest function consists precisely in the extension of their interests to what lies beyond itself."[17]

Those men who learned their Hegelianism directly from Green at Oxford or Caird at Glasgow, and whose chief theoretician was Bernard Bosanquet, might be called the second generation of

---

[14] H.J.W. Hetherington and J.H. Muirhead, Social Purpose (London, 1918), pp. 84-85.
[15] H. Jones, The Principles of Citizenship, p. 72.
[16] Ibid., p. 64.
[17] Hetherington and Muirhead, Social Purpose, p. 95.

British Hegelians.[18] There was a loss - perhaps it was inevitable - of philosophical power and sheer intellectual excitement. The enthusiasm remained high, but it was spread pretty thin. Attempts were made to assimilate new intellectual specializations, in some cases with disappointing results, and a welter of social reform and relief activities were entered into. Bosanquet himself was conscious of a loss of concentration on the "citizen spirit, the pulse-beat of the social heart,"[19] and of a danger that philosophical idealism would lose some of its adherents to other reform creeds without its coherence and comprehensiveness. He was all in favour of practical applications of the ethic of self-realization, of decentralization of effort, and of a measure of local control over the organization and administration of education, public works and even some industry. He seized upon neighbourhood improvement studies both at home and in America, and he tried to show how they and philosophical idealism could be mutually enriching. However, Bosanquet's primary and distinctive purpose was to impose some kind of order on all this activity, to relate it to a common social purpose.

The most comprehensive unifying formula was universal education, and the source of this approach could be traced to Green - if no further back. The ideal polity envisaged by Green was dubbed the "educative state" by Klaus Dockhorn. One of the undoubted success stories of British Hegelianism was organizing adult education and the beginnings of a national system of education which integrated universities, technological institutes and community colleges.[20] Of course, the educational reform movement predates the advent of Hegelianism in Britain; but earlier advocates such as Matthew Arnold and Benjamin Jowett were not totally unrelated to the growth of philosophical idealism. Its success "on the ground" owed a lot to the political power and perseverance of some of its idealist promoters. R.B. Haldane in the Campbell-Bannerman and Asquith governments (not to mention his tenure in the short-lived MacDonald Labour government) and R.L. Morant in the civil service are the two most notable examples.

Bosanquet saw his own role as primarily educational. Through such organizations as the London Ethical Society and the Charity Organization Society (in which his wife, Helen Dendy, was very active), he hoped to be able to promulgate a doctrine of reforming patriotism. While he could say that "of practical socialism, i.e. the workman's ownership of the means of production, we cannot have too much,"[21] it was more typical of him to say that he anticipated an increase in the number "of men and women of the wage-earning class who have had something of

---

[18] The two who have been most quoted in this chapter are Henry Jones and John Henry Muirhead. Henry Jones (1852-1922) was a Welsh schoolteacher who entered Glasgow University in 1875 and became a convert to the Hegelianism of Edward Caird. There he earned a fellowship in philosophy, returning to teach the subject at University College, Aberystwyth (1882-84). He was successively Professor of Philosophy and Political Economy at Bangor (1884-91), Professor of Logic, Rhetoric and Metaphysics at St. Andrews (1891-94), and Caird's successor as Professor of Moral Philosophy at Glasgow (1894-1922). He was knighted in 1912.

John Henry Muirhead (1855-1940) was another Caird disciple at Glasgow. He lectured successively at Holloway College (1889-91), Bedford College (1891-97), and Mason University College, Birmingham (1897-1900). He was Professor of Philosophy at Birmingham University from 1900 to 1922. A founding member, with Bosanquet, of the London Ethical Society, he was also active with Jones in the Workers' Education Association. He is best known in academic circles as the general editor of The Muirhead Library of Philosophy, whose catholic list of titles reflects the Cairdian ideal of reconciling divergent points of view, which inspired - corrupted, some would say - the work of so many second-generation British Hegelians.

[19] B. Bosanquet, "The Duty of Citizenship," Aspects of the Social Problem (London, 1895), p. 26.

[20] This story has been well told by Peter Gordon and John White, Philosophers as Educational Reformers (London, 1979).

[21] Quoted in W.S. Fowler, "Neo-Hegelianism and state education in England," Educational Theory (January 1959), p. 59.

a humanizing and formative training...."22 Whether the members of the "Great Society" would be servants of the state or its moral trustees was an open question for Bosanquet. As we have seen in chapter 9, he emphasized group values, even at the expense of individual values; and, like Haldane, he admired the national efficiency of Germany. It would be instructive to compare his position, as a species of pluralism, with the democratic control philosophy of the guild socialist G.D.H. Cole. In political theory the British Hegelians were resolutely prescriptive, and their goal was to heighten the sense of community purpose in order to more effectively combat entrenched privilege and more confidently drive the engine of social reform. From one perspective, their objective was a society of self-possessed individuals, and the state was the principal means to that end. However, they were the artists and the architects; they possessed the vision of the whole, knew the grand design. In the design of the world spirit, the state was not destined to wither away, and for the foreseeable future it had an extensive moral-educational role to play. What had to be learned was the necessity of something which can act for us in a way we would not if left to our own devices, and through which we can translate impotent, perhaps conflicting, aspirations into rational, because realizable, policies.

"...for a true comprehension of group life it will always be necessary to refer its inward and spiritual side to something like the general will, and its outward and visible form to a complex of institutions, and thereby to set its outward and inward aspects in their true relation to each other and to the social unity."23

It is the task of the state to express that relation, and only the state can accomplish it. It combines the widest extent with the greatest intensity of moral force. Smaller units lack its objectivity, larger ones its cohesion.

This theory of the state, drawn from "lesser and more clear-cut objects" (i.e. the Greek polis), deepened and expanded by Hegel, was applied to late nineteenth and early twentieth century British society by the philosophical idealists with some success. As they were the first to admit, the size and complexity of the modern state - its vast wealth unevenly distributed, and its remoteness from individual lives - made it extremely difficult to explain in terms of sharing a common interest and moral experience. They believed, however, that the persistent fact of the state could be explained only in these terms, and that those who failed to perceive its underlying rationality and moral purpose were incapable of seeing the wood for the trees. The British Hegelians drew encouragement in this belief from the mounting evidence that the state, far from withdrawing or atrophying, was assuming more and more social functions and responsibilities. The First World War put their theory of the state to a test which it apparently failed, because it was widely felt that the war demonstrated the moral bankruptcy of the nation-state and marked the end of its era. That feeling of moral revulsion fuelled much wishful thinking, such as can be found in Bertrand Russell's Principles of Social Reconstruction (1919). Few, however, did not remark on the extraordinary mobilization of men, material and morale effected by the belligerent states. This great fact of the twentieth century has still to find an adequate theory, one which seeks, as the British Hegelians did, to humanize political power in a manner free from moralistic illusion.

---

22 B. Bosanquet, Essays and Addresses (London, 1889), p. 28. See also H. Jones, The Principles of Citizenship, p. 117: "The State is an educational institution, and in the last resort it has to teach only one thing - the nature of the good."
23 PTS, p. xxxi.

BIBLIOGRAPHY OF BRITISH HEGELIANISM

This bibliography, like most, does not attempt to list all works consulted. If it has any special interest, it lies in coverage of the period preceding the flowering of British Hegelianism in the last quarter of the nineteenth century. There are notes on little-known authors and/or works not mentioned in the text.

In many cases the edition of the work consulted is not the first; the first edition is then given afterwards (in brackets). Where a later edition has been consulted, it is usually because it contains significant revision and/or additional material by the author. Important changes in an author's point of view that occurred between the first and some later edition of his work are discussed in the text.

I Up to about 1875.

ACTON, J.E.E.D. "Nationality," Essays on Freedom and Power, selected by G. Himmelfarb, London, 1956 (1862).
ANON. An article on Ludwig Tieck, The Oxford Magazine, vol. 1, May 1845.
---. "The German Mind," The English Review; or Quarterly Journal of Ecclesiastical and General Literature, vol. 10, December 1848.
ARNOLD, MATTHEW. Culture and Anarchy, London, 1869.
AUSTIN, JOHN. The Province of Jurisprudence Determined, 2nd ed., London, 1860-63 (1832).
BAGEHOT, WALTER. Physics and Politics, London, 1872.
BENTHAM, JEREMY. A Fragment on Government and An Introduction to the Principles of Morals and Legislation, ed. W. Harrison, Oxford, 1948 (1776 and 1789).
---. Handbook of Political Fallacies, ed. H.A. Larrabee, New York, 1952 (1824).
BLAKEY, ROBERT. A History of Moral Science, London, 1833.
---. A History of the Philosophy of Mind, London, 1848.
---. Historical Sketch of Logic from the Earliest Times to the Present Day, London, 1851. The last two works named both mention Hegel; but they make no attempt to present his philosophy in other than catch-phrases of philosophical abuse, and are of purely negative significance for the history of British Hegelianism.
BRADLEY, F.H. The Presuppositions of Critical History, Oxford, 1874.
BURKE, EDMUND. Reflections on the Revolution in France, ed. C.C. O'Brien, Harmondsworth, Eng., 1968 (1790).
CALDERWOOD, HENRY. The Philosophy of the Infinite, London, 1854. This is a critique of Hamiltonian "agnoiology," in which the author, a member of the "Scottish School," attempts to establish the possibility of rational knowledge of all being, including the Supreme Being.
CARLYLE, THOMAS. Sartor Resartus, London, 1838.
---. Chartism, London, 1839.
CHALYBAEUS, H.M. The Historical Development of Speculative Philosophy from Kant to Hegel, trans. Rev. A. Edersheim, London, 1854 (also trans. A. Tulk, London, 1854, as Historical Survey of Speculative Philosophy from Kant to Hegel). Neither translator says anything to suggest that Hegel was at that time other than a vaguely portentous mystery to the English mind.
COLERIDGE, S.T. The Friend, 4th ed., London, 1844 (1812).
---. The Philosophical Lectures of Samuel Taylor Coleridge, 1818-1819, ed. K. Coburn, New York, 1949.
---. Aids to Reflection, London, 1825.
---. On the Constitution of the Church and State, according to the Idea of each, ed. H.N. Coleridge, 1839 (1830).
---. Lay Sermons, ed. D. Coleridge, London, 1852.

---. Inquiring Spirit: A New Presentation of Coleridge from his Published and Unpublished Prose Writings, ed. K. Coburn, New York, 1951.
---. Notebooks, ed. K. Coburn, London, 1957- .
---. Marginal notes in Hegel's Wissenschaft der Logik (Coleridge's personal copy held in British Museum).
FERRIER, J.F. Scottish Philosophy, the Old and the New, Edinburgh, 1856.
---. Lectures on Greek Philosophy and Other Philosophical Remains, Edinburgh, 1866.
---. Philosophical Works of the Late James Frederick Ferrier, 2nd ed., London, 1888 (1875).
FICHTE, J.G. Addresses to the German Nation, trans. R.F. Jones and G.H. Turnbull, Chicago, 1922 (1808).
GREEN, T.H. "The philosophy of Aristotle," North British Review, September 1866.
---. "Popular philosophy in its relation to life," North British Review, March 1868.
HAMILTON, WILLIAM. Discussions on Philosophy and Literature, Education and University Reform, London, 1853.
HEGEL, G.W.F. On Christianity: Early Theological Writings, trans. T.M. Knox and R. Kroner, Chicago, 1948 (1st German eds. 1795-1800).
---. Phenomenology of Mind, trans. J.B. Baillie, 2nd. ed, London, 1931 (1910; 1st German ed. 1807).
---. Science of Logic, trans. W.H. Johnston and L.G. Struthers, London, 1929 (1st German ed. 1812-16).
---. Philosophy of Right, trans. T.M. Knox, Oxford, 1942 (1st German ed. 1821).
---. Encyclopaedia of the Philosophical Sciences (vol. III), trans. W. Wallace, Oxford, 1892 (1st German ed. 1830).
---. Lectures on the Philosophy of History, trans. J. Sibree, London, 1890 (1857; 1st German ed. 1837 by E. Gans).
---. Lectures on the History of Philosophy, trans. E.S. Haldane, London, 1892-96 (1st German ed. 1832-40 by K.L. Michelet).
---. Lectures on the Philosophy of Religion, trans. J.B. Sanderson and E.B. Speirs from 2nd German ed., London, 1895 (1st German ed. 1832-40 by P. Marheineke).
HEINE, HEINRICH. "Series of Essays on German Literature and Men of Letters," The Athenaeum; London Literary and Critical Journal, vol. 6, no. 297, July 6, 1833.
---. Religion and Philosophy in Germany, trans. J. Snodgrass, Boston, 1959 (1882; 1st German ed. 1835).
HUME, DAVID. A Treatise of Human Nature, ed. L.A. Selby-Bigge, Oxford, 1965 (1740).
---. Political Essays, ed. C.W. Hendel, New York, 1953.
---. Hume on Religion, ed. R. Wollheim, London, 1963.
---. Philosophical Works, ed. T.H. Green and T.H. Grose, London, 1882 (1874).
JOWETT, BENJAMIN. "On the Interpretation of Scripture," Essays and Reviews, London, 1860.
---. The Dialogues of Plato, trans. and ed., 4th ed., Oxford, 1953 (1871).
KANT, IMMANUEL. Critique of Pure Reason, trans. N.K. Smith, New York, 1965 (1st adequate trans., J.M.D. Meiklejohn, 1854; 1st German ed. 1781).
---. Prolegomena to any Future Metaphysics, trans. and ed. L.W. Beck, Indianapolis, 1950 (1st adequate trans., J.H. Bernard and J.P. Mahaffy, 1872; 1st German ed. 1783).
---. Kant's Critique of Practical Reason and Other Works on the Theory of Ethics, trans. T.K. Abbott, 6th ed., London, 1909 (1873-98; 1st adequate trans. Foundations of the Metaphysics of Morals, J.W. Semple, 1836; 1st German eds. Foundations, 1785, and Critique of Practical Reason, 1788).
---. Critique of Judgement, trans. J.H. Bernard, New York, 1951 (1892; 1st German ed. 1790).
---. Metaphysical Elements of Justice: Part I of the Metaphysics of Morals, trans. J. Ladd, Indianapolis, 1965 (1st German ed. 1797).
---. Kant on History, trans. R.E. Anchor, L.W. Beck and E.L. Fackenheim, Indianapolis, 1963.
LEWES, G.H. Review (unsigned) of Jean Paul's Vorschule der Aesthetik, De Quincey's Essay on the Nature, the End and the Means of Imitation in the Fine Arts, Solger's Vorlesungen über die Aesthetik, Hegel's Vorlesungen über die Aesthetik and Quatremaine de Quincey's Essai sur l'Idéale dans ses applications pratiques aux arts du Dessin, The British and Foreign

Review; or European Quarterly Journal, vol. 13, no. 25, 1842.
---. A Biographical History of Philosophy, London, 1845-46 (revised ed. 1857).
---. The History of Philosophy from Thales to Comte, London, 1867-71.
MAINE, HENRY. Ancient Law, London, 1861.
MANSEL, H.L. "A Lecture on the Philosophy of Kant," Letters, Lectures and Reviews, ed. H.W. Chandler, London, 1873 (1856).
---. The Limits of Religious Thought, London, 1858.
MARX, KARL. "Towards a Critique of Hegel's Philosophy of Right: Introduction," and "Economic and Philosophical Manuscripts," Karl Marx: Early Texts, trans. and ed. D. McLellan, Oxford, 1971 (1843-44).
MAURICE, F.D. A Treatise of Moral and Metaphysical Philosophy from the Fourteenth Century to the French Revolution, with a Glimpse into the Nineteenth Century, London, 1862. Kant is comparatively well treated in this work; but Fichte, Schelling and Hegel are afforded, as stipulated in the title, only a "glimpse" - to be precise, three pages altogether.
MILL, JAMES. An Essay on Government, ed. C.V. Shields, Indianapolis, 1955 (1820-28).
---. Analysis of the Phenomena of the Human Mind, ed. J.S. Mill, London, 1869 (1829).
MILL, J.S. Mill on Bentham and Coleridge, ed. F.R. Leavis, London, 1950 (1838 and 1840).
---. A System of Logic, 8th ed., London, 1874 (1843).
---. Principles of Political Economy (books 4 and 5), ed. D.N. Winch, Harmondsworth, Eng., 1970 (1848).
---. Utilitarianism, Liberty and Representative Government, London, 1910 (1863, 1859 and 1861).
---. An Examination of Sir William Hamilton's Philosophy and of the Principal Philosophical Questions Discussed in his Writings, 3rd ed., London, 1867 (1865).
---. Autobiography, London, 1873.
---. Essays on Politics and Culture, ed. G. Himmelfarb, New York, 1963.
MORELL, J.D. An Historical and Critical View of the Speculative Philosophy of Europe in the Nineteenth Century, London, 1846.
---. On the Philosophical Tendencies of the Age, London, 1848.
---. "Modern German philosophy: its characteristics, tendencies and results," Manchester Papers, vol. 1, February and May 1856.
NEWMAN, J.H. An Essay in Aid of a Grammar of Assent, London, 1870.
ROUSSEAU, J.-J. The First and Second Discourses, trans. and ed. R.D. Masters, New York, 1964 (1750 and 1755).
---. A Discourse on Political Economy, trans. G.D.H. Cole, London, 1955 (1758).
---. The Social Contract, trans. H.J. Tozer, ed. L.G. Crocker, New York, 1967 (1762).
---. Emile, trans. B. Foxley, London, 1911 (1762).
SANDARS, T.C. "Hegel's Philosophy of Right," Oxford Essays, 1855.
SCHELLING, F.W.J. Philosophical Inquiries into the Nature of Human Freedom and Matters Connected Therewith, trans. J. Gutmann, Chicago, 1936 (1809).
SIDGWICK, HENRY. The Methods of Ethics, 7th ed., London, 1907 (1874).
SPENCER, HERBERT. First Principles, 6th ed., London, 1884 (1862).
STALLO, J.B. General Principles of the Philosophy of Nature, Boston, 1848. This survey of mostly German philosophy includes a bare and uncritical outline of Hegel's Encyclopaedia, consisting largely of categorial headings. It is an early work by an otherwise distinguished German-American jurist and man of letters.
STEPHEN, J.F. Liberty, Equality, Fraternity, ed. R.J. White, London, 1967 (1873).
STIRLING, J.H. The Secret of Hegel, 2nd ed., Edinburgh, 1898 (1865).
---. "De Quincey and Coleridge upon Kant," Fortnightly Review, October 1867 (collected in Jerrold, Tennyson and Macaulay, with Other Critical Essays, Edinburgh, 1868).
---. Lectures on the Philosophy of Law, London, 1873.
TENNEMANN, W.G. A Manual of the History of Philosophy, trans. Rev. A. Johnson, London, 1832 (revised ed. J.R. Morell, London, 1852).
The Cambridge Review; A Journal of University Life and Thought, 1879-97. This and the Cambridge University Gazette contain occasional book reviews and other references to German philosophical literature. Hegel had become a "household word" in later issues of the

Review, but was still treated with great suspicion.
The Cambridge University Magazine, 1840-43.
The Oxford and Cambridge Magazine, 1856. "Conducted by Members of the two Universities."
The Oxford and Cambridge Review, 1845-47.
The Oxford University Magazine, 1834.
The Oxford University Magazine and Review, 1869.
Undergraduate Papers (Oxford), 1857.
VERA, AUGUSTO. An Inquiry into Speculative and Experimental Science, London, 1856.

II From 1875 to about 1925.

ARNOLD, MATTHEW. "Democracy" and "Equality," Mixed Essays, London, 1879.
BAILLIE, J.B. The Origin and Significance of Hegel's Logic: A General Introduction to Hegel's System, London, 1901. Baillie's 1910 translation of Hegel's Phenomenoogy stood as definitive until very recently.
BARKER, ERNEST. Political Thought in England, 1848 to 1914, London, 1915.
BONAR, JAMES. Philosophy and Political Economy in some of their Historical Relations, London, 1893.
---. Disturbing Elements in the Study and Teaching of Political Economy, Baltimore, 1911. Bonar was a "charter member" of the British Hegelians by virtue of his contributing to Essays in Philosophical Criticism (1883).
BOSANQUET, BERNARD. "Logic as the Science of Knowledge," Essays in Philosophical Criticism, ed. R.B. Haldane and A. Seth, London, 1883.
---. Knowledge and Reality, London, 1885.
---. Essays and Addresses, London, 1889.
---. "The Duty of Citizenship," Aspects of the Social Problem, London, 1895 (1891).
---. The Civilization of Christendom and Other Studies, London, 1893.
---. A Companion to Plato's Republic for English Readers, London, 1895.
---. The Psychology of the Moral Self, London, 1897.
---. The Philosophical Theory of the State, 4th ed., London, 1923 (1899).
---. Logic; or the Morphology of Knowledge, Oxford, 1911.
---. The Principle of Individuality and Value, London, 1912.
---. The Value and Destiny of the Individual, London, 1913.
---. Three Lectures on Aesthetic, London, 1915.
---. Social and International Ideals, being Studies in Patriotism, London, 1917.
---. Some Suggestions in Ethics, London, 1918.
---. Three Chapters on the Nature of Mind, London, 1923.
---. The Meeting of Extremes in Contemporary Philosophy, London, 1924.
---. Science and Philosophy and Other Essays, ed. R.C. Bosanquet and J.H. Muirhead, London, 1927.
---. Bernard Bosanquet and his Friends; Letters Illustrating the Sources and the Development of his Philosophical Opinions, ed. J.H. Muirhead, London, 1935.
BOSANQUET, HELEN (DENDY). The Standard of Life and Other Studies, London, 1898.
BRADLEY, A.C. "Aristotle's Conception of the State," Hellenica, ed. E. Abbott, London, 1880. A.C. was a younger brother of F.H. and Oxford Professor of Poetry.
BRADLEY, F.H. Ethical Studies, 2nd ed., Oxford, 1927 (1876).
---. The Principles of Logic, 2nd ed., Oxford, 1922 (1883).
---. Appearance and Reality, 2nd ed., London, 1897 (1893).
---. Essays on Truth and Reality, London, 1914.
---. Collected Essays, ed. M. de Glehn and H.H. Joachim, Oxford, 1935.
CAIRD, EDWARD. A Critical Account of the Philosophy of Kant, Glasgow, 1877.
---. Hegel, Edinburgh, 1883.
---. The Social Philosophy and Religion of Comte, Glasgow, 1885.
---. The Critical Philosophy of Immanuel Kant, Glasgow, 1889.
---. Essays in Literature and Philosophy, Glasgow, 1892.

---. *The Evolution of Religion*, Glasgow, 1893.
CAIRD, JOHN. *Introduction to the Philosophy of Religion*, Glasgow, 1880.
CROCE, BENEDETTO. *What is Living and What is Dead in the Philosophy of Hegel?*, trans. D. Ainslie, New York, 1912 (1907).
CUNNINGHAM, G.W. *Thought and Reality in Hegel's System*, New York, 1910.
DICEY, A.V. *Lectures on the Relation Between Law and Public Opinion in England During the Nineteenth Century*, 2nd ed., London, 1962 (1905).
DICKINSON, G.L. *A Modern Symposium*, London, 1905.
---. *Justice and Liberty, a Political Dialogue*, London, 1908.
GREEN, T.H. *Prolegomena to Ethics*, ed. A.C. Bradley, 5th ed., Oxford, 1906 (1883).
---. "The Witness of God" and "Faith": Two Lay Sermons, ed. A. Toynbee, London, 1883.
---. *Works*, ed. R.L. Nettleship, London, 1885-88.
---. *Lectures on the Principles of Political Obligation*, reprinted from *Works* (vol. II), London, 1941 (1895).
---. *The Political Theory of T.H. Green*, ed. J.R. Rodman, New York, 1964.
HALDANE, J.S. *The Sciences and Philosophy*, London, 1929.
--- with J.H. MUIRHEAD. *The Life and Philosophy of Edward Caird*, Glasgow, 1921.
HALDANE, R.B. *The Pathway to Reality*, London, 1903-04.
---. *Universities and National Life*, London, 1910.
---. *The Conduct of Life and Other Addresses*, London, 1914.
---. *The Philosophy of Humanism*, London, 1922.
---. *Human Experience: A Study of its Structure*, New York, 1926.
---. *Selected Addresses and Essays*, London, 1928.
---. *An Autobiography*, London, 1929.
HOBHOUSE, L.T. *The Metaphysical Theory of the State: A Criticism*, London, 1918.
HUXLEY, T.H. *Selections from the Essays*, ed. A. Castell, New York, 1948.
JOACHIM, H.H. *The Nature of Truth*, London, 1906.
JONES, HENRY. "The Social Organism," *Essays in Philosophical Criticism*, ed. Haldane and Seth, London, 1883.
---. *Idealism as a Practical Creed*, Glasgow, 1909.
---. *The Working Faith of the Social Reformer and Other Essays*, London, 1910.
---. *The Principles of Citizenship*, London, 1919.
JOWETT, BENJAMIN. *The Republic of Plato*, trans. and ed., 3rd ed., Oxford, 1927 (1888).
---. *Sermons on Faith and Doctrine*, ed. A. Fremantle, London, 1901.
---. *The Four Socratic Dialogues*, trans. and ed., Oxford, 1903.
---. Jowett notebooks in Balliol Library: Nos. 1 (undated) and 25 (August 9, 1881, entitled "Philosophy"), one entitled "Miscellanea 49-50" and one entitled "Analysis of Hegel's Logic and Philosophy of Law." For the opportunity to examine these I am grateful to the Balliol librarian, E.V. Quinn, who informed me that many of the Jowett papers had been destroyed.
KER, W.P. *Collected Essays of W.P. Ker*, ed. C. Whibley, London, 1925. Ker, like Bonar, was a contributor to *Essays in Philosophical Criticism* (1883), and, like A.C. Bradley, made his reputation as a literary scholar and maintained a loose association with the Hegelians.
LEWES, G.H. "The Course of Modern Thought," *Current Discussion: A Collection from the Chief English Essays on Questions of the Time* (vol. II), ed. E.L. Burlingame, London, 1878.
LINDSAY, A.D., MACKENZIE, J.S., et al. *The International Crisis: The Theory of the State*, London, 1916. Lindsay became Lord Lindsay of Birker, and as an influential Oxford don kept Green's memory very much alive there.
MacCUNN, JOHN. *The Ethics of Citizenship*, Glasgow, 1894.
---. *The Making of Character*, London, 1900.
---. *Six Radical Thinkers: Bentham, J.S. Mill, Cobden, Carlyle, Mazzini, T.H. Green*, London, 1907.
MACKENZIE, H.M. *Hegel's Educational Theory and Practice*, London, 1909. H.M. translated some of Hegel's occasional writings, and with J.S. Mackenzie was one of Hegelianism's "journeymen" in Britain.

MACKINTOSH, ROBERT. Hegel and Hegelianism, Edinburgh, 1913.
McTAGGART, J.McT.E. Studies in the Hegelian Dialectic, 2nd ed., Cambridge, 1922 (1896).
---. Studies in Hegelian Cosmology, Cambridge, 1901.
---. Some Dogmas of Religion, London, 1906.
---. A Commentary on Hegel's Logic, Cambridge, 1910.
---. Human Immortality and Pre-existence, London, 1916.
---. Philosophical Studies, ed. S.V. Keeling, London, 1934.
MAINE, HENRY. Popular Government, London, 1885.
MOORE, G.E. Principia Ethica, Cambridge, 1962 (1903).
---. Philosophical Studies, London, 1960 (1922).
MUIRHEAD, J.H. Philosophy and Life and Other Essays, London, 1902.
---. The Service of the State: Four Lectures on the Political Teaching of T.H. Green, London, 1908.
--- with H.J.W. HETHERINGTON. Social Purpose: A Contribution to a Philosophy of Civic Society, London, 1918.
NETTLESHIP, R.L. "The Theory of Education in Plato's Republic," Hellenica, ed. E. Abbott, London, 1880.
---. Philosophical Lectures and Remains, London, 1897. Nettleship was one of Green's most promising students, but his career, like that of his mentor, was cut short by an early death.
PRINGLE-PATTISON, A.S. See SETH, ANDREW.
RASHDALL, HASTINGS. "Personality, Human and Divine," Personal Idealism, ed. H.C. Sturt, London, 1902.
---. The Theory of Good and Evil, London, 1907.
RITCHIE, D.G. "The Rationality of History," Essays in Philosophical Criticism, ed. Haldane and Seth, London 1883.
---. Darwinism and Politics, London, 1891.
---. The Principles of State Interference, London, 1891.
---. Darwin and Hegel, with Other Philosophical Studies, London, 1893.
---. Natural Rights: A Criticism of some Political and Ethical Conceptions, London, 1894.
---. Philosophical Studies, ed. R. Latta, London, 1905.
SANTAYANA, GEORGE. Egotism in German Philosophy, London, 1916.
SCHILLER, F.C.S. "Axioms as Postulates," Personal Idealism, ed. H.C. Sturt, London, 1902.
---. Studies in Humanism, London, 1907.
SETH, ANDREW. The Development from Kant to Hegel, with Chapters on the Philosophy of Religion, London, 1882.
---. "Philosophy as Criticism of Categories," Essays in Philosophical Criticism, ed. Haldane and Seth, London, 1883.
---. Scottish Philosophy, Edinburgh, 1885.
---. Hegelianism and Personality, Edinburgh, 1887.
---. The Balfour Lectures on Realism, ed. G.F. Barbour, Edinburgh, 1933 (1891).
---. Man's Place in the Cosmos and Other Essays, 2nd ed., Edinburgh, 1902 (1897).
---. The Philosophical Radicals and Other Essays, with chapters on the Philosophy of Religion in Kant and Hegel, Edinburgh, 1907.
---. The Idea of God in the Light of Recent Philosophy, 2nd ed., New York, 1920 (1917).
---. The Idea of Immortality, Oxford, 1922.
SHAW, G.B., et al. Fabian Essays, London, 1931 (1889).
SIDGWICK, HENRY. Outline of the History of Ethics for English Readers, 6th ed., London, 1931 (1886).
---. The Elements of Politics, 2nd. ed., London, 1897 (1891).
---. Lectures on the Ethics of T.H. Green, Mr. Herbert Spencer and J. Martineau, London, 1902.
---. Philosophy: Its Scope and Relations, London, 1902.
---. The Development of European Polity, ed. E.M. Sidgwick, London, 1903.
---. Lectures on the Philosophy of Kant and Other Philosophical Lectures and Essays, ed. J. Ward, London, 1905.

SPENCER, HERBERT. *The Man versus the State, with Four Essays on Politics and Society*, ed. D. MacRae, Harmondsworth, Eng., 1969 (1885).
STIRLING, J.H. *What is Thought?*, Edinburgh, 1900.
STURT, H.C. "Art and Personality," *Personal Idealism*, ed. Sturt, London, 1902.
---. *Idola Theatri*, London, 1906.
---. *The Principles of Understanding: An Introduction to Logic from the Standpoint of Personal Idealism*, Cambridge, 1915.
TAWNEY, R.H. *The Acquisitive Society*, London, 1921.
TAYLOR, A.E. *The Problem of Conduct: A Study in the Phenomenology of Ethics*, London, 1901.
---. *Elements of Metaphysics*, 7th ed., London, 1924 (1903).
---. *Plato: The Man and His Work*, London, 1926.
---. *The Faith of a Moralist*, London, 1930.
TOYNBEE, ARNOLD. *Lectures on the Industrial Revolution of the Eighteenth Century in England*, London, 1927 (1884). Toynbee and Toynbee Hall are the names most intimately associated with British Hegelianism as expressed in social work among the poor, especially in London.
WALLACE, WILLIAM. *Kant*, Edinburgh, 1882.
---. *Prolegomena to the Study of Hegel's Philosophy, and especially of his Logic*, Oxford, 1894.
---. *Lectures and Essays on Natural Theology and Ethics*, ed. E. Caird, London, 1898.
WALLAS, GRAHAM. *Human Nature in Politics*, London, 1908.
---. *The Great Society, A Psychological Analysis*, London, 1914.
WATSON, JOHN. *Kant and his English Critics: A Comparison of Critical and Empirical Philosophy*, Glasgow, 1881.
---. *The Philosophy of Kant Explained*, Glasgow, 1908. Watson and MacCunn were two of Edward Caird's most industrious Glasgow disciples.
WEBB, C.C.J. *God and Personality*, London, 1919.
---. *Divine Personality and Human Life*, London, 1920.
---. "Religion, Philosophy and History," *Philosophy and History: Essays Presented to Ernst Cassirer*, ed. R. Klibansky and H.J. Paton, Oxford, 1936.

III Secondary works.

Abbott, E., and Campbell, L. *The Life and Letters of Benjamin Jowett, M.A.*, London, 1897.
Avineri, Shlomo. "Hegel revisited," *Hegel: A Collection of Critical Essays*, ed. A. MacIntyre, New York, 1972 (1968).
---. *Hegel's Theory of the Modern State*, London, 1972.
Berlin, Isaiah. *Two Concepts of Liberty*, Oxford, 1958.
Blanshard, Brand. *The Nature of Thought*, London, 1939.
---. *Reason and Goodness*, London, 1961.
---. *Reason and Analysis*, London, 1962.
Bowle, John. *Politics and Opinion in the Nineteenth Century*, London, 1954.
Brinton, Crane. *The Political Ideas of the English Romanticists*, Oxford, 1926.
Broad, C.D. *Mind and its Place in Nature*, London, 1925.
---. *Five Types of Ethical Theory*, London, 1930.
---. *Examination of McTaggart's Philosophy*, Cambridge, 1933-38.
Brudner, A.S. "The significance of Hegel's prefatory lectures on the philosophy of law," *Clio*, Fall 1978, pp. 41-48.
Burrow, J.W. *Evolution and Society: A Study in Victorian Social Theory*, Cambridge, 1968.
Carritt, E.F. "Liberty and equality," *Political Philosophy*, ed. A. Quinton, London, 1967 (1940).
---. *Ethical and Political Thinking*, Oxford, 1947.
Cassirer, Ernst. *The Question of Jean-Jacques Rousseau*, trans. and ed. P. Gay, Bloomington, Ind., 1963 (1932).
---. *Rousseau, Kant and Goethe*, trans. J. Gutmann, P.O. Kristeller and J.H. Randall Jr., New York, 1963 (1945).
---. *The Myth of the State*, New Haven, 1946.

---. The Problem of Knowledge: Philosophy, Science and History since Hegel, trans. C.W. Hendel and W.H. Woglom, New Haven, 1950.
Church, R.W. Bradley's Dialectic, London, 1942.
Clarke, Peter. Liberals and Social Democrats, Cambridge, 1978.
Cobban, Alfred. Rousseau and the Modern State, 2nd ed., London, 1964 (1934).
---. Edmund Burke and the Revolt Against the Eighteenth Century, London, 1960.
Collingwood, R.G. The Idea of History, Oxford, 1946.
Cowling, Maurice. Mill and Liberalism, Cambridge, 1963.
Crombie, I.M. Plato, the Midwife's Apprentice, London, 1964.
Cunningham, G.W. The Idealistic Argument in Recent British and American Philosophy, New York, 1933.
Dangerfield, George. The Strange Death of Liberal England, 1910-14, New York, 1961 (1935).
Dickinson, G.L. J.McT.E. McTaggart (with chapters by S.V. Keeling and B. Williams), Cambridge, 1931.
Downie, R.S., and Telfer, Elizabeth. Respect for Persons, London, 1969.
Eliot, T.S. Knowledge and Experience in the Philosophy of F.H. Bradley, London, 1964 (first draft of Harvard doctoral dissertation, 1916).
---. "F.H. Bradley," For Lancelot Andrewes: Essays on Style and Order, London, 1928.
Elliott-Binns, L.E. The Development of English Theology in the Later Nineteenth Century, London, 1952.
Emmet, D.M. "Coleridge on the growth of the mind," Coleridge: A Collection of Critical Essays, ed. K. Coburn, Englewood Cliffs, N.J., 1967.
Ewing, A.C. Idealism: A Critical Survey, 3rd ed., London, 1961 (1934).
Faber, G.C. Jowett, London, 1957.
Findlay, J.N. Hegel: A Re-examination, London, 1958.
---. "The contemporary relevance of Hegel," Language, Mind and Value, London, 1963 (1959).
---. "Hegel's use of teleology," The Monist, January 1964, pp. 1-17.
Flew, A.G.N. Hume's Philosophy of Belief: A Study of his First Inquiry, London, 1961.
Forbes, Duncan. The Liberal Anglican Idea of History, Cambridge, 1952.
Foster, M.B. The Political Philosophies of Plato and Hegel, Oxford, 1935.
Fowler, W.S. "Neo-Hegelianism and state education in England," Educational Theory, January 1959, pp. 55-61.
Geach, P.T. Truth, Love and Immortality: An Introduction to McTaggart's Philosophy, London, 1979.
Gordon, Peter, and White, John. Philosophers as Educational Reformers: The Influence of Idealism on British Educational Thought and Practice, London, 1979.
Gray, J.G. Hegel's Hellenic Ideal, New York, 1941.
Halévy, Elie. The Growth of Philosophic Radicalism, trans. M. Morris, Boston, 1955 (1928).
Hampshire, Stuart. Thought and Action, London, 1959.
Hare, R.M. Freedom and Reason, Oxford, 1963.
Himmelfarb, Gertrude. Darwin and the Darwinian Revolution, New York, 1959.
Houghton, W.E. The Victorian Frame of Mind, 1830-1870, New Haven, 1957.
Hyppolite, Jean. Génèse et Structure de la Phénoménologie de l'esprit de Hegel, Paris, 1946.
---. Studies on Marx and Hegel, trans. J. O'Neill, New York, 1969 (1955).
Joseph, H.W.B. Some Problems in Ethics, London, 1931.
Kaufmann, W.A. The Owl and the Nightingale: From Shakespeare to Existentialism, London, 1960.
---. Hegel: Reinterpretation, Texts and Commentary, New York, 1965.
Kelly, G.A. Idealism, Politics and History: Sources of Hegelian Thought, London, 1969.
Keynes, J.M. "My Early Beliefs," Two Memoirs, ed. D. Garnett, London, 1949.
Knox, T.M. "Hegel and Prussianism," Philosophy, January 1940, pp. 51-63 (see also the ensuing discussion with E.F. Carritt and J.A. Spender in April and July issues).
---. "A Plea for Hegel," New Studies in Hegel's Philosophy, ed. W.E. Steinkraus, New York, 1971.
Kojève, Alexandre. Introduction to the Reading of Hegel: Lectures on the Phenomenology of Spirit, assembled by Raymond Queneau, ed. A. Bloom and trans. J.H. Nichols Jr., New York, 1969 (1947).

Korner, Stephan. *Kant*, Harmondsworth, Eng., 1955.
Koss, S.E. *Lord Haldane, Scapegoat for Liberalism*, New York, 1969.
Krook, Dorothea. *Three Traditions of Moral Thought*, Cambridge, 1959.
Lamont, W.D. *An Introduction to Green's Moral Philosophy*, London, 1934.
Lewis, H.D. "Individualism and collectivism: a study of T.H. Green," *Ethics*, October 1952, pp. 44-63.
Lichtheim, George. *From Marx to Hegel*, London, 1971.
Lippincott, B.E. *Victorian Critics of Democracy: Carlyle, Ruskin, Arnold, Stephen, Maine, Lecky*, Minneapolis, 1938.
Löwith, Karl. *From Hegel to Nietzsche: The Revolution in Nineteenth Century Thought*, trans. D.E. Green, New York, 1964 (1941).
---. *Meaning in History*, Chicago, 1949.
Mabbott, J.D. *The State and the Citizen*, London, 1948.
Marcuse, Herbert. *Reason and Revolution; Hegel and the Rise of Social Theory*, 2nd ed., New York, 1954 (1932).
Maurice, Frederick. *The Life of Viscount Haldane of Cloan*, London, 1937.
Milne, A.J.M. *The Social Philosophy of English Idealism*, London, 1962.
Mix, M.E., Nicolai, M., and Roloff, W. *German Literature in British Magazines, 1750-1860*, ed. A.R. Hohlfeld and B.Q. Morgan, Madison, Wis., 1949.
Muirhead, J.H. "How Hegel came to England," *Mind*, October 1927, pp. 423-47.
---. *Coleridge as Philosopher*, London, 1930.
---. *The Platonic Tradition in Anglo-Saxon Philosophy; Studies in the History of Idealism in England and America*, London, 1931.
---. *Reflections by a Journeyman in Philosophy*, ed. J.W. Harvey, London, 1942.
Mure, G.R.G. *An Introduction to Hegel*, Oxford, 1940.
---. *The Philosophy of Hegel*, Oxford, 1965.
---. *Idealist Epilogue*, Oxford, 1978.
Oakeshott, Michael. *Experience and its Modes*, Cambridge, 1933.
---. *Rationalism in Politics and Other Essays*, London, 1962.
Orsini, G.N.G. *Coleridge and German Idealism*, Carbondale, Ill., 1969.
Passmore, J.A. *A Hundred Years of Philosophy*, London, 1957.
Pateman, Carol. *Participation and Democratic Theory*, London, 1970.
Paton, H.J. *The Categorical Imperative: A Study in Kant's Moral Philosophy*, London, 1947.
Plamenatz, J.P. *Consent, Freedom and Political Obligation*, 2nd ed., London, 1968 (1938).
---. *Man and Society* (vol. II), London, 1963.
Plant, Raymond. *Hegel*, London, 1973.
Pocock, J.G.A. "Time, institutions and action: an essay on traditions and their understanding," *Politics, Language and Time: Essays on Political Thought and History*, London, 1972 (1971).
Popper, K.R. *The Poverty of Historicism*, London, 1961 (1944-45).
---. *The Open Society and its Enemies*, 5th ed., London, 1966 (1945).
Prichard, H.A. *Moral Obligation*, Oxford, 1949.
Prior, A.N. *Logic and the Basis of Ethics*, Oxford, 1949.
Pucelle, Jean. *L'Idéalisme en Angleterre de Coleridge à Bradley*, Neuchatel, 1955.
---. *La nature et l'esprit dans la philosophie de T.H. Green; La renaissance de l'idéalisme en Angleterre au XIXe siecle*, Louvain, 1960-65.
Quinton, A.M. *Absolute Idealism*, London, 1972.
Randall, J.H., Jr. "Idealistic social philosophy and Bernard Bosanquet," *Philosophy and Phenomenological Research*, June 1966, pp. 499-502.
Rees, J.C. *Mill and his Early Critics*, Leicester, 1956.
---. "A re-reading of Mill on liberty," *Limits of Liberty: Studies of Mill's On Liberty*, ed. P. Radcliff, Belmont, Calif., 1966 (1960).
Rees, W.J. "The theory of sovereignty restated," *Philosophy, Politics and Society* (1st series), ed. P. Laslett, Oxford, 1956.
Reyburn, H.A. *The Ethical Theory of Hegel*, Oxford, 1921.

Richter, Melvin. *The Politics of Conscience: T.H. Green and his Age*, Cambridge, Mass., 1964.
Robson, J.M. *The Improvement of Mankind: The Social and Political Thought of John Stuart Mill*, London, 1968.
de Ruggiero, Guido. *The History of European Liberalism*, trans. R.G. Collingwood, Boston, 1959 (1927).
Schneewind, J.B. *Sidgwick's Ethics and Victorian Moral Philosophy*, Oxford, 1977.
Shklar, J.N. *Men and Citizens: A Study of Rousseau's Social Theory*, Cambridge, 1969.
Smith, N.K. *The Philosophy of David Hume: A Critical Study of its Origins and Central Doctrines*, London, 1941.
Stephen, Leslie. *The English Utilitarians*, London, 1900.
Stormer, G.D. "Hegel and the secret of James Hutchison Stirling," *Idealistic Studies*, January 1979, pp. 33-54.
Taylor, Charles. *Hegel*, London, 1975.
Ulam, A.B. *The Philosophical Foundations of English Socialism*, Cambridge, Mass., 1951.
Voegelin, Eric. *Science, Politics and Gnosticism*, Chicago, 1968 (1959).
Walsh, W.H. *Kant's Criticism of Metaphysics*, Edinburgh, 1975 (1939).
---. *Reason and Experience*, Oxford, 1947.
---. *An Introduction to Philosophy of History*, London, 1951.
---. *Metaphysics*, London, 1963.
---. *Hegelian Ethics*, London, 1969.
Warnock, G.J. *English Philosophy since 1900*, London, 1958.
Warnock, Mary. *Ethics since 1900*, London, 1960.
Weldon, T.D. *An Introduction to Kant's Critique of Pure Reason*, Oxford, 1945.
Wellek, René. *Immanuel Kant in England, 1793-1838*, Princeton, 1931.
Whitehead, A.N. *Adventures of Ideas*, Cambridge, 1933.
Willey, Basil. *Nineteenth Century Studies: Coleridge to Matthew Arnold*, London, 1949.
---. *More Nineteenth Century Studies*, London, 1956.
Williams, Raymond. *Culture and Society, 1780-1850*, London, 1958.
---. "David Hume: reasoning and experience," *The English Mind: Studies in the English Moralists Presented to Basil Willey*, ed. H.S. Davies and G. Watson, Cambridge, 1964.
Wollheim, Richard. *F.H. Bradley*, Harmondsworth, Eng., 1959.
Young, G.M. *Victorian England: Portrait of an Age*, 2nd ed., Oxford, 1953 (1936).

IV   English translations of Hegel's work in chronological order.

The Subjective Logic of Hegel. Translated by H. Sloman and J. Wallon. Revised by a graduate of Oxford, and to which are added some remarks by H.S. London, 1855.
Lectures on the Philosophy of History. Translated by J. Sibree. London, 1857.
The Secret of Hegel. With translations from the *Science of Logic* by J.H. Stirling. Edinburgh, 1865.
The Logic of Hegel. Translated from the *Encyclopaedia of the Philosophical Sciences* (vol. I) by W. Wallace. With a prolegomena by Wallace. Oxford, 1874.
The Philosophy of Art. Translated from the *Aesthetik* (part II) by W.M. Bryant. With an introductory essay by Bryant. New York, 1879.
Hegel's Doctrine of Reflection. Translated from the *Science of Logic* (part II) by W.T. Harris. With commentary by Harris. New York, 1881.
The Introduction to Hegel's Philosophy of Fine Art (Aesthetik). Translated by B. Bosanquet. With notes and a prefatory essay by Bosanquet. London, 1886.
The Philosophy of Art; An Introduction to the Scientific Study of Aesthetics by G.W.F. Hegel and C.L. Michelet. Translated by W. Hastie. Edinburgh, 1886.
Hegel's Philosophy of Mind. Translated from the *Encyclopaedia* (vol. III) by W. Wallace. With five introductory essays by Wallace (1894). Oxford, 1892.
Lectures on the History of Philosophy. Translated by E.S. Haldane, with the assistance of F.H. Simson. London, 1892-96.
The Ethics of Hegel. Translated from the *Philosophy of Right* by J.M. Sterrett. With an

introduction by Sterrett. Boston, 1893.
Lectures on the Philosophy of Religion, together with a work on the Proofs of the Existence of God. Translated by J.B. Sanderson and E.B. Speirs. Edited by Speirs. London, 1895.
Hegel's Philosophy of Right. Translated by S.W. Dyde. London, 1896.
Hegel's Educational Theory and Practice. With translations from the "School Addresses" by H.M. Mackenzie. London, 1909.
The Phenomenology of Mind. Translated by J.B. Baillie. With an introduction and notes by Baillie. London, 1910.
Hegel's Doctrine of Formal Logic. Translated from the *Science of Logic* (part III) by H.S. Macran. With an introduction and notes by Macran. Oxford, 1912.
The Philosophy of Fine Art. Translated by F.P.B. Osmaston. With notes by Osmaston. London, 1920.
Hegel's Science of Logic. Translated by W.H. Johnston and L.G. Struthers. With an introductory preface by Viscount Haldane of Cloan. London, 1929.
Hegel's Logic of World and Idea. Translated from the *Science of Logic* (part III) by H.S. Macran. With an introductory note on idealism by Macran. Oxford, 1929.
The Philosophy of Right. Translated by T.M. Knox. With commentary by Knox. Oxford, 1942.
On Christianity: Early Theological Writings. Translated by T.M. Knox and R. Kroner. With an introduction by Kroner. Chicago, 1948.
The Philosophy of Hegel. Translated from the *Phenomenology of Mind*, *Lectures on the Philosophy of History* and *Lectures on the History of Philosophy* by C.J. Friedrich, with the assistance of P.W. Friedrich and J.M. Sterrett. With an introduction by C.J. Friedrich. New York, 1953.
Reason in History: A General Introduction to the Philosophy of History. Translated by R.S. Hartman. With an introduction by Hartman. Indianapolis, 1953.
Encyclopedia of Philosophy. Translated from the *Encyclopaedia* (especially vol. II) by G.E. Mueller. With notes by Mueller. New York, 1959.
Hegel's Political Writings. Translated by T.M. Knox. With an introductory essay by Z.A. Pelczynski. Oxford, 1964.
Hegel: Reinterpretation, Texts and Commentary. With translations of the Preface to the *Phenomenology of Mind* and letters to and from Hegel by W.A. Kaufmann. New York, 1965.
Hegel: The Man, his Vision and Work. With a translation of "Eleusis" by G.E. Mueller. New York, 1968.
Hegel's Science of Logic. Translated by A.V. Miller. With a foreword by J.N. Findlay. London, 1969.
Hegel's Concept of Experience. By Martin Heidegger. Translated by K.R. Dove. With a translation of the Introduction to the *Phenomenology of Mind* by Dove. New York, 1970.
Hegel's Philosophy of Nature. Translated from the *Encyclopaedia* (vol. II) and Zusatze in Michelet's text by A.V. Miller. With a foreword by J.N. Findlay. Oxford, 1970.
Hegel's Philosophy of Nature. Translated from the *Encyclopaedia* (vol. II) by M.J. Petry. With an introduction and explanatory notes by Petry. London, 1970.
Hegel's Idea of Philosophy. With a translation of Hegel's Introduction to the *History of Philosophy* by Q. Lauer. New York, 1971.
Hegel's Philosophy of Mind. Translated from the *Encyclopaedia* (vol. III) by W. Wallace. With a translation of the Zusätze accompanying Boumann's edition of "Mind Subjective" by A.V. Miller. With a foreword by J.N. Findlay. Oxford, 1971.
Hegel's Development: Toward the Sunlight. With a translation of "System Programme of German Idealism" by H.S. Harris. Oxford, 1972.
Aesthetics: Lectures on Fine Art (vols. I&II). Translated by T.M. Knox. Oxford, 1975.
Natural Law; The Scientific Way of Treating Natural Law, its Place in Moral Philosophy and its Relation to the Positive Sciences of Law. Translated by T.M. Knox. With an introduction by H.B. Acton. Philadelphia, 1975.
Lectures on the Philosophy of World History. Introduction: Reason in History. Translated by H.B. Nisbet. With an introduction by D. Forbes. Cambridge, 1975.
"Fragments of Historical Studies." Translated by C. Butler. With an introduction by H.S.

Harris. *Clio*, Fall 1977, pp. 113-34.

Faith and Knowledge. Translated and edited by W. Cerf and H.S. Harris. Albany, 1977.

The Difference between Fichte's and Schelling's System of Philosophy. Translated and edited by H.S. Harris and W. Cerf. Albany, 1977.

The Phenomenology of Spirit. Translated by A.V. Miller. With an analysis and foreword by J.N. Findlay. Oxford, 1977.

Hegel's Philosophy of Subjective Spirit. Translated and edited by M.J. Petry. With an introduction by Petry. Dordrecht, 1977.

"A Conversation of Three: A Scene from *Julius Caesar*." Translated by C. Seiler. With an introduction by H.S. Harris. *Clio*, Winter 1978, pp. 247-51.

"On Some Characteristic Distinctions of the Ancient Poets [as Against Modern Poets]." Translated by H.S. Harris. With an introduction by Harris. *Clio*, Spring 1978, pp. 403-07.

"Prefatory Lectures on the Philosophy of Law." Translated by A.S. Brudner. *Clio*, Fall 1978, pp. 49-70.

"Two Fragments of 1797 on Love." Translated by C. Hamlin and H.S. Harris. With an introduction by Harris. *Clio*, Winter 1979, pp. 257-65.

"Commentary on the Bern Aristocracy (1798)." Translated by H. Luegenbiehl. With an introduction by Z.A. Pelczynski. *Clio*, Spring 1979, pp. 405-16.

Hegel's System of Ethical Life and First Philosophy of Spirit. Translated and edited from the Encyclopaedia (vol. III) by H.S. Harris and T.M. Knox. Albany, 1979.

INDEX

Aberdeen University 34
Antigone 10
Appearance and Reality 58, 62, 63
Aristotle 5, 9, 11, 28, 42, 43, 44, 46, 60, 85, 101
Arnold, Matthew 15, 91n.1, 101, 108
Arnold, Thomas 52n.4
Asquith, H.H. 98, 100, 108
Augustine, St. (Bishop of Hippo) 76n.20
Austin, John 12n.5, 67
Avineri, Shlomo 26, 27
Bain, Alexander 44
Balfour, A.J. 98
Balliol College, Oxford 29n.13, 30, 42n.1, 43, 45, 46, 47, 72n.1, 82n.2
Bampton Lectures 32, 33
Barker, Ernest 107
Baur, F.C. 20, 30, 58n.4
Beccaria, Cesare 54n.8
Bentham, Jeremy 12n.4&5, 54, 55, 56, 83, 103
Berkeley, George 2, 42, 65
Bosanquet, Bernard 11, 17, 33, 34, 35, 48, 49, 72-80, 81, 82, 91, 92, 95, 96, 99, 102, 105, 106, 107, 108, 109
Bosanquet, Helen (Mrs.) 108
Bradley, A.C. 107
Bradley, F.H. 15, 17, 22, 24, 34, 36, 42n.1, 47, 49, 53, 57-64, 65, 66, 69, 70, 72, 73, 74n.9&10, 77, 78, 79, 85, 86n.21, 90, 91, 95, 96, 97, 99, 104n.7, 105
Bright, John 42n.1
Broad, C.D. 1, 17n.1, 52n.4, 86, 93
Burke, Edmund 11, 64
Butler, Joseph (Bishop) 53
Caird, Edward 17, 34, 43, 46, 47, 69n.15, 72n.1, 91, 92-93, 107, 108n.18
Caird, John 34, 69, 70, 91
Cambridge University 46
Campbell-Bannerman, Henry 108
Carlyle, Thomas 18, 38
Charity Organization Society 108
Clarke, Peter i
Cole, G.D.H. 109
Coleridge, S.T. i, 20, 27-29, 30, 55
Collingwood, R.G. i, 58n.4
Comte, Auguste 19n.5
Condorcet, M.J.A.N.de C. (Marquis de) 54
Critique of Judgment 8
Crito 64
Croce, Benedetto 6, 58n.4
Crombie, I.M. 43
Cudworth, Ralph 28
Curragh Mutiny 99

Dangerfield, George 98n.1, 100
Darwin and Hegel 83-84
Darwin, Charles 27, 30, 81, 84
Darwinism and Politics 82
Dasein 5n.5
Dendy, Helen (see Bosanquet, Helen)
Descartes, René 43
Dickinson, G.L. 103
Dilthey, Wilhelm 58n.4
Dockhorn, Klaus 108
Edinburgh University 24n.33, 33n.31, 38n.1, 46n.16, 98n.1
Einstein, Albert 98
Eliot, George 19n.5
Emile 8
Encyclopaedia of the Philosophical Sciences 39, 48
Engels, Friedrich 15
Essay on Government 54
Essays and Reviews 29n.13, 30-31
Essays in Philosophical Criticism 33-34, 72, 106
Ethical Studies i, 59-63, 90, 104n.7
Ewing, A.C. 2n.2
Faber, Geoffrey 43
Ferrier, J.F. 24-25
Feuerbach, Ludwig 18
Fichte, J.G. i, 7, 17, 19, 21, 39, 48, 106n.11
Findlay, J.N. 2n.3, 99
First World War 1, 77, 98, 102, 105, 107, 109
French Revolution 10, 14
Geach, P.T. 86n.21, 87, 93, 94, 97n.25
Geist 6, 11, 96
Gifford Lectures 34, 35, 38n.1, 48, 49, 72, 75n.17, 92, 99, 106n.12
Gladstone, W.E. 100
Glasgow University 20n.10, 46, 47, 70n.17, 108n.18
Godwin, William 8
Goethe, J.W. 8, 22
Gordon, Peter and White, John i, 108n.20
Gottingen University 98n.1
Gray, J.G. 10n.1
Green, T.H. 17, 33, 34, 38n.3, 42-43, 44, 46, 47, 48, 49, 52, 55, 57n.1, 62, 65-71, 72, 73, 76n.20, 78, 81, 82, 83, 84, 85, 91, 92, 96, 99, 102, 107, 108
Grose, T.H. 17, 65
Grote, John 22, 24, 25, 26n.1
Haig, Douglas (Earl) 98
Haldane, J.S. 102, 106
Haldane, R.B. (Lord) 72n.1, 98-101, 102, 106, 108, 109

Hamilton, Sir William 17, 18, 25, 32
Harris, W.T. 41
Hartley, David 28, 54n.8
Heine, Heinrich 19
Helvétiuis, C.A. 54n.8
Herbart, J.F. 59
Herder, J.G. 7, 28
Hetherington, H.J.W. 107
Hobbes, Thomas 5, 75
Hobhouse, L.T. 67n.7, 105-106
Hölderlin, Friedrich 9n.1
Howison, G.H. 41
Hume, David 2, 17, 18, 38, 42, 55-56, 57, 65
Huxley, T.H. 81
The Idea of God 34, 35
An Introduction to the Principles of Morals and Legislation 12n.4&5
James, William 3, 36
Joachim, H.H. 47n.21
Jones, Henry 79n.29, 106, 107, 108, 109n.22
Jowett, Benjamin 10, 27, 29-32, 38n.3, 43-45, 46, 47, 58n.4, 83, 108
Kant, Immanuel i, 2, 3, 5, 6, 8, 13, 14, 15, 17, 18, 19, 20, 21, 23, 24, 25, 27, 28, 32, 33, 34, 36, 38, 39, 40, 42, 46, 52, 53, 65, 70, 81, 84, 86n.21, 92, 105
Kelly, G.A. 7n.7
Keynes, J.M. 102, 103, 104
Knox, T.M. 99
Labour Party 98, 100
Lasalle, Ferdinand 100
Laws 44, 102
Leibniz, G.W. 87
Lessing, G.E. 19, 22
Lewes, G.H. 19, 21
Liberal Party 98, 100, 101
Liberals and Social Democrats i
Lindsay, A.D. 107
List der Vernunft 13
Locke, John 18, 42, 65, 75
London Ethical Society 72n.1, 82n.2, 108
Lotze, Hermann 33n.31, 59, 98n.1
Macaulay, T.B. 12n.3, 56n.13
MacDonald, Ramsay 108
Mackenzie, J.S. 107
McTaggart, J.McT.E. 17, 26, 37, 41, 52n.4, 73, 77, 86-90, 91, 92, 93-97, 103n.6
Mansel, H.L. 22, 32-33
Marx, Karl i, 2, 6, 36, 100
Maurice, Frederick 100n.10
Maurice, F.D. 26n.1
Merton College, Oxford i, 47, 57n.1
Mill, James 54, 55
Mill, J.S. 12, 15, 32n.25, 50-52, 55, 56, 64, 83n.4

Milner, Alfred (Lord) 99
Montesquieu, C.de S. (Baron de La Brède et) 75
Moore, G.E. 95n.19, 51, 102, 103-105
Moralität 8, 63
Morant, R.L. 108
Morell, J.D. 20-21, 22
Morell, J.R. 18, 20
Muirhead, J.H. 27n.3, 38n.3, 72n.1, 79n.29, 106, 107, 108
Muirhead Library of Philosophy 108n.18
Mure, G.R.G. i, 47n.21
Natural Rights 83, 84-86
The Nature of Existence 87, 93
Newman, J.H. (Cardinal) 33n.30
Nicomachean Ethics 60, 101
Nietzsche, Friedrich 106n.11
Novalis, H.V.O. 19
Oakeshott, Michael 5n.4, 58n.4
On Liberty 50n.1, 64
On the Origin of Species 30, 81
Orsini, G.N.G. 27
Oxford University 45-46, 101
Pareto, Vilfredo 107
Parmenides 44
The Pathway to Reality 99-100
Phenomenology of Mind 59
Philosophers as Educational Reformers i, 108n.20
The Philosophical Theory of the State i, 75-77, 77, 78-80
Philosophie des Rechts (Philosophy of Right) 23, 59, 70, 98, 101
Plato 9, 31, 43, 44, 45, 46, 47, 74, 75, 76, 102
Plotinus 28
The Presuppositions of Critical History 57-58
Prichard, H.A. 67n.7
Principia Ethica 103-104
The Principle of Individuality and Value 72-74
The Principles of Logic 22, 57n.2, 58, 59
The Principles of Political Obligation i, 67-69
The Principles of State Interference 83
Pringle-Pattison, A.S. (See Seth, Andrew)
Prolegomena to Ethics 65, 71, 91
Pucelle, Jean 92n.4
Quinton, Anthony 18n.4, 20n.12, 24n.34
Rashdall, Hastings 36, 37n.47
Rechtstaat 15, 48, 76
Reid, Thomas 18
Representative Government 50n.1
Republic 31, 102
Richter (Jean Paul) 19
Richter, Melvin 42n.1
Ritchie, D.G. 33, 47n.19, 72n.1, 75, 78,

82-86, 102, 106
Robert Elsmere 91n.3
Rousseau, J.-J. i, 8, 11, 13, 67, 71, 75, 77
Russell, Bertrand 1n.1, 103, 105, 109
St. Andrews University 24n.33, 33n.31, 47n.20, 72n.1, 82n.2, 108n.18
St. Francis of Assisi 103
St. Louis Philosophical Society 23, 41
Sandars, T.C. 23-24
Santayana, George 32n.27, 106n.11
Sartor Resartus 38
Schelling, F.W.J. 17, 19, 20, 21, 23, 24, 27, 28, 29, 30, 39
Schiller, F.C.S. 36
Schiller, J.C.F. 8, 9n.1, 19
Schneewind, J.B. 25n.40
School of Ethics and Social Philosophy 72n.1
Schopenhauer, Arthur 98n.1
The Secret of Hegel 21, 23, 24, 38-40, 42
Seth, Andrew 17, 33-36, 98n.1, 105, 106
Sibree, J. 22n.20
Sidgwick, Henry 17, 25, 46, 52-53, 55, 72n.1, 83, 84, 85, 86n.21, 90, 103
Sittlichkeit 8, 13, 40, 52, 69, 71, 99
Sloman, H. 22-23
The Social Contract 67
Socrates 64, 102
Soho Radical Club 100
Sophist 31, 44
Spencer, Herbert 41, 44, 69, 82, 83n.4, 84
Spinoza, Baruch 28, 29, 87
Stanley, A.P. 29, 30
Steuart, James 10
Stirling, J.H. 21, 23, 24, 38-41, 42, 47
Strachey, Lytton 103
Strauss, David 18, 20, 22
Studies in Hegelian Cosmology i, 87-89, 89, 90, 95-6, 96, 97
Studies in the Hegelian Dialectic 89, 93-94, 97
Sturt, H.C. 36
System of Logic 12, 50n.1, 56
Taylor, A.E. 75
Taylor, Charles 6
Tennemann, W.G. 18
Tieck, Ludwig 19
de Tocqueville, Alexis 10
A Treatise of Human Nature 17, 65
Trinity College, Cambridge 24n.33, 52n.4, 86n.21
Tubingen University 30, 58n.4
Urwick, E.J. 107
Utilitarianism 50-51
The Value and Destiny of the Individual 72, 74-75
Véra, Augusto 24
Vernunft 7, 9, 14, 59
Verstand 7
Vico, Giambattista 7, 75
Vorlesungen über die Aesthetik 19
Wallace, William 42, 47-49, 72n.1, 92
Wallas, Graham 72n.1, 107
Ward, (Mrs.) Humphrey 91n.3, 100n.10
Webb, C.C.J. 37n.47
Wellek, René 17n.3, 27
Whitehead, A.N. 58n.5
Williams, Raymond 56
Winckelmann, J.J. 9n.1, 19
Wissenschaft der Logik 28, 29, 39, 47
Wollheim, Richard 59n.7
Woolf, Leonard 103
Workers' Education Association 108n.18
Working Men's College 100

For Product Safety Concerns and Information please contact our EU
representative GPSR@taylorandfrancis.com
Taylor & Francis Verlag GmbH, Kaufingerstraße 24, 80331 München, Germany

www.ingramcontent.com/pod-product-compliance
Lightning Source LLC
Chambersburg PA
CBHW081830300426
44116CB00014B/2534